Ice Blocks from Norway

Michael Freeman

Ice Blocks from Norway

THE IMPORTATION OF NATURAL ICE TO BRITAIN,
CIRCA 1870–1925

CAPPELEN DAMM AKADEMISK

© 2023 Michael Freeman.

This work is protected under the provisions of the Norwegian Copyright Act of July 1, 2018 relating to Copyright in Literary, Scientific and Artistic Works and published Open Access under the terms of a Creative Commons Attribution-Non Commercial-NoDerivatives 4.0 International (CC BY-NC-ND 4.0) License (https://creativecommons.org/licenses/by-nc-nd/4.0/). This license allows third parties to copy and redistribute the material in any medium or format for non-commercial purposes only. If you remix, transform, or build upon the material, you may not distribute the modified material. Third parties are prohibited from applying legal terms or technological measures that restrict others from doing anything permitted under the terms of the license. Note that the license may not provide all of the permissions necessary for an intended reuse; other rights, for example publicity, privacy, or moral rights, may limit third party use of the material.

This book has been made possible with support from the North Atlantic Fisheries History Association (NAFHA) and the research project 'The Last Ice Age' at the Norwegian Maritime Museum, funded by the Research Council of Norway with a contribution from Arts and Culture Norway.

ISBN printed edition: 978-82-02-79121-6
ISBN PDF: 978-82-02-75539-3
ISBN EPUB: 978-82-02-80103-8
ISBN HTML: 978-82-02-80104-5
ISBN XML: 978-82-02-80105-2
DOI: https://doi.org/10.23865/noasp.187

This is a peer-reviewed monograph.

Citation: Freeman, M. (2023). *Ice blocks from Norway: The importation of natural ice to Britain, circa 1870–1925*. Cappelen Damm Akademisk. https://doi.org/10.23865/noasp.187

Cover design: Carine Fløystad, Cappelen Damm AS
Cover image: One of the elaborate ice railways, or trunkways, taking ice from lake to fjord edge (Berg-Kragerø Museum. Creative Commons BY-ND 4.0).

All illustrations are credited in their respective captions. Images reproduced in this book may not be reused in any way without the express permission of the copyright holder.

Cappelen Damm Akademisk/NOASP
noasp@cappelendamm.no

Contents

Foreword 7

Preface and Acknowledgements 13

Chapter 1 Introduction: From Lake to Lemon Squash 15

Chapter 2 A Tale of Two Ports 27

Chapter 3 Ice Farming 55

Chapter 4 Ice Ships 79

Chapter 5 The Ice Factory 101

Chapter 6 The Iceman Cometh 125

Chapter 7 Ice Cream 151

Chapter 8 A Trade Decays 169

References 189

About the Author 193

Appendix 195

Index 197

Foreword

This monograph, *Ice Blocks From Norway*, is published under the joint auspices of 'The Last Ice Age' project and the North Atlantic Fisheries History Association (NAFHA). It concerns the Anglo-Norwegian trade in natural ice during the late nineteenth and early twentieth centuries, a business that formed an important part of the 'age of natural ice' being investigated by the project team, as well as one of the contributory factors in the development of the North Atlantic fisheries in the modern era. For 'The Last Ice Age', which is an international research investigation funded by the Research Council of Norway (RCN project number 275188) and managed by the Norwegian Maritime Museum in Oslo in partnership with the University of South-Eastern Norway, the University of Hull (UK) and Old Dominion University in Norfolk VA (USA), this book is one of a range of outputs that will include further peer-reviewed monographs on particular ice themes, an anthology of key project-generated studies, several PhD and MA theses, and numerous journal articles (see, for example, *International Journal of Maritime History* vol. 34:1, 2022, and the project website https://marmuseum.no/en/the-last-ice-age). For NAFHA, this is the fifteenth publication in its *Studia Atlantica* series, most of which are proceedings of conferences convened by the Association since 1995 in various fishing ports and locales – Akureyri, Bergen, Bremerhaven, Gothenburg, Halifax NS, Hull, Norfolk VA, Porto, Qatorqoq, Torshavn, Tromsø, Rotterdam, Westman Isles – across the North Atlantic region.

The joint sponsors are very grateful to Dr Michael Freeman of Mansfield College, Oxford, the author of *Ice Blocks from Norway*, for collaborating in the dissemination of the fruits of his research. In so doing, he enhances our knowledge and understanding of the scale, character, organisation and significance of the natural ice business of Northern and Western Europe during the period 1870–1925. By following the ice from

Norwegian lakes and ponds across the North Sea to British consumers in restaurants, shops, private households and an array of industries, not least the burgeoning inshore, offshore and distant-water fisheries, Dr Freeman sheds light on the wider contexts of transport history, technological and logistical developments, economic integration, changes in consumer patterns and environmental factors.

This is a multi-faceted story that ranges widely over time and space. In the Mediterranean world and beyond, natural ice had been used for cold storage to preserve the freshness of foods and provide cold drinks, sorbets, etc. since ancient times. In royal and aristocratic households in northern and western Europe, the use of ice for cooling can be traced back to the Middle Ages. By the late eighteenth century, a considerable local trade in ice had emerged in metropoles like London. This trade was partly triggered by a fashion for ice creams and confectionaries imported from Naples and other Mediterranean cities visited regularly by British upper-class travellers of this epoch. It was also stimulated by the development of the Scottish salmon fisheries from the 1780s, when merchants in Scotland introduced fresh salmon on ice to a growing London market as an alternative to smoked and salted salmon.

This market for natural ice emerged under climatic conditions different from the present. In most years until the second quarter of the nineteenth century, it seems that demand for ice in London, elsewhere in the British Isles and on the continent could be sated by local or regional supplies. High winter temperatures could, however, cause ice shortages, obliging ice traders to look for more distant sources of supply. The first few recorded imports of ice from Norway to Britain appeared in 1822, after a winter with extremely high temperatures and allegedly severe shortages of ice both in the London market and the Scottish salmon business.

In the following years, there were reports of imports of ice to Britain from Greenland, Iceland, the Faroe Islands and Norway, while the first imports of ice from Norway to continental ports were also recorded. In 1835 official statistics indicated that an export of 1,310 register tons of ice from Norway was customs cleared for different foreign ports. This corresponded to perhaps five or six shiploads. In some cases, during these years, ice was shipped all the way to Portugal and even to the Mediterranean, a single cargo reaching Algeria in 1839.

In the spring of 1846, after another mild winter in Britain, no less than twelve Norwegian ships were reported to have been chartered to carry ice to English ports alone. At this time, ice was also being shipped to Britain from the USA, but from the early 1850s ice exporting from Norway grew steadily, so much so that the trade in ice had become a regular industry by 1870, involving considerable investments in infrastructure, for the most part in south-eastern Norway. Ice was now an important factor in the sweeping transport and logistics revolution that changed the eating and drinking habits of broad sections of the population and led to increased economic integration in northern Europe. Fredrik Wallem, a Norwegian journalist, commented on this process while reporting from the international fishing exhibition in London in 1883: 'for fishmongers, butchers, dairies, breweries, confectioners, hotels, passenger steamships, etc. in most countries it has become necessary to have an even supply of ice […]. In the modern household, ice has become indispensable'.

In the second half of the nineteenth century, Norwegian ice also went to ports in the Mediterranean and the Black Sea. More exceptionally, Norwegian ice was shipped to Iceland, the Faroe Islands and far into the Baltic Sea to Finland and Russia, while in the 1880s a number of cargoes were sent to New York. And we know of individual cases where Norwegian ice was exported to more exotic areas like the Red Sea, Congo, Cuba, Burma and Batavia. However, ships laden with Norwegian ice primarily and most regularly sailed across the North Sea and other nearby waters. When natural ice exporting from Norway developed into a large and well-organised industry after 1850, London and the fishing ports on the east coast of England were the most important and stable markets, with substantial quantities also shipped to North-Western Europe and Scandinavia. The German market for natural ice was especially large, but in most years was mainly supplied by domestic production, with limited need for ice from Norway. Nevertheless, at least one company in the developing German distant water fisheries opted exclusively for the use of Norwegian ice.

From the 1850s, a domestic market for ice also emerged in Norway. Ice was used in the Norwegian fisheries, first to a limited extent in the urban fresh fish markets, then from the 1860s in the export of fresh fish, initially mostly mackerel and salmon, and later herring. By 1860, a nascent market for ice had emerged in other industries, and in private households in Christiania (Oslo) and other cities. But compared to Britain and continental Europe, the domestic market was limited, both for climatic reasons and due to the relatively small population and low levels of urbanisation and industrialisation. Moreover, in spite of a considerable export trade in fish, the Norwegian fisheries were slow to engage extensively in the export of fresh fish.

Overseas markets, especially in Britain, and particularly in London, therefore stimulated the expansion of the Norwegian ice business into a regular and well-organised trade. A central element in this evolution was the growing market for fresh fish in London and the rapidly growing urban industrial centres in the Midlands and north of England from the 1840s. This was facilitated and further spurred by technological changes on land and at sea, with railways opening up new markets, and sail-powered trawlers in the North Sea – and, from the 1880s, steam-powered trawlers in more distant Atlantic waters – greatly improving catches. Amidst these shifts in fishing and fish marketing, the innovative practice of taking ice to the fishing grounds allowed the catch to be put on ice immediately and kept chilled and fresh on the voyage back to the fishing ports, and thence by railway to London and other urban markets. This rendered fresh fish available to broader sections of urban society in Britain, a cheap source of protein sold as fried fish in the streets to working-class people and eventually accompanied by deep-fried potatoes and retailed as fish and chips. In essence, this was a virtuous circle, wherein the development of the British fisheries was a prime mover in the expansion of Norwegian ice imports, which, in turn, enabled trawling vessels to range more widely and return more fresh fish to more extensive markets.

In focusing on this dynamic relationship, Michael Freeman's thorough investigation of the Anglo-Norwegian ice trade, presented in this book, is not only an extremely valuable contribution to the history of the natural ice business in northern and western Europe and 'The Last Ice

Age' project, but also an important contribution to the understanding of the modernisation and expansion of the British fisheries. In thanking Dr Freeman, once more, for his commendable analysis, we would also like to express our gratitude to the publisher, Cappelen Damm Akademisk, for preparing for print and publishing the present book on a combined print-on-demand and open access online basis, thereby allowing it to reach out to a wide readership all over the world.

Per G. Norseng
Principal Investigator, 'The Last Ice Age'

David J. Starkey
Co-Investigator, 'The Last Ice Age' and Co-President, NAFHA

Ingo Heidbrink
Co-Investigator, 'The Last Ice Age' and Co-President, NAFHA

Figure 0.1. Ice loading on the Oslofjord. Photographer unknown. © Oslo Museum.

Preface and Acknowledgements

Research and writing for this study has been spread over more than a decade. However, the main basis of it was done during 2006–08, much assisted by the Governing Body of Mansfield College, University of Oxford, granting me sabbatical leave from my teaching duties for part of the academic year 2006.

Many people have helped me in locating material. Although the study is written in the first instance from a British perspective, I have been able to incorporate a range of evidence from Norwegian sources, including a fine selection of images from the Norsk Folkemuseum and also valuable primary source material from the Wiborg papers at the Berg-Kragerø Museum. In the latter case, I am most grateful to Per Norseng and the late Jean Aase for their generous help. Jean also kindly provided English translation from a part of Christian Høy's memoir. The Wiborg papers include an historical account (written in 1943) of the story of the family's ice-exporting business, together with supporting tables. Norman Meyer, a Norwegian graduate student at Mansfield College, Oxford was invaluable in helping me to translate this material for incorporation into the study.

A highly rewarding episode in later work for this study was when I was invited to attend a conference on Norway's natural ice trade held at the Norsk Sjøfartsmuseum in Oslo in early November 2009. Organised by Per Norseng and Ola Teige, it offered an opportunity to meet with many others with knowledge of the trade and to hear the results of their labours. One day of the conference was spent visiting former ice farming, ice storage and ice export sites outside Oslo. The trip was led by Per Norseng and gave life to my long sequence of historical research. Since then, Per has proved an incredibly interested and helpful international colleague. Without his support and encouragement, the present study would not have reached the point of publication.

Research for this project would not have been possible without the amazing resources of the Bodleian Library in the University of Oxford. In particular, I have benefited from being able to consult the complete run of the monthly *Cold Storage and Ice Trades Review* (beginning April 1898) that is housed in the stack of the University's Radcliffe Science Library. These large weighty volumes afford a fascinating insight into the workings of the ice trade, both natural and artificial. I am most grateful to the library staff for their patience in almost endlessly making this publication available to me and also for dealing with my many requests for photocopying via the 'mediated service' (at a time when readers were not permitted to use their own digital cameras, smartphones or iPads for copying purposes).

Michael Freeman, Ventnor, Isle of Wight, United Kingdom, 2022

CHAPTER 1

Introduction: From Lake to Lemon Squash

Figure 1.1. Illustration from *Harmsworth Magazine* (Bodleian: Per 2705 d.85/7 p. 17).

In its August number of 1901, the *Harmsworth Magazine* suggested to its British readers that, if the heat was oppressive and you were consumed by a fiery thirst, you would do best to go to your ice block and chip off sufficient to fill half a large tumbler. You then squeezed over this the juice of a whole lemon, added a teaspoonful of powdered sugar and, finally, filled the tumbler with soda water and stirred. What you had made was lemon squash. Drunk through a straw, this was reckoned at the time to be one of the most effective of all thirst-quenching beverages. In hot weather, in the 'dog days' of a July or an August, it was as indispensable as claret cup or ice cream.[1]

---

1 'From Lake to Lemon Squash: How Norway Lowers Britain's Temperature', *Harmsworth Magazine* VII (1901), pp. 17–21.

CHAPTER 1

Ten years before, lemon squash had hardly been known as a cooling drink in a British summer. What had transformed its use and popularity was the enormous development of the country's ice import trade. In London, the volume of ice landed grew twice over between 1888 and 1900, reaching some 200,000 tons.[2] The ice came almost exclusively from the lakes and fjords of south and south-west Norway, and the August 1901 issue of the *Harmsworth Magazine* took as its task the tracing of the progress of the crystal-clear ice blocks cut from the frozen lakes above the fjords in winter to the tumbler of lemon squash (see figure 1.2) that you savoured on a hot summer afternoon.

Figure 1.2. Illustration from *Harmsworth Magazine* (Bodleian: Per 2705 d.85/7 p. 21).

In today's age of automatic mechanical refrigeration, it is hard to conceive of an era when the primary means of cooling or freezing was by means of natural ice. Moreover, as an article of consumption, ice became, during the late Victorian period, a necessity of much everyday life. Food distribution, for example, increasingly relied upon it, with leading railway companies of the day constructing specially insulated meat and fish vans to handle the traffic. These vehicles all had carefully arranged ice compartments that were filled with fresh ice on a daily basis.[3] Hotels, clubs and restaurants relied on daily supplies of ice for food preservation, not to mention the use of ice in drinks. Ice cream makers, or confectioners as they were then known, needed substantial quantities of ice for their freezer drums. Hospitals had developed regular uses for ice, as had industries like brewing and fishing. In the household, ice was also growing in its applications. Whereas an

---

2   All of the statistics on the ice trade cited in this chapter are drawn from the monthly journal *Cold Storage and Ice Trades Review*, first issued in April 1898.
3   The *Cold Storage and Ice Trades Review*, in several of its earliest issues in 1898, set out in some detail the measures that railway companies were then taking to provide refrigerated transport: see, for example, I (1898), pp. 15, 25, 37.

ice-cellar or an ice-house had traditionally been the province of the upper classes, by the late nineteenth century, growing numbers of middle-class families were using ice-chests and ice safes, especially during the summer months. When a heatwave struck, even the ordinary man on the street began clamouring for ice. In London and other large cities, sudden hot spells brought fears of ice famine. In mid-June 1900, a heatwave caught the capital completely unawares and perspiring Londoners found to their dismay that iced drinks were not instantly available in hotels and eating-houses. Headlines in some quarters of the daily press speculated that ice might soon run out altogether, but wiser counsel soon prevailed as it became clear that there were extensive stocks in the capital's ice-cellars and ice-wells and it was merely a matter of extracting new supplies. One wag of a journalist went as far as to claim that the ice-clad mountains of Norway from whence ice was obtained could be reached by the District Railway in less than 30 minutes from King's Cross.[4]

Few of us today give a second thought to food preservation. We wander at leisure around supermarket stores lined with ranks of cold cabinets and chest freezers and load our trolleys with several weeks supply of provisions. Once home, our purchases are immediately re-stored in identical machines. There is hardly a home without fridge and freezer. But a hundred years ago, such a routine would have seemed incredible. Of course, many households had a larder or pantry, with stone floor, tiled walls, marble slabs for shelves and carefully sited air vents to minimize ambient air temperatures. The secret of a really effective larder was airflow, preferably from a northerly aspect. The best ventilation was achieved by means of a window fitted not with glass but with fine wire gauze or perforated zinc. When summer came, though, the larder often failed its users. In sultry weather, food quite quickly became tainted. In 1900, *The Book of the Home* described the elaborate measures that were sometimes necessary in the larder. A large pail of water, for example, assisted in reducing the effect of atmospheric heat, while inverted flowerpots placed in soup-plates filled with water and covered with wet cloths sufficiently large to

---

4   See *British Refrigeration and Allied Interests* III (1900), pp. 121–2.

CHAPTER 1

touch the water, formed a means of prolonging the life of butter and lard.[5] A cellar could be used for food storage, of course, for despite its dank reputation, it came into its own in hot weather. However, precautions invariably had to be taken against vermin.

The evident difficulties of food preservation meant that many basic foods were consumed within a day or so of their having been purchased. If you desired to keep such perishables, especially in summer, the ice-chest or ice-box became your saviour. Constructed to all manner of patent designs, the basic principle was that whole or broken ice placed in a special cage or compartment within the box would preserve for several days any item of food placed in it. There had to be a tray to collect the water from any ice that melted, but as long as the ice mass was not allowed to diminish significantly, such contraptions were generally quite effective. Butchers, fishmongers, hotels and restaurants used scaled up versions of these same chests and safes in a similar manner. In America, they were known as ice refrigerators, a term that soon found currency in Britain too. Today, we still employ the same principle in the cool-bags or cool-boxes that we take with us on picnics. A specially lined interior provides the insulation, and the cooling is achieved with sealed ice packs which we take straight from our freezers. Of course, the intention is to keep food fresh for hours rather than days, but the modern practice affords a neat reminder of what was once the primary means of food preservation.

Until the very last decade of the nineteenth century, it was natural ice that formed the mainstay of Britain's ice consumption. Although there was a long history in Britain of collecting ice from ponds, lakes and other water courses, the supply was of indifferent quality and unreliable. Instead, it was the lakes and fjords of south and south-west Norway that were the primary source of natural ice used. However, earlier in the century, a trade had developed in natural ice from America, brought across the Atlantic from Massachusetts, in particular from Lake Wenham. 'Wenham ice', so-called, was as crystal clear as its Norwegian counterpart, and its use spread rapidly. It was desired not just by butchers and fishmongers, for it became an article of necessity on the tables of society.

---

5   H.C. Davidson (ed.), *The Book of the Home* III (London, 1900), pp. 60–1.

Chefs made decorations out of it. Small lumps were placed in beverages. No restaurant or bar seemed complete without its supply of Wenham ice. In the most fashionable establishments, the ice went to make mint juleps and sherry cobblers as Britons quickly caught American ice habits.[6]

The ice trade from Massachusetts had all but vanished by 1870, forced out of existence by the rapidly growing trade from Norway which soon acquired a near monopoly in the British market. However, the technology was steadily becoming available for the production of ice by artificial means and, by 1900, London as well as many provincial centres had acquired ice factories. In the major fishing ports, dockside ice-making plants also sprang up to ensure for the expanding trawler fleets a continuous supply of crushed ice for preserving their fish stocks while at sea. By the 1920s, even small towns had acquired ice factories, especially the seaside resorts with their prodigious demands for ice for making ice cream in the summer tourist season.

Although the peak year of Norway's ice trade with Britain was 1899, when over half a million tons were landed in ports all around the country, the trade remained vigorous right up until the First World War and competed well with the rising volume of artificial ice production, not only on price but on quality and on availability. Over the 10 years from 1898 to 1907, nearly 4 million tons of Norwegian ice came into the country, with London alone accounting for some 1.9 million tons. By 1900, natural ice had become one of Norway's most important exports, involving thousands of people and hundreds of vessels.[7] The continuing attraction of natural ice was most visibly manifest in the way several of the biggest of the London ice manufacturers imported large quantities of Norwegian ice to sell alongside their factory product.

Norwegian ice also had another rather more singular feature in its favour. It brought with it a sense of the exotic, an element of the sublime. For many Victorians, the Arctic and the frozen north had long had an allure. Whereas the ice one gathered from frozen ponds and lakes in an English winter was opaque, often dirty and broken, Norwegian ice came

---

6 See *Illustrated London News* VI (1845), pp. 315–6.
7 P.G. Norseng, 'The "Last Ice Age" in Maritime History: An Introduction', *International Journal of Maritime History* 34, 1 (2022), p. 109.

CHAPTER 1

Figure 1.3. Norwegian vessels loading ice blocks at Drammen, Drammensfjord, March 1906, the ice destined for ports in Britain (Norsk Folkemuseum NF.W 04929).

in giant, shimmering, near translucent cubes. Fishmongers and ice merchants would often display examples in their shop windows. Street shoppers rarely failed to pause and gaze at them. What puzzled most was the way the blocks appeared to show little wastage from one day to the next. And it was the lasting quality of Norwegian ice, as well as its perceived purity ('nature's harvest'), that appeared to guarantee it a healthy market in the decades before 1914. For years, the early producers of artificial ice had had problems making ice that was clear in the manner of the natural product. It was air bubbles trapped in the freezing process that accounted for early factory ice being opaque. The secret was to insert a mechanical agitator, but there was then still the problem of bubbles forming in the core once the agitator had been withdrawn.

With the growth of the Norwegian ice trade to Britain over the final decades of the nineteenth century, lakes and fjords there began taking on the value that was normally attached to mines. British as well as Norwegian companies were found purchasing them much as one would purchase coal or mineral deposits. However, no ice merchant or ice trader claimed to 'mine' ice. Instead, it was 'grown' and then 'harvested'. Ice, in other words, became a resource that was farmed. And the trade soon gathered about it a whole raft of terminology that made it, if at times disconcertingly, seem to be a form of agriculture. The impact on the trade of the vagaries of weather was probably the most critical of these features. The ice harvest fluctuated according to the duration and intensity of winter cold. Equally, consumption of ice varied according to the heat or otherwise of a British summer.

For some commentators and observers, the great blocks of imported Norwegian ice were a reminder of the grand ice palaces that had once been constructed in Russian winters. The eighteenth-century poet, William Cowper, once described the structure erected for the marriage of Prince Gallitzin at St. Petersburg. Fifty-two feet long, sixteen feet wide and twenty feet high, its ice blocks were hewn from the frozen river Neva. The palace walls were sculpted with all manner of ornamentation and the furniture was also fashioned from ice. The entire structure was then defended by six ice cannon which fired hempen shot.[8]

At the start of the 21st century, we are again coming face to face with the translucent ice blocks that once went to make such palaces and which, at one time, were carried across the North Sea to Britain. For today, from the River Torne in arctic Sweden, ice is harvested annually to create an ice hotel there, not unlike the ice palace on the Neva. Even the hotel beds are made out of ice, the ultimate in 'cool' living. In parallel, London and a number of other world cities now boast ice-bars, created from the very same Swedish ice blocks. The air temperature is kept at minus five degrees centigrade. Clientèle dress in thermal ponchos and mittens. They drink vodka from glasses carved from the same ice that comprises the walls. The bar, too, is made from ice, its surface smoothed from time to time with a hot iron, while glassy ice sculptures decorate the surroundings.

If you were to roll the historical film back a century or so, the task of gathering stored Norwegian ice from a London ice well or ice cellar would not have felt or looked so different: sub-zero temperatures, ice-blocks stacked one upon another glistening in the lamplight. Or you

---

8   See *Chambers's Journal* VII (1847), p. 261.

CHAPTER 1

might have been a Norwegian sailor in early spring on board a sailing barque carrying ice from Norway to an English port on the east coast. A five-day passage over the North Sea was challenging in itself at this time of year, but not when the hold was packed with 300 tons of block ice. Every part of the ship would have been like an ice-house, whatever the air temperature outside. And if the pumps were not worked regularly, the ice blocks lying nearest the bottom of the ship's hold would melt from their base and be liable to shift in rough seas. Thus an ice-laden vessel was potentially a 'coffin ship', and the wreck lists in the maritime press often told their own sad story.

Remarkably little has been published on the shipment of natural ice from Norway into Britain. Four studies deserve particular mention. The first is Felicity Kinross's intriguing work (1991) telling the story of Carlo Gatti, a Swiss Italian emigrant who came to London in 1840 and set up an ice cream and confectionery parlour. In due course, he became a leading importer of Norwegian block ice, via the Regent's Park Canal. Kinross's book, although titled *Coffee and Ices*, actually offers a wonderful vignette of the ice trade between Norway and Britain as viewed through the lens of one company. The second study forms an MSc dissertation undertaken at the London School of Economics and published as a working paper of the Department of Economic History there in 2006. It is by Bodil Blain and offers a fascinating perspective on the rise and decline of the Anglo-Norwegian ice trade under the broad explanatory concept of 'melting markets'. The study conforms to what is traditionally expected of a Master's dissertation, in that it follows a generally prescribed academic structure. However, it includes valuable statistical series and affords a highly succinct appreciation of the underlying elements and overall dynamics of the trade. The third and fourth studies are both by R.G. David and address the place of Norwegian ice imports in the economy of the North of England from 1840 to 1914, and, more broadly, the demise of Anglo-Norwegian ice imports in the early twentieth century. The work of all three authors is detailed in the bibliography.

By contrast, there is rather more in print on what one may call the 'supply' side of the trade in ice from Norway to Britain, in other words the harvest of Norwegian lake and fjord ice and its export out of Norwegian ports. This gathered momentum with the launching of Per Norseng's 'Natural Ice Project': *The Last Ice Age: The Trade in Natural Ice as an Agent of Modernisation and Integration in the Nineteenth and Early Twentieth Century* under the auspices of the Norwegian Maritime Museum (Norsk Sjøfartsmuseum) and the University of South-Eastern Norway around 2009. Some of the collected results of this work have appeared in an issue of the *International Journal of Maritime History* 34, I (2022).

The primary source for the present study has been a British trade journal, the *Cold Storage and Ice Trades Review*, which first appeared in April 1898. Original records of the Norwegian ice trade are relatively few in Britain, but the pages of this particular voluminous monthly publication, printed in large format on glossy paper, fully illustrated, more than compensate, for they afford a penetrating narrative and extensive overview of the trade from among the many individuals and companies who engaged in it.

Figure 1.4. Masthead of the journal *Cold Storage and Ice Trades Review* (Bodleian: Per 193998 d.1/III p. 337).

Month by month from April 1898, the reader is transported back into a virtual world, the pages of each issue opening a window on just about every aspect of the natural ice trade from Norway, as well as the competitive rise of artificial ice production in Britain. There are 'natural ice notes' almost every month, sent in by correspondents, reporting on conditions in the trade across Norway. In parallel, British consular officials in Norway would submit regular updates on winter ice crops in their respective domains. Come early spring, the journal contained near continuous accounts of the progress made by ice shippers in meeting their advance contracts. London receiving merchants would be constantly on the lookout for signs of warm weather, for all in the trade remained on tenterhooks as to whether they had sufficient stocks of ice in store and had made sufficient advance orders to meet a prolonged heatwave. The truth was that fortunes could be lost or made in what was a disturbingly volatile market. Indeed, so anxious was the desire for information in real time that the *Cold Storage and Ice Trades Review* found itself with a competitor journal by the start of 1899. This was the short-lived *British Refrigeration and Allied Interests*, another monthly publication that seemed almost to trace the same ground, except that its editor, Cecil Lightfoot, was very firmly in the ice factory lobby, his name later associated with Lightfoot Refrigeration.[9]

In the meantime, the *Cold Storage and Ice Trades Review* published detailed statistics, monthly and annually, on the volume and value of Norwegian ice imports into Britain. There were correspondents in cities and towns across Britain updating the journal's editorial team on conditions of demand and supply in the local ice trade, whether it was over Norwegian imports or the artificial ice produced by local factories. A running tally seems to have been kept on new patent applications affecting technical improvements in artificial ice manufacture and refrigeration. There were also regular shipping reports and all manner of other 'market memoranda'. Leader columns would offer assessments of the future direction of the trade, and in cases where government or local authorities (the local state) had instituted inquiries bearing upon the ice trades, the results would be laid out in some detail in the journal. Equally, where notable court cases had been brought by participants in the trade, these would be rehearsed in the journal. When bound into 12-month volumes, the *Cold Storage and Ice Trades Review* frequently ran to over 400 pages, and the quality of its production may partially be explained by the fact that it had a world-wide sale, evidenced in it being available on subscription at just five shillings per annum, post-free.

In Norway, there are far more surviving business records that touch on the ice trade into Britain, for example the extensive papers of the Wiborg

---

9   By the 1920s, this company had become an international supplier of refrigeration plants, alongside its many installations across Britain: see *Cold Storage and Ice Trades Review* XXVI (1923), p. xxvi.

family which operated a large and highly profitable ice-export business from Kragerø in the south-east of the country.[10] There is also a fine collection of glass plate images depicting many aspects of the ice trade at the Norsk Folkemuseum in Oslo, many of which are accessible online. Both sources have been fully utilised in the present study.

Another critical body of evidence for the present study has come from London's *Times* newspaper, especially now that it is available in electronic archive form. Whereas once one spent days and weeks poring over its newsprint or endeavouring to read indifferent microfilm copies, *The Times Digital Archive* affords the most instantaneous of search facilities. It proved vital, for example, in tracing some of the calamities that befell ice-laden ships on their journey across the North Sea and up the Thames estuary, or others that were in passage to more northerly English, Scottish and Welsh ports.

Beyond the three sets of sources set out above, the study draws on a wide variety of other nineteenth-century printed literature, as well as more recently published material. Full details are given in the bibliography.

The organisation of the book features an introduction, followed by chapters that explore different dimensions of the ice trade. Chapter 2 takes the reader back one hundred or more years to a typical sea passage from the port of London across the North Sea to Oslo fjord and the port of Oslo, the passage taken by countless ships that traded ice, either direct from London to Oslo, or else via some of Britain's east coast ports where they would have loaded coal or coke as a return traffic. From early spring, these vessels, laden with fresh lake or fjord ice, would then have made passage back across the North Sea to face the difficult task of navigating the wide open Thames estuary and the sinuous course of the river to reach London itself. Chapter 3 focuses on the Norwegian ice farms, the source of the high quality, translucent block ice that was demanded by ice merchants in Britain. Ice farming generated a whole support system of

---

10 An idea of the range of possible Norwegian sources can be gleaned from E. Bagle, 'Ice from "Nature's Factory"', *International Journal of Maritime History* 34, 1 (2022), pp. 123–32. Bagle offers three different perspectives, one centering on the large Wiborg business enterprise around Kragerø, another on the Dahll brothers' venture, the brothers being among the pioneer ice farmers in the 1850s and 1860s at Røyken in the Oslo fjord, and, finally, a ship captain, farmer and ice exporter (Thorvald Baarsrud) whose business centred on his own property in the inner Oslofjord.

ice stores and wooden trunkways for transporting ice blocks down to the fjord sides, along with an elaborate labour force that was often diverted from fishing and forestry. Chapter 4 explores the ships that plied ice over the North Sea, the mix of sail and steam power, and the men who crewed them. Chapter 5 then examines the rise of the Ice Factory in Britain, with the production of artificial ice becoming steadily more technologically efficient, though never quite achieving the purity that high quality Norwegian block ice typically demonstrated. Chapters 6 and 7 deal with the consumption of ice in Britain, including the rapid rise of the ice cream trade that helped sustain Norwegian ice imports. Finally, Chapter 8 traces the slow decline of Norwegian ice imports during and following the First World War. A series of uncharacteristically mild winters in Norway in the 1920s and similarly cool summers in Britain acted to reinforce that decline.

CHAPTER 2

A Tale of Two Ports

Figure 2.1. Oslo (Kristiania) viewed from Ekeberg, winter 1908, the surface of much of the fjordhead frozen over (Norsk Folkemuseum NF.W 08092).

The Oslo fjord is about seventy miles long and at its head, at the foot of pinewood hills, lies the city and port of Oslo, Norway's capital. Before 1925, and therefore at the time that this book is set, it was known as Kristiania, at the head of Kristianiafjorden. At a latitude of almost sixty degrees north, Oslo lines up with the southernmost point of Britain's

Shetland Islands. Its summers are relatively short and its winters long. On account of its position at the end of the Skagerrak (the sound separating Norway from Denmark), Oslo is also colder in winter than many other fjords. One hundred years ago, moreover, navigation at its head was typically restricted by ice for three or four months, a feature that is much less usual today. In December, though, a sunless sky still often hangs over the country around, as it did a century back. If the atmosphere is clear, the moon takes the place of the sun, the aurora borealis sending streams of light towards the heavens. Visitors from one hundred years back saw nature here as in a deep sleep, with some rivers and streams falling silent, lakes freezing over, and giant icicles appearing on mountainsides and ravines. Pine trees would droop under a heavy mantle of snow, and thick fogs creep across fjord heads. Come summer, however, the contrast with winter could not have been more stark. In Oslo the summer sun dips below the horizon at night for a very short time, and twilight takes the place of the normal darkness of night. Gardens soon erupted in flower, fields were cultivated, fjord sides were clad in the vegetation of spring, and tourists started to arrive to take in the sunshine and the grand scenery.[11] The fjords of Norway, both the Oslo fjord and the fjords the length of Norway's western coast, were as popular among late nineteenth-century visitors as they are today.

Making sea passage from London to Oslo

From the port of London, it is a 650-mile sea passage to Oslo (then Kristiania). By sail, at the end of the nineteenth century, this meant a four or five-day voyage, varying according to the state of the sea or the direction of the winds. By steamship, it was then two to three days, but the hazards were not necessarily any the less. Having dropped down with the tide to the outer Thames estuary, boats made a north-easterly passage, past the treacherous, wreck-strewn Gunfleet Sands and the Suffolk coast, before striking out over the North Sea off Lowestoft or Flamborough, or

---

[11] For a contemporary description of the situation of Kristiania and its fjord, see P. B. Du Chaillu, *The Land of the Midnight Sun: Summer and Winter Journeys through Sweden, Norway, Lapland and Northern Finland* I (New York, 1882), pp. 297ff.

else off one of the north-east ports. Even in summer, Atlantic winds can penetrate to the North Sea and the Skagerrak and make for a heavy crossing as great swells build from the west and sharp squalls send spray flying from the crests of waves.

In autumn and winter, the south coast of Norway, too, can be stormy, with unpredictable currents that set towards the coast, the shores rocky and desolate, perpetual prey to roaring breakers.[12] The sea appears never to rest here, for this is where the shallow North Sea gives way to much deeper water and where the tides of the Skagerrak and the North Sea meet. This generates an almost perpetual swell which, when aided by strong winds, makes for heavy seas, forcing many smaller vessels to run for shelter. One British Admiralty pilot describes navigation off this coast as difficult, requiring 'great caution and promptitude'.[13] A century ago, ships' pilots, including those aboard steamships, often had to cut engines in hostile sea and weather to clear their bearings. In 1871, an article for prospective tourists in the London *Times* described any voyage to Norway as a matter requiring serious thought. You were tempting a 'proverbially stormy sea', liable even in early summer to sink ships. There were tales of overladen North Sea steamers having gone down in winter gales. Few passengers escaped seasickness.[14] One seasoned traveller later recalled a dreary December day near this portion of Norway's south-western coast. He was aboard a steamer bound for Kristiania, and there was a fierce gale blowing from the south-east, with snow, hail and sleet falling in alternate succession. Among the other passengers were a dozen sturdy Norwegian captains going home to spend Christmas. These men knew almost every inch of the barren and rocky shore, yet even they seemed anxious and watchful, listening out for the sound of breakers that would signal too close a proximity to the shore and potential shipwreck.[15]

For the vessels that engaged in the ice trade from Norway to Britain, the return passage across the North Sea back to Kristianiafjorden was

---

12 See the account in W.A. Ross, *A Yacht Voyage to Norway, Denmark and Sweden* I (London, 1848), pp. 3ff.
13 See Hydrographic Dept. of Admiralty, *Norway Pilot* (7th ed., London, 1948), p. 29.
14 See *The Times*, 14th October 1871.
15 Du Chaillu, *op.cit.*, II, p. 2.

quite often made in ballast. But at other times shipowners instructed their captains to call at north-east ports to pick up a return cargo of coal or coke. This made for a longer turn-around, but as the shipping route from London to the south of Norway skirted that part of the British coast anyway, it did not represent a serious diversion.[16] Whether in ballast or in coal, however, the ice ships still faced the same hazards as every other vessel crossing the North Sea. Storms and gales tested the competence of crews as well as the seaworthiness of ships. The special ice steamers that were introduced for some of the traffic in the last decade of the nineteenth century certainly had much better chances in heavy weather, but, as will later become clear, sailing vessels remained prominent in the ice trade right up until 1914.

Having completed passage across the North Sea, the port of Kristiansand eventually affords a welcome refuge to seafarers, its harbour well sheltered from outside sea and gale, and one hundred years ago an easy place for ice ships to shelter and to repair. In clear weather, this first real spectacle of Norway's coast never failed to impress (and nor does it today): peaks capped with snow, piercing an atmosphere of the intensest blue. Leaving Kristiansand, it is still no easy passage along Norway's south-eastern shores. But, a century ago, aided by Norwegian pilot-boats that had a reputation to be able to swim the waves like ducks, the entrance to Kristianiafjorden would soon have appeared to its late nineteenth-century navigators, the tall, tapering lighthouse of Faerder Fyr ready to throw out its welcome beam. The Norwegian sea pilots were then a remarkable body of men. Numbering some 500 in total, they mostly fished or worked in the forest in winter, but in summer joined one of the many pilot stations. Any vessel of more than 30 tons burden was required by Norwegian law to take on a pilot, and as many as 17,000 vessels could be piloted in any one year, the ships engaged in the ice trade affording no exception.[17] With a pilot aboard and once under the lee of the fjord, itself

---

16   This was the case, for example, at Shoreham harbour on the south coast of England where Norwegian ice was regularly imported for supply to ice merchants in the nearby resort of Brighton: see R.G. Martin, 'Ice houses and the commercial ice trade in Brighton', *Sussex Industrial History* 14 (1984–85), pp. 22–3.
17   See M.A. Wyllie, *Norway and its Fjords* (London, 1907), pp. 3–4.

A TALE OF TWO PORTS

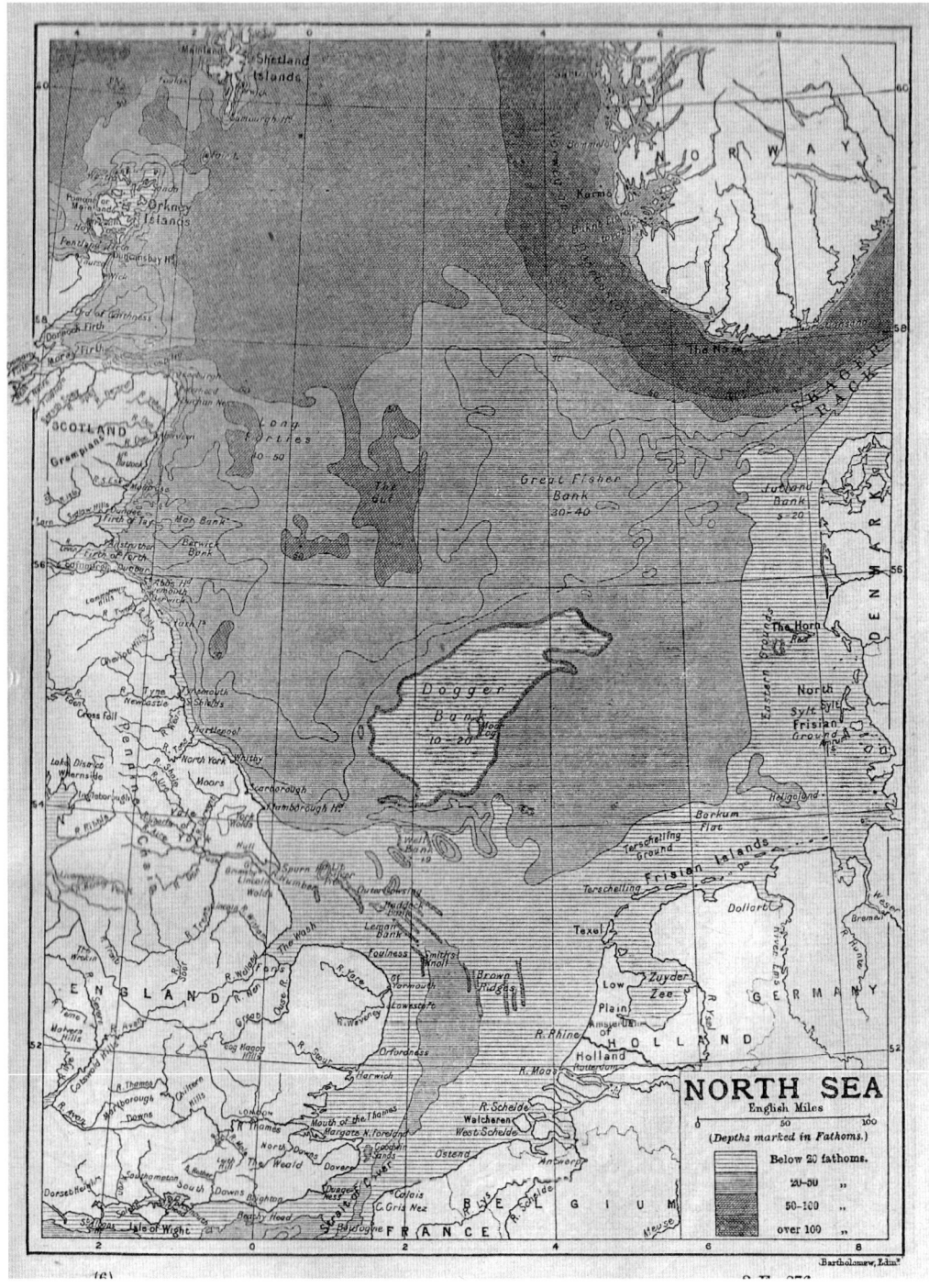

Figure 2.2. A period map that highlights the shallowness of much of this sea area, but also the deep water off the Norwegian coast (*The Harmsworth Encyclopaedia VI*, London, c. 1903).

significantly less deep than many fjords of Norway's western coast, the journey to Kristiania lay northward, past hundreds of rocky, ice-worn islands. On all sides, the sloping shores were (and remain today) covered with thick forests of fir, as far as the eye can see. By the town of Drøbak, where the many inshore pilots lived, the fjord narrows to about a mile broad. Later, though, it expands into an irregular basin and the shores steepen. Then, wind and tide permitting, vessels approached the old harbour of Kristiania, fronted by an array of small islands. Westward, the stark white tower of Oscarshall, the royal summer palace, came to view on the island of Bygdøy, while, in the centre, stood the ancient fortress of Akershus, dominating the foreground promontory. Finally, one saw the elegant late nineteenth-century city stretching out northward, some of its buildings standing on terraces reminiscent of Calton Hill in Edinburgh. One hundred years back, this part of the fjord regularly froze over from the end of December until early spring and all vessels were in danger of becoming imprisoned in the ice. However, ice-breakers subsequently began to maintain a navigation channel, but, alongside them, local men would have been out cutting ice on the otherwise frozen water. For this was then the season of the ice harvest.

Over these winter months, some of the ships that carried the harvested ice blocks to London and other British ports would have lain scattered about the shores and inlets around the fjord head. Many of the sailing vessels, largely an assortment of wooden barques and brigs, would have had their rigging dismantled and some would have been held fast in the ice. A number, though, would already have been taking ice on board, despite being imprisoned in the frozen fjord. For it was as practical to store ice in a ship's hold in winter as it was to carry it to a nearby ice store. There was also the advantage that, as soon as the thaw set in, these ships could make immediate passage to British ports and begin fulfilling spring contracts with ice import merchants there.

Visitors to Kristiania at such times never ceased to be amazed at the hive of animation that the areas around the head of the fjord presented on fine winter days. It was not just the presence of small armies of men out cutting the ice and hauling the giant blocks of ice on to the fjord surface with all their attendant horses and sleds. Equally striking were the bands of ordinary inhabitants walking to and fro across the ice. There were also people skating, and others riding small hand sleighs, propelled along with the aid of special ski sticks.[18] If you ventured further inland, it soon became apparent that lakes were also an important contributor to the ice harvest. In fact, as much ice was probably cut from lakes around Kristianiafjorden as came from the fjord itself, and the

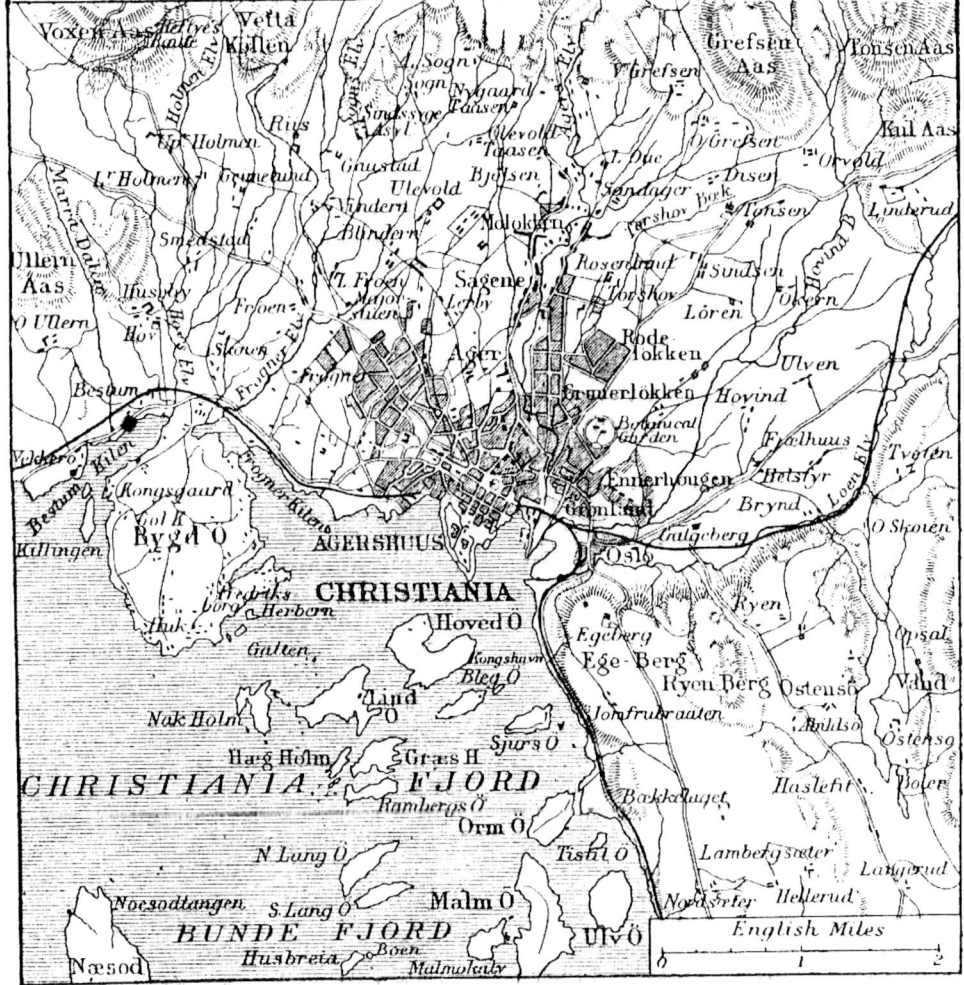

Figure 2.3. Kristiania and the head of Kristianiafjord at the turn of the century, the spelling anglicised in this British map (*The Harmsworth Encyclopaedia VI*, London, c. 1903).

---

18   Du Chaillu, *op. cit.*, II, p. 3.

ice from these lakes had often started to form earlier and was thicker. The difficulty was finding means of conveying it to waiting vessels, but, as will later be seen, Norwegian ice exporters evolved some ingenious solutions for the task.[19]

The earliest time in the year that ships fully laden with ice usually left Norwegian shores to make passage to Britain was at the beginning of March. In the southern part of Kristianiafjorden, some ports and loading places remained almost ice-free in an average winter, and the same was true on the south and south-east coasts of Norway. In such cases, departures might be possible at the end of February, but for areas further inland ice impeded navigation, for sailing ships especially. Moreover, the earlier an ice-ship left Norwegian shores, the more likely it was to meet bad weather. And the nature of ice as a cargo, as will later become plain, made the voyages of all ice ships especially hazardous. *The Times* regularly reported disasters at sea and nearly all those that related to ice ships occurred when they were in passage to British or other European ports laden with ice. In the spring of 1892, for example, the schooner *Telegraph*, en route from Drøbak in Kristianiafjorden to Bristol with an ice cargo, went aground on the Goodwin Sands. Fortunately, lifeboats observed her distress signals, and she was eventually assisted into Dover by a steam tug.[20] Seven years later, in the spring of 1899, the Norwegian schooner *Iduna*, on its way to Newhaven on the south coast of England with an ice cargo, foundered on rocks off Aberdeen. Its crew saved themselves by escaping in boats to reach the Lemon and Owen lightship, where they were later taken off by another vessel and conveyed safely ashore.[21]

The autumn season also brought its share of disaster for ice ships. In early November 1878, the Norwegian brig, *Matilda*, was wrecked with a cargo of ice on the Lincolnshire coast near Donna Nook. She had sailed from Larvik and was destined for Hull to supply the fishing fleet there.

---

19 See, for example, the commentary in A.F. Mockler-Ferryman, *Peeps at Many Lands: Norway* (London, 1909), p. 12.
20 *The Times*, 19th March 1892.
21 *Ibid.*, 28th March 1899.

Happily, all the hands were saved by the local lifeboat.[22] In November 1895, however, the crew of the Norwegian brigantine, *Isbaaden*, was much less fortunate. Bound from Kragerø to Lowestoft with a cargo of ice, again for the fishing trade, the vessel became unmanageable in a severe storm, after having lost most of her sails and spars. She drifted on to the Norfolk shore south-east of Cromer at a point where it was impossible for any rocket apparatus to reach her. As a result, all 10 hands perished, the vessel breaking up rapidly on the beach.[23] The storm trials suffered by some ice ships can often defy imagination. In September 1899, the Norwegian schooner *Marie*, with a cargo of ice, had spent 16 days struggling to make passage across the North Sea, running before fierce gales for nine of them. She was eventually sighted by a British steam trawler and towed into Yarmouth.[24]

Navigating the Thames estuary to the Port of London

As if the perils of the North Sea were not enough for the crews of ice ships, the approach to the estuary of the Thames offered its own peculiar hazards. Compared to the deep water off the coasts of Norway, the sea approach to the port of London could not be more different. Shallow as they are, the North Sea and the English Channel become still shallower in the outer estuary of the Thames. As the tide retreats, there is revealed a vast delta, mile upon mile of mud and sand bisected by an ever-growing array of meandering channels.[25] There are areas of the outer estuary thirty or forty miles from shore that are fully exposed at some states of the tide. They rejoice in names like Barrow, North Shingle, Long Sand and Kentish Knock. In September 1909, the Norwegian brig, *Bein*, with a cargo of ice, was driven in a northwesterly gale on to the Mouse Sands off Foulness. There she sprang a leak, but, with the aid of the ship's pumps,

---

22 *Ibid.*, 11th November 1878.
23 *Ibid.*, 26th November 1895.
24 *Ibid.*, 25th September 1899.
25 Some of the hazards are admirably demonstrated in E.E. Middleton's *The Cruise of the Kate* (2nd ed., London, 1888).

succeeded in sailing five miles further up the estuary, only to capsize in Long Reach, her cargo a total loss but her crew managing to scramble ashore.[26]

At its most seaward, the mouth of the Thames estuary is all of thirty miles wide. To the eye, though, such a measure is meaningless, for there is a perpetual difficulty in distinguishing what is water from what is land. A century ago, the country around the estuary was wide-open and remains so to a large extent today. As Charles Dickens remarks in *Great Expectations*, the river here appears as just one black horizontal line and the marshes just another, if not quite so broad and so black. The estuary is marked by no natural gateway. There are no bluffs or promontories on which ancient fortifications once deterred foreign raiders. Instead, there are merely great flats, desolate marshes as far as the eye can see, unbroken by house or tree, with not a soul to be seen on them. The run up the lower Thames estuary appears like a sail through Fenland. You might even be in Dutch country, as lines of sea walls and sea dykes are all that catch the eye. Almost the whole area is subject to inundation. For much of its lower course, the Thames stands higher than the surrounding country. Some of the dykes or embankments date back more than a thousand years. In a few places they stand as much as fifty feet above low tide. But over the centuries, the river has still periodically burst through, the Barking and Dagenham levels perhaps seeing the worst and most regular of the floodings.[27]

At the close of the nineteenth century, there was no more difficult place in the world for a foreign navigator to find sea passage.[28] Many Norwegian sea captains were old hands at negotiating the outer estuary, but there remained the difficulty that the sandbars and mud banks were constantly shifting. In bad weather, even the most accomplished of seamen could lose their bearings. Although lines of buoys stretched out everywhere across the wide estuary, marking out the so-called 'deeps',

---

26 *The Times*, 11th September 1909.
27 See T. R. Way and W.G. Bell, *The Thames from Chelsea to the Nore* (London, 1907), pp. 90–1; also H. Belloc, *The River of London* (London, 1912).
28 One gets a clear sense of this from a perusal of S.A. Moore, *The Thames Estuary: Its Tides, Channels, Ports and Anchorages* (London, 1894).

Figure 2.4. The wide expanse of the sea approach to the estuary of the lower Thames (Bodleian: 201226 e.3, fold-out map).

CHAPTER 2

they were sometimes so close that it was easy to end up crossing from one marked channel to another and run the risk of going aground. In strong westerly winds, there was no other course than to lay anchor and wait, sometimes for days. Tides presented another hazard. Catch the flood unawares and you could end up marooned in mud or sand. In places, there were double tides to drive you along deeper into the estuary mouth. Eventually, though, you saw signs of civilization. First was the famous Nore light, three miles north-east of Sheerness, marking the Nore sandbank. The light shows fifty feet above high water. But from here it is still forty-seven miles to the port of London. In June 1797 the Nore acquired revolutionary associations when there was mutiny in the fleet anchored there. Its ringleader, Richard Parker, proclaimed the fleet a 'Floating Republic', but his fame was brief. Within the month he had been hanged from the yardarm of his own ship.[29] Beyond the Nore, you are in Sea Reach, where the estuary is two-thirds of a mile across and the navigation channel broad and deep. Here around 1900, in the hours immediately before and after high water, observers would have seen a constant procession of vessels inward and outward bound. They ranged from Atlantic leviathans and tramp steamers to all manner of sailing ships and river barges, ice ships not least of them. This was also a major place of anchor, for what was known as 'lying-off'. On some days whole squadrons of vessels could be seen riding here, lazily swinging round on their anchor chains with the ebb and flow of the tides, as if under orders from some invisible admiral.[30]

London's first land defences made their appearance on the shores above the Nore. At Sheerness, forts and batteries, some of them floating, then guarded the entrance to the Medway and Chatham dockyard beyond.[31] Cruisers and other ships of war could be seen constantly coming and going. Above Sea Reach, as the river makes a ninety degree southward bend, the granite-faced Coalhouse Fort and battery would have come into view to starboard.[32] It was just above here, at Coalhouse Point, that

---

29 C. Dickens, *Dictionary of the Thames, from Oxford to the Nore* (London, 1880).
30 See Way and Bell, *op. cit.*, pp. 102–3.
31 See C. Dickens, *op. cit.*, p. 66.
32 See M. Brown, *Coalhouse Fort Wing battery, East Tilbury, Essex* (London, 2003).

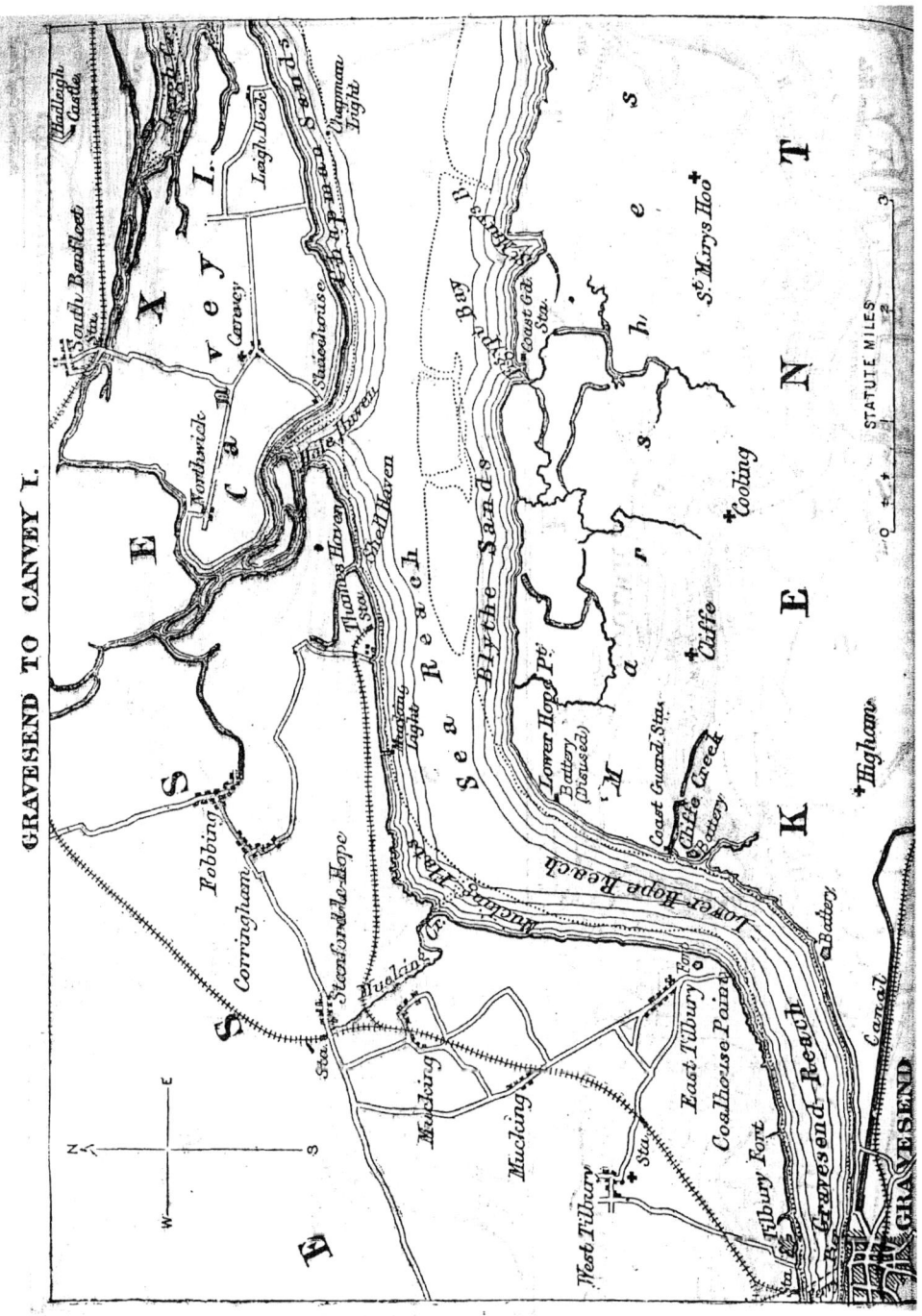

Figure 2.5. The lower reaches of the Thames from a late nineteenth-century map (Bodleian: G.A Eng. Rivers 16' 33 pp. 130-1).

the Norwegian sailing barque, *Crro* [sic], with a cargo of ice, had to be beached in July 1907, having sprung a leak downriver and taken on 11 feet of water in her hold, fatal for any ship that had ice aboard.[33]

Continuing the journey upriver, there were yet more forts and batteries to port, lining the eastern shore: first Cliffe Fort, then Shornehouse Fort.[34] At Coalhouse, heavy guns could be brought to fire downriver, across the river, as well as upriver in the direction of Gravesend. But if this was not enough to deter an enemy ironclad, Cliffe Fort also had a torpedo launcher, designed to target enemy vessels as they slowed to make the turn from Lower Hope into Gravesend Reach. Finally, moored to the riverbed, was a network of mines that could be detonated electrically from Coalhouse and Shornehouse Forts.[35]

Eventually, at Tilbury, Henry VIII's famous fort, with its elaborate earthworks and seventeenth-century water gate, stood as lowly sentinel, built at the point in the river where its width first fell within the range of early cannon shot.[36] It was near here, in the fields of west Tilbury, that Queen Elizabeth reviewed her forces before they left to take on the Spanish Armada.

At Gravesend, the main channel of the river, almost 60 feet deep, makes contact with the land for the first time. Here has long been the first river ferry. It is here, too, that sea pilots were exchanged for river pilots. In 1900, there were around 200 stationed in the town, all engaged in steering vessels through the tide-swept reaches, a facility for which the masters of ice ships were doubly thankful.[37] In April 1910, nevertheless, a pilot still failed to prevent a steamer running down the Norwegian sailing barque *Berean*, anchored with a cargo of ice in Gravesend Reach, waiting on the flood tide. The barque was so damaged that she had to be beached on the north shore below Tilbury, her cargo destined to become a total loss.[38] The town of Gravesend itself rises rapidly from the riverside, and there were then chalk cliffs and wooded hills visible to lend to the view.

---

33 *The Times*, 18th July 1907.
34 See Brown, *op. cit.*
35 Ibid.
36 See P. Pattison, *Tilbury Fort, Essex* (London, 2004).
37 A.J. Philip, *Gravesend, the Watergate of London* (3rd. ed., London, 1906), p. 69.
38 *The Times*, 9th April 1910.

On the north bank, meanwhile, to the west of Tilbury fort, were the new Tilbury Docks, opened in 1886. Built largely as transit docks, with little in the way of warehouse accommodation, they would have appeared as giant rectangular ponds in an otherwise featureless marsh. At their head, a small half-timbered building may have caught the eye, its roof formed from thatch. But this was no remnant of marsh farming. It was the dockworkers' canteen. However, the docks had remained surprisingly empty since their opening in 1886.[39]

From Gravesend, it remains a lengthy passage to the port of London, for this is the Thames in its flood plain and the river meanders crazily, in places turning through as much as 180 degrees.[40] The meanders give rise to depositional shoals, particularly where the river widens its banks. Shoals also form below the mouths of the larger tributary streams and can encroach on the centre of navigation. For sailing vessels, movement on the river is now entirely dependent on wind and tide. In a few places the channel is wide enough for tacking, but when the winds are contrary or when the depth of water is suspect, the tide becomes the key to movement. At low water, there are parts of the river where the available draught reduces to fifteen feet, whereas at London Bridge, for example, there is a twenty-foot rise to high water. In favourable winds, passage is possible from Gravesend to the Pool of London on a single rising tide. But, more often than not, vessels have to make stops on their passage. The flood typically yields only about four hours of flow, but at little more than two miles an hour. The draughts of many of the larger ice ships would have given them little sea room over this long stretch of the Lower Thames. Moreover, by the end of the nineteenth century, sailing space on this portion of the river would have been crowded with lighters and barges. On a clear afternoon, the sun lit up the rich colours of the barge sails: crimson, red, and purply-brown. But in rain or fog, they became hazy shadows, requiring a vigilant look-out.[41]

---

39 J. Pudney, *London's Docks* (London, 1975), p. 105.
40 For a full account of the river above London, see L. Rodwell Jones, *The Geography of London River* (London, 1931).
41 See F. Cowper, *Sailing Tours: The Coasts of Essex and Suffolk* (London, 1892), pp. 11ff.

Soon the Thames' river banks would have started to show signs of more regular settlements.[42] Those at Greenhithe and Erith were built on estuarine bluffs. On clear days, open windows and balconies commanded grand views of the water and of river life. Woolwich had a naval dockyard, while at Greenwich there was Wren's magnificent palace, a river vista to compare with St. Petersburg. At Gallion's Reach, the new Albert Dock, all of three quarters of a mile long, came into view, formed, like its neighbouring Victoria Dock to the east, from the barren Plaistow marshes. Now the banks on both shores were increasingly lined with houses and stores. Tavern bay-windows peered out across the water. All seemed to perch precariously on the river's edge, streets often ending abruptly in water steps or wooden jetties. Behind them lay soaring warehouses and steaming factories. The river's meander bends would now have been honeycombed with shipyards and dock basins of all shapes and sizes. By Rotherhithe, the banks consisted of a continuous mass of brick and stone. Here was the London river of Dickens's *Old Curiosity Shop*: forests of masts, steamships beating the water impatiently with their heavy paddles, long black tiers of colliers, fleets of barges coming lazily on like lumbering fish. There were vessels discharging cargoes, while others spread out their sails to dry. It was the flood tide and the water and all upon it were buoyant, a mass of motion.

For the crews of the ice ships, the port of London was a second home. In spring and autumn, it offered respite from an often arduous passage. The seamen frequented the dockside pubs and bars, exchanging stories of their voyages. By the early 1900s, there were typically 20 or more ice ships from Norway discharging their cargoes in the port of London every 24 hours in the ice import season. One of the largest recorded individual shipments was 910 tons. It was imported in 1899 and was destined for the ice stores of Messrs. Leftwich & Co., the firm that brought the very first cargo of Norwegian ice to Britain in 1822.[43] Sometimes cargoes of over 1,000 tons were landed, although this was not always aboard a single vessel.

---

42 See Rodwell Jones, *op. cit.*
43 *Cold Storage and Ice Trades Review* II (1899), p. 35.

Figure 2.6. The upper pool of the Thames (Bodleian: G.A Eng. rivers 4' 26 plate XI).

The port had no single point of landing for Norwegian ice once the vessels that carried it had completed the circuitous passage upriver. The Regent's Canal Dock at Limehouse was, historically, among the first destinations. At its north-eastern quay, Slaters occupied a long-established site for ice imports. As early as 1893, it was landing more than 25,000 tons annually.[44] Here ice blocks were trans-shipped on to barges for delivery to ice stores and ice wells at various points along the line of the canal, particularly as

---

44   A. Faulkner, *The Regent's Canal: London's hidden waterway* (Burton-on-Trent, 2005), pp. 131–2.

CHAPTER 2

Figure 2.7. The entrance to the Regent's Canal dock at Limehouse. Illustration: J. Pudney, *London's Docks* (London, 1975), p. 47 (Bodleian 247921 d.3090).

it threaded north and west across the capital. Carlo Gatti, who founded what in due course came to be one of the largest ice importing companies, brought his first consignment of Norwegian ice to London via the Regent's Canal, and had ice wells at 12–13, New Wharf Road, alongside the canal's Battlebridge basin just north-east of King's Cross station.[45] The man that founded the Norway ice trade into London, William Leftwich, had large ice wells by the canal at Camden.[46] The Great Cumberland market also drew its supplies from the Regent's Canal, via the Cumberland Market Basin, where it boasted a huge underground ice store with a capacity of 1500 tons.[47]

The Thames at Limehouse aside, the famous Wenham Lake Ice Company had an ice store further upriver at St. Katherine's Dock just below Tower Bridge, while Slaters, who by 1900 claimed to be the largest ice merchant in England, had established further depots in the London Docks at Shadwell as well as much further upriver at Battersea.[48] The last site would not have been accessible by the vessels that brought the ice from Norway's lakes and fjords. The ice would have had to be trans-shipped to river barges at Shadwell or at the Regent's Canal Dock.

45 F. Kinross, *Coffee and Ices: The story of Carlo Gatti in London* (Sudbury, 1991), pp. 26–7.
46 See *Cold Storage and Ice Trades Review* II (1899), p. 36.
47 S.P. Beamon and S. Roaf, *The Ice-Houses of Britain* (London, 1990), p. 52.
48 See the company advertisement in *Cold Storage and Ice Trades Review* III (1900), p. 182.

Figure 2.8. Full-page advertisement for the North Pole Ice Company's Norwegian ice imports (Bodleian: Per. 193998 d.1/IX p. 97).

The early years of the twentieth century saw Slaters face serious competition from the newly formed North Pole Ice Company which both manufactured ice and imported it.[49] The new company had a Thames jetty on the Greenwich Marshes on the south side of the river. It was linked by tramway to their ice factory in Blackwall Lane nearby. The jetty was for some time the loading place for its manufactured ice, for distribution by barge to places upriver. At the same time, though, it was also an easy point of landing for imported block ice from Norway, given the natural depth to the river at the seaward end of Blackwall Reach. However, the company also had an ice depot in Great Tower Street, close to the Tower of London. From here they advertised natural block ice delivered twice daily.

Another destination for imported ice by the turn of the century was the Surrey Commercial Docks, formed within one of the tight south bends of the river. They handled up to about 25,000 tons annually.[50]

---

49   For a detailed profile of the company, see *Cold Storage and Ice Trades Review* IV (1902), p. 314.
50   *Ibid.*, VI (1903), p. 233.

CHAPTER 2

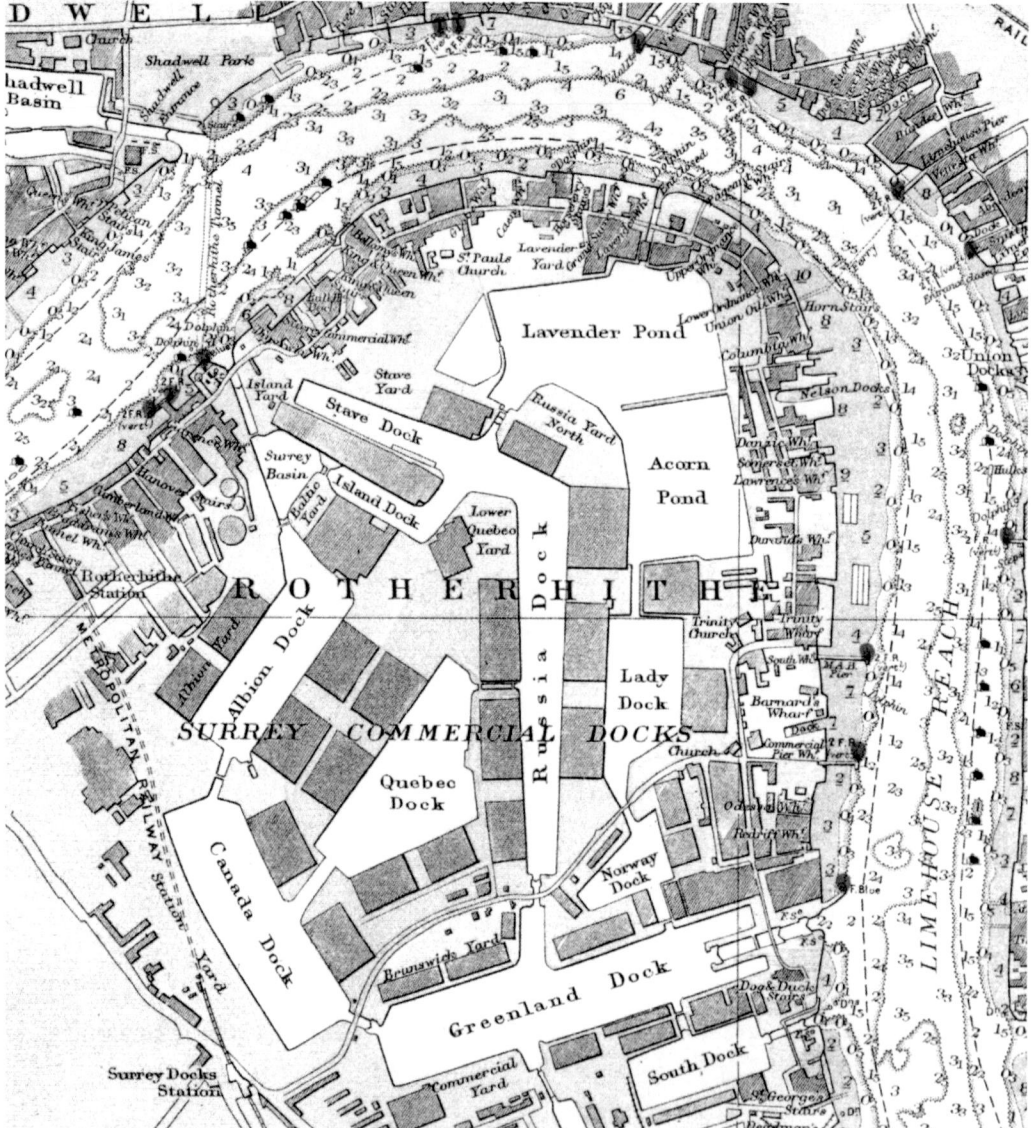

Figure 2.9. London's Surrey Docks, formed within a tight south bend of the Thames. Limehouse and the Regent's Canal Dock are just off the map due north, and the Shadwell Basin is plainly visible north-west (Admiralty Chart no. 3337, 1903 – Creative Commons CC0 License).

There was even a Norway Dock, although it is not necessarily the case that Norwegian ice was actually landed there. Of course, some Norwegian ice was not off-loaded at docks at all. It was transferred direct to river barges anchored in the stream. Such practices were common with quite a range of coasting and foreign traffics, although it made for serious congestion at times, particularly within the Pool of London just below Tower Bridge. It was generally reckoned that there was more wastage of ice with transhipment of this sort. Indeed, in a court case of 1912 involving ice transferred to Thames lighters from the North Pole Ice Company's Blackwall factory, the cargo in question was claimed to have decreased from 44 to 28 tons through the bargeman failing to pump waste water from the lighters regularly.[51] This was an infinitely heavier rate of loss than normally occurred on passage over the North Sea.

Several of the individuals who started up London's trade in Norwegian ice in early to mid-century went on to amass substantial fortunes. Carlo Gatti was one of them.[52] He had arrived in England in 1847 from Ticino in Switzerland and, like so many Italian-speaking Ticinese, he ultimately prospered abroad, becoming one of London's most famous restaurateurs. The young Gatti started his career by running a street stall in London, selling coffee, hot chestnuts and a confection rather like a sugared waffle. Within a couple of years, though, Gatti had joined in business with a Swiss-Italian *chocolatier* and together they set up a café-restaurant in Holborn Hill. It was here, sometime around 1850, that Carlo Gatti began making ices for his customers. By 1851 he had opened premises as a pastry cook in the Great Hall of Hungerford Market off the Strand and this was where he soon established his legendary Refreshment Hall, a real continental-style café, and eventual venue for the launch of the famous 'penny ice'. At first, Gatti obtained the ice for the freezing mixture for making his ice creams from local ponds, lakes and canals. But finding limits to the quantities he could obtain, especially after mild winters, he set upon importing ice from Norway. Among the earliest cargoes was a 400-ton shipment from Kragerø in the spring of 1857. By this time, Gatti was already styling himself as an ice merchant and had acquired a selection of wells and cellars for storing the article. Within a few years he had become the capital's largest ice trader, his employees delivering supplies around central London in a fleet of carts and wagons. He died in 1878, but

---

51 *Ibid.*, XV (1912), p. 304.
52 See Kinross, *op. cit.*

his company lived on, becoming part of a giant ice-importing combine for London in 1901.

Carlo Gatti had a major rival as an ice merchant in the Leftwich family, whose company operated from London's Little Albany Street. William Leftwich, the founder member, had, as we have seen, pioneered the import of Norwegian ice to Britain. Chartering a sailing ship called *The Spring*, he accompanied it to a location north of Trondheim and there loaded 300 tons of ice. The ship left Yarmouth for Norway on March 17th 1822 but it was not until May 8th that she arrived back in London. The explanation for the extraordinary duration of the voyage was that she had faced an exceptionally stormy passage and had suffered a leak that necessitated the crew manning the pumps in fear of the vessel being completely overwhelmed. Even on arrival in the Thames, she still had four feet of water in the hold. She was also held up by British customs officials who could not at first decide what duty was payable on such an unusual cargo.[53]

William Leftwich was descended from an old Cheshire family that was able to trace its line of descent back to feudal times. He began business as a wholesale confectioner in London's Fleet Street and in Kingston.[54] He would thus have made ice cream in summer seasons and would have needed large quantities of ice for the purpose, just like Carlo Gatti. Importing ice from Norway was a logical step and when the first cargo was eventually landed, there was no shortage of confectioners as well as fishmongers ready to purchase it. Leftwich's profits from the carriage of ice were initially small and it was ten years before he had any competitors in the trade. Subsequently, though, the firm grew steadily, drawing its custom principally from among families of the upper classes, and from a range of clubs and hotels. By the 1890s, it was regarded as London's premier firm of ice importers, with the *Cold Storage and Ice Trades Review* running a feature article on it in June 1899.[55]

---

53 There is a detailed account in the Wiborg ms: T Wiborg, 1913, Berg-Kragerø Museum, Norway.
54 See E. David, *Harvest of the Cold Months: The Social History of Ice and Ices* (Harmondsworth, 1996), p. 344.
55 *Cold Storage and Ice Trades Review* II (1899), pp. 35–6.

Ports outside London that shared in the ice trade

The ports of Kristiania and London were not the sole axis of Norway's ice exports to Britain, but they assumed primary status at an early point in the growth of the trade in natural ice. As early as 1867, it was noted how large quantities of ice were exported from Kristiania to leading British ports.[56] One London ice company had already taken a lease on an island in the fjord on which there was a small lake from which ice was gathered each winter season.[57] The trade subsequently grew in leaps and bounds and, at its height, in the late 1890s, London alone was receiving from Norway around 200,000 tons each year, accounting for between forty and fifty per cent of the total trade.[58] From Kristiania, ice exports seem to have peaked at around 76,000 tons in 1898 which would account for only about one sixth of all ice exported to Britain from Norway. However, the proportion is much higher if Kristianiafjorden is treated as the point of export. For whilst the Kristiania district was a place where ice was loaded aboard ship and where ice from hosts of small ice farmers was stored, much ice (especially in winter) was loaded directly into vessels at the fjord edge – usually at the point nearest to the lake or fjord area from which it had been cut. There were also other ports in the fjord that participated in the trade. Most prominent was Drøbak, from where ice cut for the Wenham Lake Ice Company was loaded. It came from the nearby Lake Oppegård which the Company had renamed Lake Wenham to maintain the association with imported American ice from Wenham Pond in Massachusetts.

There were branches of Kristianiafjorden where ice was loaded. Drammen, at the head of Drammensfjord, was among them. Here, by the early 1900s, it was a common sight to find steamers moored right alongside the rocky shores taking on cargo that came sliding down wooden chutes from the lakes in the hills around. By this mechanism, blocks of

---

56   J. Bowden, *Norway: Its Peoples, Products and Institutions* (London, 1867), p. 129.
57   Ibid.
58   Details of all Norwegian ice imports into Britain were recorded each month in the *Cold Storage and Ice Trades Review*. The figures were typically summarized at six and twelve-monthly intervals, with commentaries on the state of the trade and its prospects.

CHAPTER 2

Figure 2.10. An ice block on a wooden switch-back railway near Kragerø as it approaches the shoreline, ice workers and ice-steamer awaiting loading (Berg-Kragerø Museum, Creative Commons BY-ND 4.0).

ice could be directed straight into the ships' holds.[59] As will later be seen, the chutes were the terminal points of switchback ice railways. Observers remarked how at first it was almost impossible to make out the nature of the cargo that came down from the hillsides, appearing and re-appearing on its roller-coaster course. It was only when the sun's rays caught a block on its swift course downward that it was revealed as a great lump of ice, now, according to the traveller, turned into a shimmering jewel.

---

59   M.A. Wyllie, *Norway and its Fjords* (London, 1907), p. 7.

Outside of Kristianiafjorden, ice was also despatched to Britain from a number of places on the southern or south-eastern fjords, including Skien, Brevik and Kragerø. But ultimately it was the Kristiania and Drøbak districts that dominated Norwegian ice exports, for here was found ice of the best and most uniform quality, and typically thicker than that from the fjords of the North Sea coast.

In Britain, whilst London was the chief port of entry for Norwegian ice, there were many other ports that shared in the trade. For a while, Grimsby headed that list, in many years unloading as much ice tonnage into its stores as was loaded in a year in Kristiania. Much of it was destined for Grimsby's large fishing industry. The first regular cargoes of Norwegian ice arrived in the port in 1857 aboard the sailing barques *Amphion* and *Lehman*. The 460-ton consignment originated from Drøbak on Kristianiafjorden. There was already a thatched ice-house on the dockside for storage.[60] Hull had a similar but smaller trade, also allied to fishing. Elsewhere, Liverpool and Glasgow were importing some 37,000 tons between them in both 1899 and 1900, in this case connected not with fishing but with general public demand in summer.[61]

By the year 1900, there were in total no less than 49 separate ports of entry for Norwegian block ice, embracing a startlingly wide array of destinations (see Appendix for details of their names and tonnages). Ireland, for instance, took some 23,000 tons in that year, and included small south-west ports like Galway, Limerick, Tralee and Skibbereen. Tralee alone took nearly 4,300 tons, as much as each of the North Sea ports of Hartlepool and Goole.[62] Tralee, though, was twice the sea distance from the Norwegian fjords, as were many of its neighbouring ports. The ice was destined for use in the prosperous fishing then to be had in the Atlantic off south-west Ireland, particularly for mackerel and herring. But the sea freight on the ice would have been prohibitive unless cargoes came by sail rather than steam. This is confirmed by a case in the Liverpool County Court in November 1901. It told of an episode in March of that year when a 604-ton cargo of Norwegian ice aboard the sailing barque *Lorenzo* had

---

60 E. Gillett, *A History of Grimsby* (Oxford, 1970), p. 231.
61 Figures drawn from summary tables in the *Cold Storage and Ice Trades Review*.
62 *Ibid.*, III (1901), pp. 344–5.

been delayed discharging in Berehaven harbour in Bantry Bay. The 482-ton vessel had been chartered by a Liverpool ice merchant from a ship-owner in Arendal on Norway's south-eastern coast. The original plan had been to discharge the ice into a hulk anchored in the harbour, but the depth of water was inadequate for the barque, with its 17-foot draught, to tie up alongside. The reason for the court case was that the shipowner claimed demurrage (storage) costs for the extra time that the cargo had to remain on board the ship.[63]

The wide array of ports of entry for Norwegian ice, with some regularly landing only a few hundred tons a year, reflected the difficulties of transferring ice for any distance inland, especially if there was no inland water communication. Individual consignments of ice were regularly carried by railway wagon, but bulk transfer of Norwegian ice was far less common, largely due to problems of handling, packing and insulation. By the last years of the nineteenth century, therefore, even some of the smallest coastal towns had seen the formation of ice-importing companies, their ice supplies arriving once or twice a year, invariably by sailing ship since it was sail that offered the cheapest freights. Falmouth, in south-west Cornwall, for instance, had an ice company from 1898, even if it continually struggled to pay its way. It had rented a hulk and had invested in crushing apparatus. As it imported only a few hundred tons each year, any delay in the arrival of a cargo could mean the difference between profit and loss. Its managers appear to have taken no pay. In effect, they ran the company largely for public benefit.[64]

Britain was not in fact the only country in Europe to import natural ice from Norway. Denmark, Germany, the Netherlands, Belgium and France at various times all traded in the commodity. In 1901, taking ice exports just from the district of Kristiania, 53,432 tons went to Britain, but a mere 1,324 tons to Germany and 2,354 tons to France.[65] However, the Wiborg papers indicate that Boulogne in France and Ostend in Belgium were some of the most important destinations for ice exported

---

63 See *Cold Storage and Ice Trades Review* IV (1901), p. 234.
64 Ibid., I (1898), p. 9; idem., VII (1904), p. 54.
65 Ibid., V (1902), p. 175.

from Kragerø by around 1910. Germany boasted ice farming of its own and the call for Norwegian imports generally came only after an exceptionally mild winter there when little ice formed on its lakes and water channels. The Weser districts, for example, were producing 150,000 tons a year in the early 1900s.[66] When this ice harvest failed, as it did in 1906 and 1910, that was roughly the volume of ice that was shipped in from Norwegian stores.

---

66 *Ibid.*, IX (1906), p. 49.

CHAPTER 3

Ice Farming

A tale is often told of an enterprising American sea captain who, familiar with the magnificent procession of icebergs that issued into the mid-Atlantic from the Arctic Circle, settled upon the idea of grappling one of them and towing it to harbour where he anticipated a rich reward from dealers and merchants who sold ice. In tugging the shimmering mass into harbour, however, he completely forgot that the submerged portion of the berg was eight times the scale that the berg projected above the waterline. As a result, he failed to get his convoy anywhere near port. Had he been able to do so, the polar seas would have become akin to coal mines, affording a bountiful supply of ice in summer, just as the coalfields provided bountiful fuel in winter.[67]

For Britons, the tale was not necessarily quite the fantasy it at first seemed, for in a very cold winter season, huge ice floes could sometimes be seen on the shores of major river estuaries. In London in February 1895, for instance, when there had been extensive ice formation on the Thames, blocks of ice 20 feet high were visible at low tide near the Surrey Docks, on the river's south side.[68] Indeed, that same month there were so many floating ice masses in the lower Thames estuary off Sheerness that the naval gunnery school there had to suspend sending gun-boats to sea for their regular target practice.[69]

Whether any London ice merchants collected some of this river ice to replenish their ice stores went unrecorded. However, for centuries ice had been regularly gathered from frozen lakes and ponds during winter and stored in special underground chambers. Ice-houses had long been

---

67 See *The Times*, 11th September 1868.
68 *Ibid.*, 15th February 1895.
69 *Ibid.*

familiar structures on country estates, both large and small, and over the years increasing attention had been paid to refinement of their design.[70] In Norfolk in a hard winter, ice was collected in some quantity from the Broads and loaded aboard wherries for use by Lowestoft's fishing fleet.[71] In cities and towns, fishmongers and confectioners had long used 'rough ice' as a mainstay of their trade. It was collected not just from lakes and ponds, but from canal cuts and dock basins, their deadwater channels forming ice much more quickly than rivers ever did. Carlo Gatti, the great London ice merchant, restaurateur and confectioner, for a time leased a section of the Regent's Canal close to his premises for the exclusive right to use the ice that formed there in a hard winter.[72] At Aston in Birmingham, a large nineteenth-century boating pool was a major source of ice in the winter months, when it was gathered and stored in nearby underground chambers.[73] In 1933, when labourers were engaged on the Cockfosters extension of the Piccadilly underground line, they uncovered a series of eighteenth-century ice stores 70 or more feet deep. They had been used by one of the first merchants to supply ice to Billingsgate fish market, the ice obtained from local lakes and canals.[74]

The difficulty with these various sources of ice was that supplies were fitful, dependent, both as to time and quantity, upon the accidental occurrence of severe frost that was prolonged over a number of days. At Deddington Manor in north Oxfordshire in the nineteenth century, the Reverend Coton Risley was always at pains to record in his diary occasions when the severity of the frost enabled the men to fill his ice house. Equally, he recorded winter seasons when no ice was to be had in any quantity and the ice house went unreplenished.[75] In Britain, then, the notion that ice might be farmed was remote. The fickleness of the seasons meant that nothing as regular in its activity as farming could be imagined. In Norway, by contrast, ice was farmed, as was also the case in parts

---

70   See S.P. Beamon and S. Roaf, *The Ice-Houses of Britain* (London, 1990).
71   See R. Maltster, *Lowestoft East Coast Port* (Lavenham, 1982), p. 116.
72   F. Kinross, *Coffee and Ices: The Story of Carlo Gatti in London* (Sudbury, 1991), p. 25.
73   *Cold Storage and Ice Trades Review* VII (1904), p. 314.
74   Ibid., XXXVI (1933), p. 70.
75   Coton Risley, W., *Early Victorian Squarson: The Diaries of William Coton Risley, Vicar of Deddington, Oxfordshire*, 2 vols (Banbury, 2007–12).

Figure 3.1. The satirical magazine *Punch* records the traditional ice harvest: collecting broken ice from a nearby lake or pond (*Punch's Almanac*, XXVIII (Jan–June 1855), January).

of North America. Norway had two harvest seasons in every year: the harvest of ice in winter and the harvest of crops in summer. Of course, there was no ground to cultivate in ice farming, nor any seed to sow. But the startling feature of the Norway ice trade around the close of the nineteenth century was the lexicon of terminology that cast it unambiguously as a species of farming. Norway had its 'ice-fields' and its 'ice-growers'. Ice was 'reaped' just as if it were corn. There were implements known as 'ice-ploughs' and 'ice-hooks'. Out of season farmhands were employed in the trade. What most distinguished the trade as a species of farming, though, was the way those involved in it had an almost constant eye to weather conditions. There was nothing to compare to the anxiety with which the Norwegian ice farmer or ice merchant looked to early frosts or steady cold.

CHAPTER 3

The ice harvest

On the ice farms of southern Norway, the ice harvest normally began sometime in January and continued for the next two or three months, depending on weather conditions.[76] The task started with the farmers and merchants skimming the frozen lakes or fjord creeks in their light one-horse sleighs. Attired in thick furs and long boots to keep out the cold, the tinkling of their sleigh bells carrying far away through the sharp air, they faced the critical decision as to when to begin the ice harvest. The ideal for a good ice season was an early frost to eliminate the latent heat in the lakes and fjord-heads. Thereafter, one needed a steady cold temperature once the initial surface ice had formed. Then, within two months or so, usually by early to mid-January, the ice would be frozen to a depth of between 14 and 24 inches, or sometimes as much as 30 inches in the higher and more remote areas. It was at this stage that fjord heads and lakes that for some time had been deserted became at once scenes of animation. As men and horses crowded the area, their first task was to clear away the covering of snow, achieved either manually or else using a mechanical contraption like a plane. When drawn across the ice, this collected the snow in a large box. They were pulled by horses, and it was often necessary to go back and forth several times to clear away all the snow. Any compacted snow that remained had also to be removed, but this was done manually with broad-bladed hatchets after the ice had been cut. Sometimes such compactions were so great as to treble the costs of cutting and shipping to the outports.

The actual work of cutting the ice began with horses drawing a light plough across the lake or fjord surface. The plough worked to a depth of about twelve inches and ran in parallel lines roughly two feet apart. The same action was then repeated at right angles so that the lake or fjord surface began to take on the appearance of a large chessboard.

---

76 Information on Norwegian ice farming has been drawn largely from the following sources: N. Wiborg, 1943: Wiborg ms., Berg-Kragerø Museum, Norway; 'From Lake to Lemon Squash: How Norway Lowers Britain's Temperature', *Harmsworth Magazine* 7 (1901), pp. 17–21; T. Morton, 'The Harvest of the Ice', *Pearson's Magazine* VIII (1899), pp. 206–10. Morton's article was summarized in *Cold Storage and Ice Trades Review* II (1899), p. 76.

ICE FARMING

Figure 3.2. Ice-ploughing at Kragero, February 1908 (Norsk Folkemuseum NF.W 08544).

Figure 3.3. Ice-cutting near Kristiania, February 1912 (Norsk Folkemuseum NF.W 13882).

59

CHAPTER 3

Men subsequently cut right through the ice using long six-foot handsaws in an upward and downward motion. The sawn ice blocks were then prized away with a crowbar specially designed for the purpose. Finally, an implement known as an ice-hook was used to pull the floating ice blocks on to the surface. The blocks normally measured twenty to twenty-four inches square and weighed several hundredweight. Rope handles were sometimes frozen into the blocks for facility of movement. In some cases, the blocks were conveyed away by horse-drawn sled to be loaded aboard vessels waiting at quaysides or in the channels that steam ice-breakers had made in the fjord. In others, the ice blocks were floated along narrow 'ice canals' especially cut for the purpose and then hauled up slides that extended into the water from the fjord bank or from lake edge. Here the blocks could be transferred to the elaborate wooden ice railways that fed ice direct into ships' holds as they lay at anchor. As we have seen, some of these vessels were themselves held fast in the ice so that their ice cargoes waited until the spring thaw before they could be moved. Ice blocks not immediately required for export were conveyed to special ice stores nearby. Around the turn of the century, the Norway Lake Ice Company of Kristiania had 14 loading places for its large export trade to British ports and an associated storage capacity of 150,000 tons.[77] On the west coast of Norway, the Sogns Iskompagni, on Sognefjord, had an ice-house at Skjolden with a capacity of 30,000 tons, and it was not unusual there to ship 2,000 tons a day during the main ice export season.[78]

Strangers who visited the Norwegian lakes and fjords during the period of the ice harvest invariably came away with impressions that lingered long in memory. It was not just the throng of men and horses and the shouts that accompanied their labours that remained fixed in people's minds. Much more significant were the extraordinary sounds that accompanied their activities. The great six-foot handsaws hissed as they were forced through the ice. The iron ploughs gave out continuous low grating sounds as they were drawn over the frozen surface. But the most startling sounds of all came when the ice cracked or split. Travellers familiar with Mary

---

77 *Cold Storage and Ice Trades Review* I (1898), p. 124.
78 'From Lake to Lemon Squash', *op. cit.*, p. 19.

Shelley's account of the Arctic in her novel *Frankenstein* (1818) may have recalled her description of the apocalyptic sounds that came from the frozen arctic seas as the water rolled and swelled beneath the ice-pack. Much the same sounds reverberated across Norway's fjord heads and lakes as ice blocks not fully separated by handsaws were finally prized apart. The great splitting sounds that accompanied this action made it seem as if the entire surface was breaking up, about to precipitate men and horses into the ice-cold deep.

Visitors were equally fascinated by the miles of ice railways that, for so many of the fjords and lakes, became vital for the success of the ice harvest there. Constructed entirely of timber (always in plentiful supply in Norway), they involved engineering expertise that would not have been out of place on a conventional railway. Properly known as trunkways, some were relatively short affairs, lightly inclined and reliant solely on free gravity to deliver ice blocks to the fjord shore for loading directly aboard ice-ships or for transfer to ice store. Others were longer, steeper and more sinuous affairs that required men to be positioned at intervals along the tracks to check the motion of the ice blocks.

Figure 3.4. One of the elaborate ice railways, or trunkways, taking ice from lake to fjord edge (Berg-Kragerø Museum. Creative Commons BY-ND 4.0).

On the steepest inclines, rope pulleys were attached to 'trains' of ice blocks to steady their motion down to the fjord edge. The track-beds consisted of long timber 'sleepers', fashioned from pine poles. They were laid in longitudinal fashion, three, four or five abreast. To ensure level grading, the sleepers often required elaborate vertical supporting timbers, especially where tracks skirted valley sides. In places, timber trestles carried tracks across valleys. Curved sections of track needed to be carefully banked if ice blocks were not to end up 'derailing'. What surprised so many observers was the speed at which some of the ice blocks moved and how they seemed to remain on the tracks with only the minimum of guidance. The great problem with these ice railways, though, was that they required constant maintenance, especially after harsh winters. The timberwork also needed periodic renewal. Even so, when the British press ran illustrated feature articles on Norwegian ice imports, it was these remarkable ice railways or trunkways that invariably won centre stage, either in the form of photographs or as artists' impressions.[79]

Figure 3.5. A 'train' of ice blocks, controlled by pulley, descending to the fjord shore (Bodleian: Per 2705 d.85/7 p. 18).

The task of loading ice aboard ship was one that occupied days rather than hours. In March 1865, a 225-ton cargo consisting of blocks 10, 12 and 18 inches thick required seven working days for loading aboard the galiot *Phoenix*. The ice was brought by horse and cart from a lake two miles distant.[80] At the same time, a 412-ton cargo took just nine days to be loaded aboard the barque *Achilles*, but the ice in this instance came from a

---

79 See, for example, *Daily Mail*, 20th June 1900.
80 R.W. Stevens, *On the Stowage of Ships and their Cargoes* (7th ed., London, 1894), p. 335.

lake only half a mile away and was slid down by trunkway.[81] The value of such 'ice railways' for the economy of loading is plainly highlighted in this comparison. It almost halved the time taken, the trunkway operating as a sort of continuous conveyor.

Norway's ice farms, as we have observed, were almost exclusively located on either lakes or fjord heads. When Britain's Wenham Lake Ice Company sought to replace its North American ice supplies with cheaper imports from Norway, the proprietors located a lake a few miles from the port of Drøbak, on Kristianiafjorden, that was fed entirely by natural springs. Upon testing, the lake water proved to be exceptionally pure, so the company settled upon purchasing not only the lake itself but the farms surrounding it, thus securing it from any contaminating local drainage.[82] Where it was not lake ice that was farmed, it was areas at the heads of fjords that became primary sources of ice. Small fjord creeks, fed by surface streams, were often artificially dammed by ice farmers to speed up the process of winter ice formation. In Telemark, at the end of the nineteenth century, ice farms or ice fields of this kind littered the heavily indented coastline.[83] These were mostly made by small proprietors who produced grass in summer and ice in winter. Many would engage in the ice trade for a few years and then withdraw from it. This was in sharp contrast to the ice farmers who took their supplies from lakes. These were typically larger business ventures altogether, occasionally syndicates, with the 'ice-growers' taking leases on lakes, or, as in the case of the Wenham Lake Ice Company, purchasing them outright.

Whatever the scale of the business involved in ice production, it was essential that the fjords or lakes being farmed were not too distant from the regular ice-shipping ports. Otherwise the expense of transport became too great. In 1898 and 1899, when ice was unusually thin on the fjords and lakes where it was regularly harvested, it became necessary to take ice from lakes higher inland, involving heavy additional costs of

---

81 *Ibid.*
82 *The Times*, 11th September 1868.
83 See T. Ouren, 'The Norwegian Ice Trade', in D.V. Proctor (ed.) *Ice Carrying Trade at Sea*, proceedings of symposium at National Maritime Museum, September 1979, published as No. 49 of *Maritime Monographs and Reports* (Greenwich, 1981), pp. 31–42.

Figure 3.6. Ice-hooks being used to haul ice blocks to the surface, Christiania, January 1906, with an ice-store in the left distance (Norsk Folkemuseum NF.W 13666).

transport.[84] In such cases, it was vital that there was a fair covering of snow on the hills and in the forests that the drivers of the ice-laden sleds had to traverse. For a largely snowless winter or an early thaw made the costs of overland transport prohibitive. Where ice blocks were to be stored prior to export, they were stacked to a height of 20 feet or more and around them was erected a wooden structure, typically made of pine, with double walls two feet apart, the cavity between them filled with sawdust. Some of these timber structures were little more than large wooden huts, but as Norwegian ice exports grew, they began to take on the appearance of industrial sheds, with huge ice storage capacity. Many were constructed

---

84 *Cold Storage and Ice Trades Review* XI (1908), p. 122.

on or adjacent to principal harbours. Others were erected on fjord shores, where ice could readily be loaded aboard small sailing vessels for transfer to the main loading ports. In Kristianiafjorden, ice stores were found scattered all the way down from the fjord head to the Skagerrak.[85]

Figure 3.7. Ice store in process of construction on a fjord edge (Bodleian Per. 2705 d.69 p. 206).

Mild winters in the lakes and fjords spelt disaster for the trade and for the merchants who engaged in it. The editor of one refrigeration journal acutely observed in 1899 that Norwegian winters, like people nearer home, had an awkward way of upsetting calculations by now and then taking a long day off.[86] In a mild season, moreover, any ice that did form would lack the requisite thickness to ensure the legendary lasting quality of Norwegian block ice. Occasionally Norway experienced little in the way of winter weather at all. January and February 1913, for instance, saw persistently mild south-westerly gales with alternate rains and snows. On many lakes and fjords, ice was half its normal thickness and when the ice harvest was finally started in mid-February, it was soon abandoned in some districts on account of the ice already loosening and melting.[87] In some years, a lengthy cold spell (in which ice formation was plentiful) would be succeeded by a temporary thaw. Then the choice was either to

---

85   See Bowden, *op. cit.*, p. 129.
86   *British Refrigeration and Allied Interests* 1 (1899), p. 14.
87   *Cold Storage and Ice Trades Review* XVI (1913), p. 62.

CHAPTER 3

Figure 3.8. Sailing vessel at anchor in Drammensfjord during the ice harvest, 1905 (Norsk Folkemuseum NF.W 17978).

harvest the ice immediately and accept the deterioration in quality, or to wait and hope for a return to cold weather that might never come. If the decision was taken to harvest, the ice farmer immediately required large numbers of hands for the task and wages could sometimes double. Normal winter conditions, though, could bring their own particular hazards.

Heavy and persistent snow, for instance, could make the ice harvest impossible. Over Christmas 1901, an exceptional winter storm blanketed the whole of southern Norway with over two feet of snow, its weight in places forcing the ice to become submerged.[88] Thick snow was also liable to reduce the rate of ice formation by protecting it from the effects

---

88   *Ibid.*, IV (1901), p. 296.

of atmospheric conditions. Especially severe winter weather, whilst often conducive to an excellent ice crop, could also impede despatch of ice at the ports. In February and March 1900, for instance, so severe was the frost in southern Norway that all loading ports were inaccessible, with the result that shippers were delayed by up to six weeks in the fulfilment of their spring contracts with British buyers.[89]

Figure 3.9. A solitary horse struggles to pull a sled laden with ice blocks across the snow-covered fjord surface (Norsk Folkemuseum – unidentified).

All of these various features made for a highly unpredictable trade in which changing weather conditions played a critical part. This was vividly illustrated in the way the trade's premier journal, the *Cold Storage and Ice Trades Review*, reported them on a month-by-month basis. In September 1900, it was amazed to discover that, so great was public interest in the country's ice supply, that some fifty daily and weekly journals were regularly quoting its details of ice imports from Norway. The same journal even maintained correspondents in Norway. At times their reports carry shades of the pioneer wheat farmers of the American plains or of

---

89   *Ibid.*, III (1900), p. 65.

CHAPTER 3

South Australia. All life, all prosperity seemed to hinge on the weather. The ice crop could fail in a mild winter just as the pioneers' wheat stands could wither in a spring or summer drought. Prospects for a favourable ice crop could be good one month, but then deteriorate rapidly the next. In November 1899, one correspondent recorded in a tone of despondency how no ice at all had by then formed on Norway's lakes and fjords. In March 1904, despair ruled once again, for a spell of mild weather had spoilt most of the remaining ice, and, to make matters even worse, persistent westerly winds had hindered vessels sailing with their cargoes of ice to British ports. Some of the correspondents were British consular officials. Moreover, the consul in Kristiania submitted an annual report on Norway's trade, with the ice export business to Britain always figuring

Figure 3.10. Symmetrical blocks of ice freshly harvested at Drammenfjord in 1905 (Norsk Folkemuseum NF.W 07980).

prominently. He was clear by 1910, though, that the rise of cold storage in Britain, together with the rise of the ice factory there, held a serious threat for the continuance of the Norwegian trade.[90]

After a good harvest, the ice merchant, much like his counterpart in the corn trade, could often gauge the quality of the product just by looking at it. A good season made for hard and clear ice, known as steel or crystal ice. A bad season produced ice that was streaked and murky, the outcome of alternate frosts and thaws and repeated snows. The ice block thus carried the weather's signature within it. One look was sometimes enough to determine its commercial value.

The fickle nature of the demand for Norway's ice blocks

When farmers grew corn, they were reasonably assured of a market for it. Corn is a food staple all over the western world and, save for fluctuations in prices related to the specific conditions of demand and supply in any one harvest season, both the farmer and the merchant in corn could rely on a residual level of consumption for the commodity that each was involved in supplying. Corn as a necessity of life gave a certain security even against the vagaries of weather, crop disease, purchasing power and taxation. For the ice farmer or the ice merchant, however, the residual certainties of the corn trade did not exist. In Britain, there was no public taste for general use of ice. In other words, for eight or nine months of the year there was no demand for it among the ordinary populace. Come hot weather, though, this altered dramatically, as the *Cold Storage and Ice Trades Review* recorded in verse:

> O Iceman! My iceman! Summer at length is here,
> The gladdest, gayest time for you all of the circling year;
> For when beneath a sultry sun the milk is turning sour
> And butter's rank and meat goes bad, then is the Iceman's hour.[91]

Hotels, clubs and eating houses soon pressed ice depots for larger and more regular supplies. A confectioner needed two hundredweight of ice

---

90 *Ibid.*, XIII (1910), pp. 29, 251–2.
91 *Ibid.*, III (1900), p. 101.

daily to make his twenty quarts of ice-cream. The ice was not an ingredient but used in the freezing mixture. In London, in a heat wave, some ice depots were distributing over twenty tons of block ice each day. *The Times*, in September 1868, remarking on the 'late tropical weather', described ice as forming a real power in the community, just as in winter coal became an absolute necessity. In city streets, hawkers sold ice in summer much as they sold coals in winter. The London ice merchant, Slaters, experimented with selling ice in this way in the abnormal heat of July 1900.[92] In some places, ice was also taken round like milk, delivered from door to door. Ice demand was thus critically dependent on the manifold chances and changes of a British summer. In fact, some commentators could conceive of no more uncertain a trade from beginning to end.

When a cool day followed hot, demand could fall on a scale equivalent to a whole 500-ton sea cargo. A heat wave, by the same token, could result in demand outstripping local stocks several times over. After abnormally high temperatures in August and September 1898, some British cities were facing an ice famine.[93] In London, some parts of the press talked of ice fetching £5 per ton, although retailers actually seem to have been paying 40 to 50 shillings a ton. In Liverpool, ice merchants were forced to bring in ice from other Lancashire towns. Much the same pattern prevailed in the months of July and August 1899. At one point, Norway block ice was double the price of coal in London.[94] Within a matter of days, though, once the weather had turned, ice demand could be at a standstill. In 1900, for example, the summer season was grim. In May, so cold was the weather that firms making artificial ice had to stop their machinery so that Norwegian block ice arriving as spring contract cargoes could be found storage space.[95] Then, in the July of 1900, as we have previously seen, there was a heat wave, but it proved short-lived. For a while, there was a scarcity of ice and importers had to telegraph Norwegian ports for prompt steamer cargoes, which in some cases fetched 20 shillings a ton. By the time they had arrived, though,

---

92 *Ibid.*, III (1900), p. 153.
93 *Ibid.*, I (1898), p. 78.
94 *Ibid.*, II (1899), p. 64.
95 *Ibid.*, III (1900), p. 102.

the demand had largely collapsed. Ice merchants then found that they were becoming overstocked, with still more new cargoes arriving for which there was no ready sale. One steamer cargo ended up being sold at auction for 7 shillings per ton.[96] By that year's end, Norway was reputed to have had 70–80,000 tons of ice unsold.[97] Two years later, in 1902, the summer was non-existent and the ice market chronically depressed as an outcome. In London that August, ice sales were almost at a standstill. The weather was like October on some days, and the ice importers wished they could have cancelled some of their contract cargoes.[98] September proved no different. Some London merchants even despatched odd cargoes to France and Belgium at very low prices.[99]

Fishmongers all across the country demonstrated a more regular need for ice than did consumers at large, helping to explain why so many became involved in the general public sale of ice on the high street, whether in or out of season. On this account, many also styled themselves as ice merchants. The fishing industry itself was a large, regular user of ice for preservation of its catches, especially at leading fishing ports like Lowestoft, Grimsby, Hull and Aberdeen. However, even here there were significant fluctuations in demand. In summer months, inevitably, fish spoil more readily if there is an insufficiency of ice. Thus demand was typically lower in the months from December to February and higher over June to August. But, supplementary to this, demand also fluctuated from day to day. At Grimsby, over the month of August 1906, for instance, it varied between around 180 and 400 tons.[100] Changing weather conditions were part of the explanation, but so were the vagaries of fish shoals, eluding the fleets one day, filling nets to overflowing the next. At all events, ice stocks needed to be sufficiently large to be able to cope with daily or weekly peaks. This meant very extensive stores and a very careful laying in of ice stocks in spring and early summer.

---

96   *Ibid.*, III (1900), p. 205.
97   *Ibid.*, IV (1901), p. 136.
98   *Ibid.*, V (1902), p. 175.
99   *Ibid.* V (1902), p. 208.
100 *Ibid.*, X (1907), pp. 125–6.

Not surprisingly, the largest fishing ports soon resorted to artificial ice manufacture to help meet the peaks in demand. But this was not necessarily a complete solution, as the artificial product had a shorter lifespan than the best natural ice, and early ice-making plants were subject to a variety of inefficiencies of production. Trade or labour disputes in the fishing industry could also cause havoc to even the best-laid plans for ice supply. In the autumn of 1901, a strike paralysed the Grimsby trade to the extent that only 50 or so boats were regularly going to sea. A single trawler might take between 5 and 25 tons of ice depending on its size and the duration of its trip. For the new ice factories that had just been brought into commission at Grimsby by that time, this strike was a serious setback to profitability.[101]

Figure 3.11. Logo from the journal *British Refrigeration and Allied Interests* which provided its readers with regular monthly reports on the trade (Bodleian: N.193998 c.1/1 p. 14).

The volatility of the market for ice made for a speculator's paradise. Sudden surges in demand afforded opportunities for quick profits. Norwegian ice merchants with plentiful ice in their stores could raise prices with impunity, and, moreover, sit on their stores in the hope of an ice famine in Britain which would bring still higher prices. Shipowners, likewise, could share in the bounty as demand for cargo space temporarily outstripped supply and so higher freight rates could be charged. When, in late July 1900, the ice trade in London surged in a spell of hot weather, demand for prompt cargoes rose considerably. But owing to a scarcity of sail as well as steam tonnage at the time, freight rates from Norway increased by 100 per cent in some cases and many orders were frustrated for want of cargo

---

101 *Ibid.*, IV (1901), p. 195.

space.¹⁰² In Britain, ice merchants still with large stocks in their depots or wells could raise prices to consumers. Ultimately, though, if such a surge in demand was sustained, they themselves could find their profit margins being squeezed as it became necessary to replenish stocks from Norway at grossly inflated prices.

All speculative booms, of course, ultimately burst, and whilst some ice farmers and some ice merchants enjoyed rich rewards, others, especially the later entrants, could end up recording heavy financial losses when demand collapsed almost as rapidly as it had risen. The press had a habit of fuelling such speculative activity. In the summer of 1906, when an exceptional heat wave struck in August and September, it was claimed in some papers that ice consumption in an average 85°F week amounted to £1 million, with London's share as £400,000. Both figures were grossly inflated and prompted the editor of the *Cold Storage and Ice Trades Review* to describe such statements as 'out-heroding Herod'.¹⁰³ A number of papers added to the ferment by remarking how artificially-made ice was invariably inferior to the natural product, thereby encouraging the speculative interest in the Norwegian trade. A more measured assessment came in April 1910 from the Chairman of London's United Company. He argued that a difference of one degree in the average annual temperature made a difference, plus or minus, of 10,000 tons of ice sales in the capital.¹⁰⁴

The roller-coaster nature of investment in the ice trade is evident from occasional sale notices that appeared in the trade columns of London's *Times* newspaper. In March 1880, for instance, it advertised 'Ice Lakes in Norway' for sale. They were styled as being part of 'an establishment in one of the best Kristianiafjorden districts'. The lakes in question reputedly yielded 6,000 tons of ice a year and the concern came complete with five ice houses, along with wharves and every other convenience for landing the ice. The annual ground rent for both lakes and houses was only £20 and the vendor was keen, according to the advert, to dispose of the entire establishment 'cheap to a cash purchaser'. Located near Drøbak,

---

102 *Ibid.*, IX (1906), p. 212.
103 *Ibid.*, IX (1906), p. 261.
104 *Ibid.*, XIII (1910), p. 105.

the business benefited from year-round navigation and no less than three export vessels could load at any one time.[105]

The high volatility of the ice trade meant that investors needed significant cash reserves to ride out the lean years. It was no business for small men, aside from the Norwegian farmers who grew crops in summer and ice in winter. In the case of this particular sale opportunity, any interested parties were invited to apply to the British Consul in Drøbak, suggesting that the vendor was in fact an English ice trader. And it is clear that, as the trade in natural ice grew over the next decades, more and more English investors staked capital in Norwegian ice farming. In 1886, for example, a notice in *The Times* revealed the launch of the Anglo-Norwegian Ice Company Ltd. Its objective was supplying and dealing in natural ice and acquiring an ice business for this purpose in south-east Norway, including leases in perpetuity on various lakes near Kragerø and Kristiansand. The annual rent for a projected total of nine lakes, including lake ice-dams, ice stores, ice-runs, jetties and plants amounted to £130. And the price of purchasing the entire business outright was £12,000, with £9,000 in cash, the rest in fully paid-up shares in the new company. The calculation was that cutting, storing and loading the ice could be done at 1/3d per ton. With freights to England at 6–8/- per ton, the new company anticipated a profit of 10/- per ton given the prevailing dockside price in England of £1 a ton. The potential ice yield from the nine lakes in even a mild winter was reckoned at 200,000 tons, giving a potential profit of £100,000 annually.[106] Here was the ice trade as big business, even if the prospects were plainly being hyped so as to attract investors.

As competition mounted in the Norway trade in the early 1900s, especially from plants making artificial ice in Britain, ice farmers looked to concentrate their business enterprise on creeks and fjords rather than inland lakes. Newly constructed networks of dams facilitated ice formation at these sites and the otherwise quite heavy costs of overland transport were avoided. In due course, this diminished the prominence of the Kristiania district in favour of Skiensfjord where less

---

105 *The Times*, 23rd March 1880.
106 *Ibid.*, 1st December 1886.

ice was drawn from inland areas. Where the trade experienced a run of lean years, there was inevitably less capital to repair and renew ice stores, ice chutes, ice railways and loading piers. Weather conditions sometimes forced the complete renewal of such facilities at intervals of only a few years. Where renewal was not possible, lakes and creeks had to be abandoned.

Norway's ice farms in the eyes of the British public

For all its appeal to the capitalist entrepreneur, public familiarity with ice farming was considerably greater than one might at first have imagined. In part this stemmed from the fact that, in the mid-nineteenth century, there was a history of lake ice being imported from America. And when the eventually famous Wenham Lake Ice Company first began bringing ice cargoes into English ports in the mid-1840s, newspapers and magazines were very quick to report on the nature of the trade, including the manner in which ice was recovered from the frozen lakes. The *Illustrated London News*, for example, gave extensive space to the ice harvest on Wenham Lake in Massachusetts in an issue of May 1845. And that venerable organ of the satirical presses, *Punch*, quickly found in ice importation an excellent source of copy. In early 1846, for instance, it claimed to be mystified by the ice cargoes that were continually arriving from America. There was far too much for making ice-creams and far too much for the ginger-beer that greengrocers kept perpetually on ice for the public to consume in summer. *Punch's* surmise was that there had to be another planned usage. One idea was that it might be substituted for the controversial wooden pavements that had been installed on some London streets. The ice would have all the same slippery qualities, but have many more other desirable attributes. Henry David Thoreau, the famous American essayist and poet, used to watch the ice farmers at work from his home on the edge of Walden Pond in Massachusetts. He described how in the winter of 1846-7 a hundred ice cutters descended upon the pond, 'ploughing, harrowing, rolling, furrowing' the ice. On a good harvest day, they could clear a thousand tons an acre, the ice yield stacked 35 feet tall. Prior to being packed around with hay to reduce wastage, the stacks looked like vast blue forts of Valhalla.[107]

When ice imports from America's Lake Wenham declined a few decades later, to be replaced by imports from Norway, the press again lost no time in apprising readers of the change. In 1868, *The Times* published a long article on the natural ice trade generally, and on the Norway trade in particular. It remarked how Norwegian ice stores sometimes contained ice blocks that were two and occasionally three years old. It seemed absurd, so the article's writer recorded, to 'keep the hand of time' from so perishable an article, but it was nevertheless a fact that much of the table ice supplied in London by local ice merchants was ice that had been 'reaped' in the year 1866 – that is, two years before.[108] As the scale of imports of Norwegian block ice mushroomed in the final decades of the nineteenth century, so accounts of ice farming multiplied. *Longman's Magazine* of February 1884, whilst focusing largely on the story of the ice harvest in the Hudson River in New York State, was unambiguous about the scale of the parallel activity in Norway.[109] And in August 1899, *Pearson's Magazine* treated its readers to a heavily illustrated account of work on the ice-fields of Norway. The piece opened by inviting its readers to contemplate the origin of those glistening lumps of ice that slipped, clinking, to the bottom of glasses in the heat of August days. It urged them to watch the refreshing dew they found on the outside of the glass as the lumps of ice gradually dissolved. What was the history of that ice that had now become such a regular ingredient of summer drinks? It went on to observe how the trade in natural ice, almost exclusively drawn from Norway's lakes and fjords, had been increasing by as much as five per cent per year. Manufactured ice seemed to be having only the slightest effect on the imported variety, for it was still reckoned to be always cheaper to transport natural ice over hundreds of miles than make it on the spot where it was consumed.[110] By June 1900, the nation's ice supply had found its way on to the pages of national newspapers, the story of the Norwegian ice harvest snatching precious columns

---

107   *Cold Storage and Ice Trades Review* XXXIII (1930), p. 260.
108   *The Times*, 11th September 1868.
109   *Longman's Magazine* 3 (1884), pp. 410–17.
110   T. Morton, *op. cit.*

from reportage of the Boer War. Articles came complete with picturesque views of ice-clad lands, the source of much of the nation's ice supply in the 'broiling dog-days'.[111] Even as late as 1909, there were books for children in which the story of ice farming on Norway's lakes was being recounted. *Peeps at Many Lands* reminded readers how the huge blocks of ice that were displayed in fishmongers' shops had come from across the North Sea from Norway's lakes and fjords. Meanwhile, among English tourists there was Murray's famous *Handbook for Travellers* to draw to their attention the way the frozen lakes around Kristianiafjorden were planed, ploughed, sawn and split to keep England supplied with summer ice.[112]

The ultimate testimony, though, to the place that the ice trade by this time occupied in public awareness came from within the nine columns that James Murray devoted to the word *ice* in his great Oxford English Dictionary in 1899. Among so-called 'general combinations', he offered ice barge, ice-basket, ice-crusher, ice-cutter, ice-folk, ice-leveller, ice-market, ice-marker, ice-pick, ice-preserver, ice-scraper, ice-shaver, ice-spade, ice-tongs and ice-tool. Among 'special combinations', he listed ice-box, ice-chest, ice chamber, ice claw, ice-elevator, ice-farm, ice-machine, ice-pail, ice-pit, ice-pitcher, ice-safe and ice-station. Many of these uses had materialized directly in association with the growth of the natural ice trade, both in North America and in Scandinavia. Some usages were less obvious in their meaning than others: ice-station, for instance, had nothing at all to do with a conventional railway; it referred merely to a place where ice was collected for shipment or for storage. Ice-farm, meanwhile, was defined as 'a place where the business of procuring ice for commercial purposes was carried on'. Together with special treatments accorded to combinations like ice-plough, Murray, like so many contemporary commentators, plainly had no doubts at all about the ice trade as forming a species of farming.[113]

---

111 Daily Mail, *op. cit.*
112 *Murray's Handbook: Denmark, Norway and Sweden* (London, 3rd ed., 1871), p. 61.
113 *Cold Storage and Ice Trades Review* II (1899), p. 89.

CHAPTER 4

Ice Ships

> O clear ice! Ice! Ice!
> Crystal cargoes oversea!
> When freights are low, Norwegians know
> How merry iceman be.[114]

Figure 4.1. Loading ice blocks on a steamer at Sønderstøen, on the Nesodden peninsula, Kristianiafjorden, 1907 (Norsk Folkemuseum NF.08958-004).

Britain's ice trade with Norway was conducted largely in Norwegian ships. It could not be anything other than a unidirectional trade and so ship-owners, as has been seen, sometimes looked for return cargoes at

---

114   *Cold Storage and Ice Trades Review* VII (1904), p. 336.

the principal unloading ports, or at ports on Britain's north-east coast where coal or coke were the most obvious return traffics. At Shoreham in Sussex in the early 1900s, a fleet of small steamers was handling the ice trade into the port, most of it destined for the nearby resort of Brighton.[115] The ice came from Kristianiafjorden and some of the ice steamers followed a triangular trading pattern, calling at Newcastle or adjacent ports on the return leg to pick up coal or coke. In such cases, the round voyage from Kristianiafjorden could take two to three weeks. Return traffics were more common in winter than in summer months, for in the 'high' season, the demand for cargo space was usually sufficiently buoyant to make returning in ballast an economic proposition for the shippers.

Christian Høy, as a young Norwegian sailor in the 1890s, has left a memoir of his time on ice ships that plied to Britain from his home port of Langesund on Norway's south-east coast.[116] His father was for a time the English Consul there and had regular dealings with the English captains who arrived in the fjord to load ice blocks for delivery at various ports on Britain's coasts. When the trade had first got fully under way, in the 1870s, the vessels were largely English-owned. Soon after, however, he observed how the trade came to be handled largely in Norwegian ships, though often financed by English merchants. By the 1890s, the trade was an all-year-round one. Høy spent most of his sea time crewing sailing vessels on the Grimsby ice trade, for the port's fishing fleet was then sizeable and very active in winter. The Grimsby ships tended to race each other across the North Sea. Captains were paid £25 per voyage, with a premium if they managed to overhaul another Grimsby-bound ice ship. Discharging took two to two and a half days and then it was out to the mooring buoys to take on ballast for the return voyage. The ballast would be thrown overboard near Larvik and, over the years, hundreds of thousands of tons had been flung out

---

115   R.G. Martin, 'Ice Houses and the Commercial Ice Trade in Brighton', *Sussex Industrial History* 14 (1984–5), pp. 22–3.
116   C. Høy, *Vinden er en lunefull venn. Seilskuteliv* (Oslo, 1972).

there, but without apparently making the waters any shallower. Back in the fjord, loading of ice blocks would begin again. It usually took a day or so to complete. Tugs would then tow the heavily laden vessels out to sea, sometimes with their decks nearly awash.

Høy remarked how the ice export trade was carried on from the coast as far as Porsgrunn and Barkevik in the east and as far as Vindafjorden in the west. This is, of course, aside from the extensive trade from Kristianiafjorden extending north to Kristiania. Ships sailed in all weathers, despite the sometimes fearsome reputation of the North Sea in bad winters, with all its hazardous banks and shallows. The vessels on which Høy crewed were mostly ships that had first-class tackle. Sails were kept in fine repair by the sailmakers at the home ports. Provisioning on the ships was also excellent. He recalled that if there were contrary headwinds when vessels were due to depart Grimsby, the practice was to hug the English coast northward and load coke or coal from one of the north-east ports, seeking the best possible freight rate back to Norway and then hoping for more favourable winds. His worst recollection of bad weather was one year when they were sailing home just after Christmas with a cargo of coal out of Blyth. After a very stormy passage, the ship froze in, towards Skien after a dramatic fall in temperature. Her waterlogged planking slowly froze and developed huge bulges. She needed large-scale repair work afterwards.

For insurers, 'cargo ice' rarely inspired confidence among brokers and the result was that insurance rates became a significant part of the costs of the Norwegian ice trade to Britain. Failure to pump out meltwater properly was perhaps the most critical issue, for this could cause the cargo to move and render a vessel unstable. Ice-ships that were in less than good condition was another potential problem. Then there had to be added the usual hazards of bad weather and high seas, mechanical failure, together with basic failings of seamanship. In October 1900, the 295-ton steamship *Veritas*, based at Drammen in southern Norway and carrying ice from Kragerø for a merchant in Liverpool, burst its port furnace off the Isle of Man. The vessel was towed by another steamer to an anchorage in the Mersey only to be almost immediately run down by the 10,000-ton liner *Devonian*, whereupon it was once more put in tow towards the Cheshire shore, but then broke cables, drifted, struck a steamer anchored in the estuary, then struck part of the Liverpool landing stage, then turned turtle, before finally running aground. As one commentator who reported the incident observed, the *Veritas* had a truly wild career.[117] Earlier, in August 1898, two ice ships had collided at night in calm seas near the Gabbard Light off the east coast of England. One vessel was outbound in ballast, the other inbound with a full cargo of ice blocks. The Norwegian brigantine *Vera* was the in-bound vessel, in passage from Kristiania with ice for Newhaven. It was run down by the Norwegian brig *Pollux*, returning to Norway across the North Sea. The crew of the *Vera* saved themselves by jumping on board the *Pollux* and the damaged brig then limped back into Yarmouth Roads before getting assistance from a tug. The *Vera*, however, was apparently a total loss, including her cargo.[118]

It was almost universally the case that ice was carried aboard wooden ships. They afforded much better insulating properties than iron ones. In the cases where iron-hulled vessels were used, they had to be specially adapted and fitted out, including wooden decks and bulkheads, as well as wooden linings ('ceilings') for the hold. They also had watertight compartments to prevent sinking.[119] In general terms, a ton of ice occupied forty cubic feet of hold space.[120] And the greater the ice mass the greater the lasting quality of the cargo. The wooden vessels, as we have seen, increasingly comprised a mixture of sailing ships and steamers. By the early 1900s, a whole fleet of wooden steamships had come into being, most of them owned by shippers in Bergen and Stavanger, for which the ice trade was their primary traffic.[121] There was little other trade that they could carry against the competition of iron-hulled steamships. Thus the fortunes of this group of shipowners necessarily rose and fell with the ice trade itself.

Some of the shipping companies operated a form of equity-sharing – that is, vessels part-owned by different shippers. The same companies would also hire extra tonnage in busy seasons, especially in a hot summer in Britain or on the European continent. By 1910, about forty per cent of

---

117 See *The Times*, 15th October 1900; 21st May 1901; also *Cold Storage and Ice Trades Review* III (1900), p. 279.
118 *The Times*, 29th August 1898.
119 'N. Wiborg 1943', Wiborg ms., Berg-Kragerø Museum, Norway.
120 See *Cold Storage and Ice Trades Review* I (1898), p. 124.
121 *Ibid.*, VIII (1905), p. 151.

the net registered tonnage in the ice trade was accounted for by wooden steamers.[122] The remaining sixty per cent consisted of a variety of sailing vessels. Many were three-masted barques, the two leading masts square-rigged, the after mast fore-and-aft rigged. But there were also schooners, barquentines, brigs and brigantines involved in the trade. Much of this sail tonnage was in the hands of owners in Kristiania, Arendal and smaller ports on the south-east coast.[123] Christian Høy's memoir very much reflects this pattern. Steam tonnage, as previously indicated, was more the preserve of Bergen and west coast ports, although Kristiania held an important share. At Kragerø, the Wiborg family's ice export business afforded a fairly typical profile of the mix of vessels engaged in ice shipment. Their records indicate that they had five brigs, ten barques, four schooners and one sloop in use at different times over a period of four or five decades. Alongside there were some 18 steamships, together taking an increasing share of the trade from the sailing ships by the turn of the century.[124]

The Ice steamers and the sailing ships that conveyed ice varied in size from around 200–250 to 400–450 net registered tons. To calculate deadweight tonnage (that is, the cargo-lading potential) sailing ships took roughly one and a half times their net registered tonnage, steamers roughly double. So a steamer that was 400 tons on the net register might carry an 800-ton cargo of ice, in other words 800 tons deadweight. Most of the wooden ice-steamers in use by 1910 had deadweight capacities of 600–800 tons.[125]

In an age of steam power at sea, it is logical to ask why, even when deadweight tonnages are considered, roughly half of all the ice trade was being handled by sailing ships. One explanation was the very tight margins within which the trade typically operated, making the cost of freight critical to profitability. The wind was free but coal was not. So sail always had a built-in advantage over steam. And if a cargo was being shipped to an English merchant for placing in his ice-store, the additional time

---

122 Ibid., XIII (1910), p. 252.
123 S. Konow and K. Fischer (eds.), *Norway: Official Publication for the Paris Exhibition* (Kristiania, 1900), p. 433.
124 'Familien Wiborgs skib', Wiborg ms., Berg-Kragerø Museum, Norway.
125 See *Cold Storage and Ice Trades Review* VIII (1905), p. 31; ibid., XIII (1910), p. 251–2.

CHAPTER 4

that a sailing barque took on its voyage across the North Sea was largely immaterial. Another reason for the general prevalence of sail over steam was that there was much sailing capacity still in existence, and much of it underutilized. Indeed, in small ports where there were no ice stores or wells, redundant wooden sailing ships were even anchored in harbour and used for ice storage, as ice hulks.[126] Providing there were no undue delays in trans-shipment from the supply vessel, and providing a suitable drainage layer was put in place in the hold, wooden hulks could provide effective ice stores for many months. Where the ice-steamer came into its own was when ice was required for almost immediate consumption, typically in high summer. At such times, cargoes needed to be shipped in haste. London merchants would telegraph for prompt steamer shipment in the months of June, July and August if their stocks of ice were being seriously depleted in a heatwave, or an 85-degree week, as commentators labelled such weather events. The higher freight costs would obviously be reflected in the retail price, but this was no problem in a rising market.

Figure 4.2. Waterside jetty with ice blocks waiting to be loaded aboard a sailing vessel, Kragerø 1908 (Norsk Folkemuseum WO8556).

---

126 The port of Falmouth, for example, used a hulk for ice storage. See *Cold Storage and Ice Trades Review* I (1898), p. 9.

Notwithstanding the continuing importance of sailing ships in the ice trade generally, by 1914 some ports handled more steam-borne tonnage than they did sail. In 1898, for instance, the Lowestoft Ice Company was importing 18,000 tons of Norwegian ice annually, mainly for packing in the fishing trade, and it was shipped almost exclusively in ice steamers, some 40 or 50 of them, each with a deadweight capacity of about 500 tons.[127] That sailing barques had at one time figured in the Lowestoft trade, though, is plain from late-nineteenth century photographs showing small barques unloading ice at the thatched ice-house in Lowestoft harbour.[128] The most likely reason for the predominance of steamers by 1898 was that the ice demands of the fishing trade were significantly more regular than was true for ice consumption at large. There were certainly seasonal fluctuations in fish stocks, but there was not the major hiatus in demand in the autumn and winter months that characterized public consumption, the times when stores were re-stocked at leisure. It was the relatively sustained ice demands of the fishing industry that prompted Lowestoft to establish artificial ice-making in the late-1890s. In 1897, the Lowestoft and East Coast Manufacturing Company made nearly 6,000 tons of artificial ice, alongside importing 3,000 tons of ice from Norway.[129]

In London, however, the largest ice combine was still using sailing vessels for some of its Norwegian ice imports as late as 1909. For in April of that year, the City of London Court heard an action against United Carlo Gatti, Stevenson and Slaters from the owners of the sailing barque *Nore* for recovery of demurrage on 9,000 tons of ice delivered in a series of spring cargoes.[130] The vessel owners lost the case, but it serves to illustrate how even one of the largest importers of Norwegian block ice was still utilizing sailing tonnage well into the twentieth century. The *Nore*, according to Lloyd's Register, was Swedish-built in 1873, at a net register of 469 tons. With a 15-feet draught, she was larger than most sailing ships engaged in the ice trade, capable of loading nearly 700 tons of ice. It was such

---

127 *Cold Storage and Ice Trades Review* I (1898), p. 124.
128 See R. Maltster, *Lowestoft East Coast Port* (Lavenham, 1982), p. 117.
129 *Cold Storage and Ice Trades Review* I (1899), p. 124.
130 Demurrage refers to unanticipated storage on board the vessel while in dock or harbour. See *Cold Storage and Ice Trades Review* XII (1909), p. 134.

capacity that accounted for her use alongside the smaller ice-steamers, for it afforded significant economy of scale. At the fishing port of Grimsby, too, rather in contrast to the case of Lowestoft, Norwegian ice was still being brought in by sailing vessels as late as 1901.[131] At that time, the fishing trade of the port was largely paralysed owing to a lock-out. Whereas there had typically been 450 fishing boats plying their trade to and from the port, the number fell to 50 during the time of the dispute. The port's ice merchants suffered, and the import of Norwegian ice fell dramatically. In common with Lowestoft, though, Grimsby had already taken steps to supply itself with artificial ice, up to a capacity of 600 tons a day.

Over the three or four decades during which Norwegian ice was being imported into Britain in large quantities, the ice merchants in London and other receiving ports were locked in an almost perpetual contest with ship-owners over the cost of sea freight. In some ways it proved an archetypal arena of capitalist competition, with ship-owners and ice importers at various times seeking power in combination in an endeavour to move prices more in their favour. Where shipping capacity was in plentiful supply, and especially when wooden steamers specially fitted out for ice entered the trade, the importing merchants rather held the upper hand. When capacity was tight, though, particularly when the slow decline in the volume of ice traffic began after 1900, the ship-owners enjoyed more bargaining power as some of their number abandoned ice altogether for other traffics. In the spring of 1905, Bergen and Stavanger owners agreed minimum rates for ice steamers of between 7 shillings and 10/6d per ton.[132]

For the importers, the cost of freight was critical, for it bore heavily on the price of ice on the dockside. In 1899, when spring freights were running at 6/6d-7/0d per ton, and summer freights 8/6d-9/6d (and even more by steamer), the deadweight value of ice was only around 1/9d per ton. This gave an average dockside price (including insurance) of 10/10d.[133] Over the several decades of the expansion of Norwegian ice imports to Britain, the dockside price had fallen from around 18 shillings a ton in

---

131 *Cold Storage and Ice Trades Review* IV (1901), p. 195.
132 Ibid., VIII (1905), p. 151.
133 Ibid., II (1899), p. 90.

1884 to under eleven shillings in 1897, much of the reduction explained by the competitive bargaining by the import merchants.[134]

Another reason for falling freight costs was to be found in the use of spring contract and charter arrangements.[135] Spring contracts were an increasing feature of the London trade and consisted of advance orders for ice made between British and Norwegian ice merchants in the autumn of the preceding

Figure 4.3. Ice-blocks being loaded aboard a steamship at Drammen in March 1906, with a sailing barque and another steamship in the middle distance waiting to load (Norsk Folkemuseum NF.W 04929).

---

134 *Ibid.*
135 *Ibid.*, XI (1908), pp. 122–3.

year. The Norwegian exporters usually made the shipping arrangements and were able to obtain highly competitive prices because they were offering ship-owners successive cargoes over three if not four months. Vessels were thus kept constantly employed with a guaranteed traffic. Charters were agreements between British ice importers and Norwegian ship-owners direct in which cargoes of ice would be brought across the North Sea on a regular, usually weekly, basis. The largest ice importers in London typically had ice in transit in this way for much of the high season. When the Bergen and Stavanger owners fixed minimum freights in 1905, they set no fixed rate for chartering except in the case of new wooden steamers, where the price was set at £200–250 a month, varying according to net registered tonnage.

The movement towards combination among vessel owners was something of an act of desperation as it was by then becoming widely accepted throughout the Norway ice trade that the article was being carried by shippers at near or less than cost. Even so, there were still British ice merchants who saw potential to get ice carried at below the ship-owners' minimum rates. One way that ship-owners could trim their costs further was for ice steamers to tow sailing barques, laden with ice, across the North Sea. In June 1905, this is exactly what happened at Brevik, on Norway's south-eastern coast, when two ice steamers, between them towing three ice-laden sailing vessels, set out for London.[136] Towing was a risky business, especially if bad weather set in on the 600-mile passage. But it clearly altered cost margins very significantly, especially wages of the crews.

At about this time, the London County Council received a report it had commissioned into the use of ice and cold storage in London.[137] The fundamental purpose of the inquiry had been to survey the risks of contamination within the various branches of the trade, but the report that was delivered turned out to provide a much broader survey, encompassing the entire manner and extent of its operation. As part of their fact-finding, the report's authors visited the Thames docks and inspected one of the vessels that carried ice imported from Norway. It was a sailing ship with a cargo

---

136 *Cold Storage and Ice Trades Review* VIII (1905), p. 204.
137 W.H. Hamer, *Ice and Cold Storage in London: report for London County Council* (London, 1904); a detailed summary appeared in *Cold Storage and Ice Trades Review* VIII (1905), pp. 4ff.

capacity of 640 tons, in other words around 420 tons on the net register. It had a crew of nine men, all of whom were housed on deck rather than in the icy hold area. The vessel concerned sometimes took return traffics, notably coke from ports in the north-east of England. When this happened, the hold would be thoroughly washed out before another cargo of ice was loaded. The particular ship in question, so it turned out, had not voyaged across the North Sea under its own power. It was one of the ice-ships that had been brought over under tow. This had cost the owner £1 for towage out of the fjord, £10 for towing across the North Sea, and finally £3 for the Thames pilot. The entire round trip from London to the fjords and back normally occupied 24 days under favourable weather conditions. However, fog, contrary winds and rough seas could extend that time considerably. There were cases of such ships waiting as long as 14 days off Gravesend in the face of strong westerly winds. The vessel inspected by the authors was apparently moored in Regent's Canal Dock, where its cargo of ice blocks was being unloaded either into barges or direct into ice stores on the quayside. Although described as an 'old ship', the vessel was equipped with wind pumps so as to ensure that there was no accumulation of water in the hold.

The unloading of ice blocks at Thames docks was something that the *Harmsworth Monthly Magazine* turned into spectacle in its feature article on the Norwegian ice trade in 1901.[138] Opening of the hatch covers of an ice ship was among the most attractive sights to meet the eye on a sultry summer's day, so the writer claimed. The tightly packed blocks gleamed in the sunlight and the cargo exhaled a refreshing coolness. Almost immediately, the crew set to work to shift the ice into adjacent barges or else into vans or wagons drawn up along the dockside. 'Ice-dogs' in the form of large grappling irons were attached to the ice blocks and lifted out of the hold with the aid of dock cranes. Clambering about on the ice was no task for ordinary dockworkers. The crew of the ice-ship, though, had this down to a fine art, rarely slipping or losing their balance. The average ice block weighed about two hundredweight, but

---

138 'From Lake to Lemon Squash: How Norway Lowers Britain's Temperature', *Harmsworth Magazine* 7 (1901), pp. 17–21.

CHAPTER 4

much depended on the thickness of ice at harvest time. In a good harvest year, it was not at all unusual to see blocks weighing nearly four hundredweight.

The sailors who crewed ice ships on a regular basis had to be a tough breed. Even when their quarters were located on the ship's deck, the passage was inevitably a cold one, and if it was a sailing vessel, the only heat came from the galley fire. The first spring cargoes were the ones that presented crews with the harshest of sailing conditions, though probably none as devastating as the case of the sailing schooner *Presto* which left Brevig on Norway's south-east coast in early February 1907 with a cargo of ice for West Hartlepool.[139] The ship encountered fearful blizzards within a few days of being at sea and her decks and rigging were quickly coated with layers of ice. Weighed down in this manner, the captain found that the vessel was making no headway in the fierce contrary winds and the hapless sailors were being perpetually soaked to the skin by the seas breaking over it. Their clothes soon froze stiff on them and

Figure 4.4. Ice blocks being unloaded from ship to barge in a Thames dock (Bodleian: Per 2705 d.85/7 p. 20).

---

139 *The Times*, 4th March 1907.

they succumbed to frostbite, one seaman suffering the misfortune of being washed overboard, his companions too weak to give him any assistance. After almost a month adrift in the North Sea, with captain and crew fearing for their lives, the stricken vessel was sighted by a Grimsby trawler, which took it in tow. Once ashore, the surviving crew members rallied after receiving medical treatment.

The most difficult passage for ice ships was undoubtedly the one that took vessels to ports on the west coasts of Britain and Ireland. Whilst the sea route from southern Norway round the north of Scotland was a direct one, largely following a constant line of latitude, it involved negotiating some of the stormiest waters of any part of Europe's Atlantic seaboard. In February 1870, the Norwegian brigantine *Henry*, having sailed from Kristiania with a cargo of ice, was wrecked on the Orkneys after becoming waterlogged in a gale. Only three of her crew were saved.[140] A similar fate befell the Norwegian ice steamer *Italia* in December 1913. Bound from Porsgrunn for Glasgow with an ice cargo, the 576-ton wooden steamer got stranded in a gale on the Arnish Reef off the Hebrides, her stern almost submerged. The expectation was that she would become a total wreck in the prevailing wind conditions. However, her crew appear to have survived.[141]

As well as competition between exporting merchants in Norway and importing merchants in Britain, there was also competition among the ice-shippers themselves. As we have seen from Høy's memoir, premiums were to be had for fast passages, especially in the summer season. Thus many captains and their crews engaged in out-running each other in the voyaging across the North Sea, especially to London.[142] The best crews would then celebrate their success in Thames-side ale-houses. In the off-season, some of the sailors spent their time helping to win the ice harvest. They were thus among the men who in the months of January to March were out on lakes and fjords cutting ice. Others found work loading ice directly aboard the ships on which they sailed, or else in moving the ice to water-side ice stores. All of this labour was largely casual

---

140 *Ibid.*, 12th February 1870.
141 *Ibid.*, 18th December 1913.
142 See F. Kinross, *Coffee and Ices: The Story of Carlo Gatti in London* (Sudbury, 1991), p. 30.

CHAPTER 4

work, of course, highly seasonal and dependent on favourable weather conditions. Some sailors found casual winter employment in the timber trade which generally dwarfed the ice trade both in volume and value. However, the ice trade could bring higher wages for sailors if there was a heatwave in Britain. It was not just that ice became at a premium, but shipping capacity as well.

At Kragerø, in the Wiborg family's ice export business, ships' captains were, by 1880, making return journeys with ice cargoes for the east coast port of Lowestoft inside 14 days. One particular vessel, the *Geir*, a wooden brig of 231 registered tons, built in 1867, proved an exceptionally fast ship. Borresen, its captain, served the Wiborg business over many years, taking family members to and fro across the North Sea on an annual basis to arrange new contracts with clients for coming seasons. By the 1890s, when steamships were much more common in the Wiborg fleet, vessels were making the return passage to English ports inside 10 days. The company's green-painted vessels with their yellow funnels, became a common sight in London, Liverpool and other ice-landing ports. The *Embla*, for instance, a wooden ice steamer of 497 registered tons, was built for the trade in 1892 and became one of a dozen or so similar vessels that increasingly dominated the ice trade out of Kragerø. The biggest of these, the *Nico* and the *Vale*, iron-hulled rather than wooden, were built in 1913 and came in at just over 700 tons. By this time, Kragerø's ice exports, largely in the hands of the Wiborgs, were running at 120,000 tons a year – and not just to Britain, but to France, Germany and other countries of the continent. It was said that if you lined all Wiborgs' exported ice blocks end to end they would stretch all the way from Liverpool to New York.[143]

There were a few British-owned sailing vessels engaged in the Norwegian ice trade. At Grimsby in the third quarter of the nineteenth century, they mostly belonged to the Grimsby Ice Company and were crewed by men and boys from the town, perhaps as many as 100 in total in the 1870s. The company, though, had a difficult record of labour relations. By 1886 it was cutting the wages of sailors on its ice barques by 10 shillings a month,

---

143 See Wiborg ms., 1943, Berg-Kragerø Museum, Norway.

a move that precipitated a strike among the crewmen. But its directors responded by bringing in labour from Hull.[144] All this was a foretaste of even more difficult labour relations to come, early in the twentieth century. In the company's defence, though, there is no doubt its directors were having to respond to cut-throat competition among shipping proprietors. By the twentieth century, as a result, it was rare for British-owned ships, whether sail or steam, to figure in the Norwegian ice trade.

The power of combination in the ice trade was most manifest among London's ice importers. It came to a head in 1901 with the amalgamation into one huge combine of the firms of Carlo Gatti Stevenson, and Slaters. In 1901–2, the London Butchers' Trade Society reacted against what it perceived as unjustifiably high retail prices for ice charged by the new combined company by seeking to bring the product from Norway on its own account and arranging storage at an appropriate location in the capital.[145] However, this became unnecessary after the entry of a new competitor into the London market, the North Pole Ice Company, which became sufficiently large to temper the monopoly exercised by the new combine. The new company contracted to supply ice at 19/- per ton to

Figure 4.5. Norwegian ice barques tied up in Grimsby docks in 1897, the famous Italianate water tower in the distance (Bodleian: G.A. Lincs 8' 297 Plate opposite p. 30).

---

144 E. Gillett, *A History of Grimsby* (Oxford, 1970), pp. 234–5, 269.
145 See *Cold Storage and Ice Trades Review* IV (1901), pp. 246–7.

butchers within a four-mile radius of its Charing Cross and Deptford works.[146] Even so, some Norwegian exporters and shippers were still complaining in 1905 of the lack of healthy competition within the London trade. The combine was regarded as an 'amalgamated monster' in the way it had London agents of the Norwegian suppliers and shippers powerfully within its grasp. During the summer of 1905, the dockside price of ice in both London and Liverpool was down to 6 or 7 shillings a ton, leaving next to no profit for shippers and exporters.[147] It was no wonder that the combine could report a net trading profit of £26,000 for the year 1904.[148] However, it is clear that the benefits of amalgamation fell somewhat short of expectations. Whereas the combine's directors had looked to a ten per cent dividend, the years 1902 to 1907 yielded only 5.6 per cent. The failure to meet profit expectations was, according to one director, due to 'ruinous' competition within the trade, indicating that the North Pole Ice Company, or ice exporters and shippers in Norway, had had some success in taming the power of the so-called 'monster' firm.[149]

The saving grace for ice exporters and shippers came, as already indicated, when exceptional summer temperatures in Britain caused a run on the supplies of ice in the ice stores in the capital. In early August 1900, for instance, cargoes of Norwegian ice were selling at the dockside for 20 shillings a ton. At channel ports, they were even higher, at 27/6d.[150] This followed from a very hot and sticky July when the mean monthly temperature reached 17.7°C, a figure that had barely been approached in the month of July for any of the preceding 20 years. In July 1905, though, when the mean rose to 17.2°C, exporters and shippers did not benefit in anything like the same measure. Although there was a price boom, the difficulty was that there was just not enough ice in Norwegian stores available to be shipped.[151] It became a lost opportunity. Even contract shipments ended up having to wait for the new season's ice crop to be cut in December. At Kragerø, one of the Wiborg family recalled the effects

---

146 *Ibid.*, IV (1902), p. 314.
147 *Ibid.*, VIII (1905), p. 148.
148 *Ibid.*, p. 93.
149 *Ibid.*, XI (1908), p. 77.
150 *Ibid.*, III (1900), p. 205.
151 *Ibid.*, VIII (1905), p. 313.

of a hot summer in England on their ice export business. All its employees, from the youngest to the oldest, would be working from early in the morning to late at night. Vessels as well as ice had to be ordered, then loading and discharge arranged and co-ordinated. The importers seemed to want ice shipments all at the same time. The business continued weekdays, Sundays, night as well as day. At some of the largest ice farms around Kragerø, it was not unusual for three vessels to be loaded in a single day at peak periods.[152] But the danger in such boom times was that entire ice stocks could be cleared, leaving nothing to be carried over for the succeeding year.

The ice shippers not uncommonly found that it was not just over freight rates that they crossed swords with British ice merchants. A secondary bone of contention was over demurrage. In the early summer of 1901, partly due to poor weather in Britain, the ice market in London was exceptionally slack. The result was that the incoming spring contract cargoes, mostly on board sailing ships, had to be left lying in the Thames for up to 16 days, waiting for space in London's ice stores and ice wells.[153] The problem with ice on demurrage was that it could deteriorate rapidly if attention was not paid to maintaining its condition. Waste water had to be pumped out frequently, for example. The costs of demurrage could also be considerable. On a 400-ton cargo, it could amount to £7 a day. The shippers would see this as a charge on the importer and, if re-imbursement was not forthcoming, the importer faced court action.[154]

In London in high summer, it was not unusual for there to be a score of ice ships unloading in the docks on any one day.[155] Among the larger ice importers in Britain, it was common to have at least one vessel laden with ice inbound across the North Sea, just to maintain an adequate level of insurance stocks. Since the size of ice cargoes varied according to a ship's registered tonnage and whether it was steam or sail, it is not easy to estimate the total number of voyages made by ice ships in any one year. But in the case of London, with some 220,000 deadweight tons of

---

152 See Wiborg ms., 1943, Berg-Kragerø Museum, Norway.
153 *Cold Storage and Ice Trades Review* IV (1901), p. 75.
154 *Ibid.*, IV (1901), p. 234.
155 *The Times*, 26th July 1911.

ice imported in 1899, a fair estimate would be 500 to 600 return passages, mostly concentrated between the months of March and October. So whilst ice ships were never as common as colliers on the Thames off Gravesend, they would have been a regular daily traffic.

One of the particular difficulties faced by ice-ships entering the Thames was the sheer volume of estuary and river traffic. The different speeds of sail and steam tonnage added to the hazard, as did the need for many sailing vessels temporarily to lay anchor in wait for a flood tide. In June 1876, the 133-ton Norwegian brig *Gem*, with a cargo of ice from Drammen, was riding at anchor near the Deptford buoys when a Hamburg-bound steamer, the *Virgo*, of 1,013 tons, coming down river at six knots, struck the *Gem* amidships. The brig was so severely damaged that she very soon sank, and her owners brought a suit against the steamship proprietors. In court, however, the judge dismissed the case as an unfortunate accident. A combination of an ebb tide and a strong south-west wind had caused the brig to lay athwart the river and when the steamer tried to take sharp evasive action, her steering gear broke, resulting in the collision.[156]

A much more spectacular accident, though, occurred in April 1910 near the anchorage grounds off Gravesend Reach, at the mouth of the river. The German steamship *Julia*, of 1,227 tons, making four and a half knots downriver, collided with the 526-ton British sailing barque, *Berean*, anchored with a cargo of ice. The barque was so damaged that she had to be beached near Tilbury Fort. In court, it transpired that the collision had been precipitated after another steamer, the *Belvedere*, of 1,001 tons, a London County Council sludge boat, had struck the *Julia* in the process of trying to overhaul her and then cut a passage between the vessels lying at anchor in Gravesend Reach and a P. & O liner that was turning in the river with the assistance of tugs. The manoeuvre by the *Belvedere* and the subsequent collision forced the *Julia* off-course, whereupon she ran into the ice-laden *Berean*. Once more the setting was compounded by an ebb tide with a force of two and a half knots. Judgement was eventually delivered against the owners of the *Belvedere*,

---

156 *Ibid.*, 18th November 1876.

for as the overtaking vessel it had been her duty to keep out of the way of the *Julia*.[157] But wherever responsibility ultimately lay, the accident affords a powerful illustration of how very crowded the Thames had become by this time.

On a 650-mile sea voyage, it would be anticipated that some of the ice in the ships' holds would melt. Within the trade, the general reckoning was that six per cent was the average loss. However, wastage invariably varied according to the time of year that cargoes were shipped and the care that was taken to pump out meltwater during the passage, not to mention the sea conditions, the length of the voyage and the manner of stowage. In the best cases, cargo loss could be minimal. In February 1865, for instance, the Norwegian barque *Achilles* loaded 412 tons of ice at Kragerø. A space of two feet was left between the deck and the surface of the cargo. Wood, four inches in depth, had been laid as insulation in the bottom of the hold and the blocks of ice were stowed close together, with both ends of the ship not quite full. The cargo was destined for Plymouth and, when discharged, around three weeks later, made out 406 tons, in other words an exceptionally small wastage.[158] In the very same year and the very same month, though, the Norwegian galiot *Phoenix* loaded 225 tons of ice at Lengner. There were 12 inches of wood insulation in the hold and it was filled, with the exception of four feet forward. On arrival at Plymouth, the vessel off-loaded 208 tons, representing a rather more significant level of wastage. The explanation was partly that the vessel had to wait for discharging orders at Plymouth and, the weather being warm, some of the ice melted.[159]

Sometimes court cases shed light on the measure of ice wastage. In a dispute that came before the Poole County Court in the late summer of 1908, the captain of the Norwegian sailing ship *Duin* reported that he had originally loaded his 240-ton vessel with 360 tons of ice. Upon arrival in Poole, the cargo was down to 300–320 tons, although on earlier voyages the captain stated that he had often cleared 350 tons. In the latter case, this represented a wastage of only about three per cent, whereas the

---

157 *Ibid.*, 4th July 1910.
158 R.W. Stevens, *On the Stowage of Ships and their Cargoes* (7th ed., London, 1940), p. 335.
159 *Ibid.*

voyage which the court was examining involved a wastage four times that level. The cargo was ultimately destined for Bournemouth, and its deadweight had been reduced to 240 tons by the time it arrived there, with only 200 tons capable of being put into store. It appears that in the conveyance of the ice from Poole to Bournemouth by railway, the ice-blocks had been poorly packed and left uncovered, or, at least, that was the central substance of the plaintiff's claim. The plaintiff won a judgement partially in his favour, but at the same time announced that his company was being dissolved, a comic echo of the dissolving ice in its transit along the south coast.[160]

Figure 4.6. A heavily laden wooden barque under partial sail off the west coast of Norway in the early 1900s (Bodleian: 2044 e.42 plate opposite p. 6).

Many of the specially built ice steamers and a few of the sailing ships were fitted with windmill pumps to ensure that meltwater was continuously removed. But where a vessel had to rely on hand pumps, the level of waste water was more difficult to control. Cargoes would then deteriorate even faster and, more seriously, be prone to shift in a heavy swell.

---

160 *Cold Storage and Ice Trades Review* XI (1908), p. 225.

In August 1920, a motor schooner laden with ice began to roll violently in bad weather in the southern North Sea. The cargo eventually shifted and forced the crew to abandon ship. However, this was not the end of the crew's misfortune. The ship's boat subsequently capsized twice and the members that survived had to wait 30 hours before they were sighted by a Lowestoft steam trawler and rescued.[161]

Some of the wooden sailing ships engaged in the ice trade were plainly close to the ends of their working lives. Travellers aboard steamers en route to Norway frequently remarked on the sight of such vessels, masts seemingly sloping all ways at once, yards creaking from right to left, sails old and patched. When fully laden, solid green water periodically swirled across the decks, the windmill pumps everlastingly at work to keep the ship afloat. The vessels in worst condition had yawning seams and seemed to have an almost perpetual list. It was no wonder, then, that they were sometimes seen beached or floating bottom up. In 1921, when the editor of the *Cold Storage and Ice Trades Review* began speculating on the potential for the ice trade to recover in the wake of the First World War, readers were reminded of how the pre-war ice trade was often carried in the 'roughest of hulls' and it was unlikely that such vessels would any longer be familiar sights on the Thames. Only the specially fitted-out wooden ice steamers held out any prospect of the trade's renewal.[162]

---

161 *The Times*, 26th August 1920.
162 *Cold Storage and Ice Trades Review* XXIV (1921), p. 189.

CHAPTER 5

The Ice Factory

> Happy those early days, when I
> Shipped ice from Norway, nor did try
> Excessively to make the pace,
> Or other traders to displace;
> Nor scanned in vain my books to see
> A credit large in l.s.d.
> When on some glorious mountain peak
> I now and then could spend a week
> Ne'er dreaming man would e'er turn out
> Ice half so pure or clear throughout.[163]

These lines are an extract from an English ice merchant's lament, penned in 1907. They record the halcyon days of Norwegian ice imports into Britain when profits were high and competition thin. In most years, importers would visit their suppliers in Norway and take in the glorious summer scenery of lakes and mountains. They were familiar with artificial ice-making machinery, but it seemed an absurd proposition that one day such contraptions would be able to supply ice to a metropolis.

Chemical means of inducing artificial cold had long been known.[164] Dissolving saltpetre in water was one long-tested method. By this means, anything that was immersed in the resulting liquid was cooled to a low temperature. Known as frigorific mixtures, such liquids act by the abstraction of heat. Mechanical or machine methods of producing cold are, by contrast, much more recent in origin. In the eighteenth century, the French chemist Antoine Lavoisier and others had experimented with

---

163 *Cold Storage and Ice Trades Review* X (1907), p. 330.
164 For a useful history of the various methods of inducing artificial cold, mechanical as well as chemical, see B.H. Springett, *Cold Storage and Ice-Making* (London, 1921); see also *Cold Storage and Ice Trades Review* I (1898), pp. 9–11; see also A.J. Wallis-Taylor, *Refrigeration, Cold Storage and Ice Making* (London, 1902), pp. 415–64.

CHAPTER 5

evaporating liquids within a vacuum as a means of abstracting heat. However, the modern compression systems of refrigeration did not materialize until after Jacob Perkins constructed an ice machine in London in 1834. There then followed a whole succession of technological improvements and refinements that eventually allowed commercial production of artificial ice by the closing decades of the nineteenth century. One critical issue was the liquid to be used in compressors. The first commercial machines used ether, but they quickly became obsolete, to be replaced by ammonia machines. Ammonia has a much higher latent heat and its use enabled major reductions in the size of the compressor needed. Experiments were also made with carbonic acid and sulphur dioxide, but by 1900 ammonia had become far and away the favoured choice.

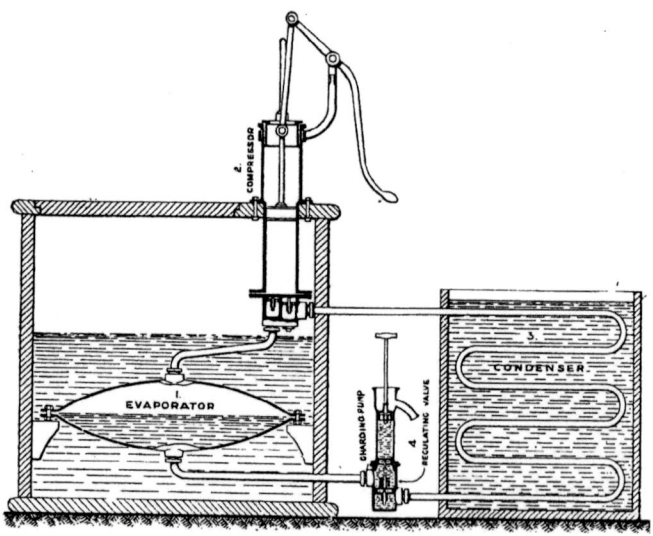

Figure 5.1. The first Perkins ice machine (Bodleian: 193998 e.18 p. 5).

All the early factory-made ice was opaque or cloudy in appearance, as compared with the normally highly transparent natural product. The cloudiness arises because, in stagnant water conditions, bubbles of air adhere to the newly-formed ice and then become imprisoned as ice formation continues.[165] When water is in a gentle state of agitation (as in lakes, for example),

---

165   B.H. Springett, *op.cit.*, p. 74.

the bubbles are washed away and the ice remains clear. In natural ice of the best quality, you could place a newspaper beneath an individual ice block two feet thick and still be able to read the small print. Opaque ice was fine for use as crushed ice – that is, for use on board fishing trawlers for packing fish, for filling the ice-boxes of refrigerated railway wagons, or for filling the freezer drums used by confectioners when making ice cream. But it was not acceptable for wider public consumption and use. Thus successful ice factories had to find means of agitating the water during the freezing process in order to obtain the necessary level of translucence to meet a wider market.

In London, the first firm to produce ice by machine means was the Shingleton Ice Company in 1870. It was based in Blackfriars in the City of London and operated an ammonia absorption plant type that was capable of making 9 tons of ice a day.[166] Norwegian block ice then fetched £8 per ton, a price that seriously limited its sale. However, artificial ice was viewed in some quarters as a dangerous chemical product and many potential customers were very reluctant to use it on that account. There was a widespread belief that the ammonia used in its manufacture came into contact with the water from which the ice was formed. In fact, it was to take 30 or 40 years for such prejudice to fade and for factory-made ice to make significant inroads into the natural ice market. The journal, *British Refrigeration and Allied Interests*, in one of its first issues in 1899, commented on the cheerful idiots who still thought that ice was manufactured by dropping some obnoxious chemical into a pail of water and stirring.[167]

The Shingleton Ice Company was soon joined by two other ice manufacturers: the General Ice Company with an ether plant at Lambeth, and the British Ice Company at Southwark using another ammonia absorption machine, both locations south of the river.[168] Within a couple of decades or so, London had acquired a total of five ice factories which, according to a reporter for the *Daily Graphic* in 1898, could together put out 200 tons

---

166 See *Cold Storage and Ice Trades Review* II (1900), p. 154.
167 *British Refrigeration and Allied Interests* I (1899), p. 14.
168 *Cold Storage and Ice Trades Review* II (1900), p. 154.

a day, even if regular production fell well short of that level.[169] The most prominent of the factories was the Linde British Refrigeration Company's ice plant on the Thames river bank at Shadwell, by the dock basin there. Equipped with three Lancashire boilers and two horizontal steam engines of 300 and 150 horse-power respectively, it had been erected in 1887 and was quickly doing a trade in ice with passing vessels, not to mention the adjacent Shadwell fish market. The plant was capable of being in continuous production and yet it could be operated by only four men. From its inception, the owners seemed to have recognized the value of producing ice for different markets. The fish market and the Thames fishing vessels used ice of the lowest quality. The best ice from the factory, known as crystal ice, went to hotels, clubs, restaurateurs and domestic customers.[170]

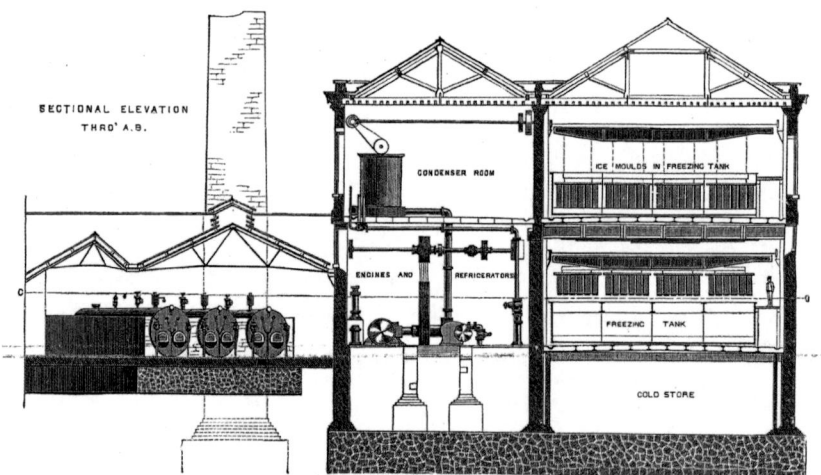

Figure 5.2. The design of the Shadwell ice factory as it existed in 1899 (Bodleian: Per 193998 d.1/II p. 59).

In late June 1900, in the wake of a sudden heatwave in the south of England, the *Daily Mail*, as previously observed, ran a major feature article on Britain's ice supply.[171] It included details of a visit by one of the newspaper's reporters to the Shingleton Ice Company's factory that had

---

169   *Ibid.*, I (1898), p. 66.
170   *Ibid.*, II (1899), pp. 58–60.
171   *Daily Mail*, 20th June 1900.

by then been in operation at Blackfriars in London for 30 years. He saw the huge engine that drove the compressors, along with the condenser room. But the most remarkable spectacle was the huge loft with its many tanks of water in which the artificial ice was made. Ice cold brine, collected in chambers around the tanks, effected the freezing process in about three days. By lifting the hatch-covers off the tanks, you could watch the ice slowly forming. Fern-like crystals and long needles, resembling hoar-frost, began to shoot out from the tank sides and, as time passed, gradually coalesced. Then, towards the end of the freezing process, loops of rope were placed in the centre of each block to allow their removal by travelling crane.

Over the last decade of the nineteenth century, plants making machine ice began springing up in cities, towns and fishing ports all around the country. Many were associated with the erection of cold stores as the technology of refrigeration was steadily consolidated. London in 1887 had but one cold store, but by 1899 there were no fewer than 17.[172] In its January 1900 issue, the *Cold Storage and Ice Trades Review* listed some 22 new companies in Britain that had come into being in 1899 for the purpose of manufacturing ice, often including the provision of cold storage. The tally embraced coastal centres as far flung as Exeter, Swansea, Fleetwood and Dundee, as well as an array of inland towns such as Bath, Coventry, Birmingham and Huddersfield.[173] The further a town was from a port, the greater were the costs of obtaining natural ice, not least owing to higher transport costs, but also due to higher losses through melting. The city of Manchester ceased to bring in Norwegian ice after 1899 owing to uncompetitive freight rates on the Manchester Ship Canal. Ice manufacture had begun as early as 1874.[174]

The economic and social backcloth to this runaway expansion of factory-made ice was the steep rise in urbanisation in Britain in the Victorian age. In 1831, there were just seven urban centres outside London

---

[172] *Cold Storage and Ice Trades Review* II (1899), p. 17.
[173] *Ibid.*, p. 151.
[174] See R. G. David, 'The Ice Trade and the Northern Economy, 1840–1914', *Northern History* 36 (2000), p. 119.

with populations of 100,000; by 1901 there were near forty.[175] This was far and away ahead of any country of continental Europe and it altered fundamentally the various exigencies of food supply to the nation's inhabitants and, within that, how the life of food could be extended.

Some of the ice-making companies proved wildly successful, while others had a rather short-lived existence. The Shingleton Ice Company's two early competitors in London ceased trading after relatively short periods.[176] In Aberdeen, though, the North Eastern Ice Company was returning a 15 per cent dividend to its shareholders by 1901 and the Aberdeen Ice Manufacturing Company a heady 20 per cent.[177] Between them, these two particular businesses seem to have squeezed out the bulk of the traditional import traffic in Norwegian ice which by 1899 was regarded locally as both unprofitable and unsatisfactory. It was Aberdeen's rapidly growing fishing fleets that were the principal users. And as other leading fishing ports discovered, their interests were best served by making ice on site, then using Norwegian ice as supplementary stock for when demand outstripped available supply. Thus Hull, Grimsby and Lowestoft matched Aberdeen's example.

Grimsby's first ice factory, The Great Northern Ice Company, was launched as early as 1885 and its directors reckoned on an estimated dividend to investors of 15 per cent.[178] At the time, imported Norwegian ice was costing the fishing trade 22/6d per ton. The new company reckoned to manufacture artificial ice for 5/- a ton and to sell it at 15/-. By 1900, construction was in progress at Grimsby on the erection of several more ice plants that, with existing capacity, were expected to be capable of supplying the port with up to 600 tons of ice daily.[179] With over 700 trawlers operating out of the port around that date, this was not an overly optimistic output. One of the new ice plants (the Grimsby Co-operative Ice Co.), located in a triangle of land on the north side of the fish dock, comprised a building 240 feet long, with a 120-foot-high chimney. Each of its

---

175 F.M.L. Thompson. *The Rise of Respectable Society: A social history of Victorian Britain, 1830–1900* (London, 1988), p. 28.
176 *Cold Storage and Ice Trades Review* II (1900), p. 154.
177 Ibid., V (1902), p. 63.
178 *The Times*, 30th August 1886.
179 *Cold Storage and Ice Trades Review* III (1900), p. 235.

ammonia compressors were powered by 300 horse-power triple expansion steam engines and could produce 75 tons of ice each day. The ice made was opaque and came in blocks eight inches thick, weighing about two hundredweight apiece.[180]

Grimsby had succeeded in stealing a march over its fishing-port rival, Hull, after the new and highly competitive Manchester, Sheffield and Lincolnshire Railway had constructed a special six-acre Fish Dock there, opened in 1857. Grimsby-landed fish now became one of the new railway company's primary traffics, destined not just for London but for the growing cities of the industrial Midlands and the North. It was not long before the Company's Fish Dock had to be enlarged.[181] And Grimsby was later to become England's leading fishing port.

Figure 5.3. The Grimsby Co-operative Ice Company's factory stands to this day, but operations ceased in 1990. The complex is a listed building, and it was once the largest ice factory in the world (Wikipedia – CC BY-SA 2.0).

Although large ice factories were initially the preserve of the major fishing ports, cities were not long in following their example. In London, the newly-formed North Pole Ice Company was, by 1902, operating

---

180 *Ibid.*
181 E. Gillett, *A History of Grimsby* (Oxford, 1970), pp. 230–232.

a factory at Blackwall, on the river's north bank, east of Limehouse. It had a capacity of up to 200 tons a day, with further scope for enlargement. Londoners would not fail to have noticed its 150-foot chimney with 'North Pole' emblazoned in large letters stretched from top to bottom, appearing like a new goal for arctic explorers.[182] The ice was made in a chamber in which there were 110 separate tanks, each producing 5-ton ice blocks, 12 inches thick.

Figure 5.4. The tank room at the North Pole Ice Company's Factory (Bodleian: Per 193998 d.1/ II p. 99).

These were then cut to form two-hundredweight blocks ready for despatch and use. It was claimed that the ice so manufactured was 'free from core', the bugbear of factory-made ice whereby a small mass of opaque ice was left in the centre of each ice block, formed as a result of the withdrawal of the central agitator in the final stage of the freezing cycle. The veracity of this claim was ably demonstrated in the issue of the *Cold Storage and*

---

182   *Cold Storage and Ice Trades Review*, IV (1902), p. 314.

Ice Trades Review of April 1905 when two men were pictured standing behind a 5-ton crystal ice block at the company's premises, their images largely unblemished by any imperfections in the ice mass.[183] By this time, the company had secured a substantial share of the London market and was combining its ice-making with the importing of natural ice from Norway. To ensure continuity of supply, the ice plant was operated 24 hours a day and stopped for a week for cleaning only twice a year.[184] In January 1902, a reporter from the *Cold Storage and Ice Trades Review* had been given a guided tour of the new plant by one of the company's managers. It was equipped with all the latest technology, including superheated steam boilers, water-softening apparatus and electrically-operated cranes for lifting and moving the huge ice blocks. What most intrigued the magazine's reporter, though, was the method for cutting the 5-ton ice blocks. This was achieved by means of a tube frame laid on top of the ice block in its horizontal position. Steam was passed through the tubes and by this means the frame slowly ate its way through the large block, ultimately producing regularly cut, two-hundredweight blocks.[185]

In Glasgow, large-scale ice manufacture was begun in 1902 when William Milne, a prominent local ice merchant, erected a plant with an ice-tank capacity of 180 tons and a projected daily ice output of 60 tons. The premises, in Old Wynd in Glasgow, were housed in an impressive brick building and included cold storage for perishable foodstuffs as well as extensive storage for ice. It was hoped that the latter would help to alleviate, if not remove altogether, the chronic ice shortages that were a regular feature of Scotland's first city in hot summer seasons.[186]

In Liverpool, the story of artificial ice manufacture was much the same as in London. In 1880, natural ice realized 40 shillings a ton in the city. By 1905, both natural and artificial ice averaged 15 shillings a ton and there were five companies manufacturing ice with an aggregate daily capacity of up to 200 tons.[187] Among them was the Riverside Cold

---

183 *Ibid.*, VIII (1905), p. 99.
184 *Ibid.*, pp. 98–100.
185 *Ibid.*, IV (1902), p. 314.
186 *Ibid.*, IV (1901), p. 251.
187 *Ibid.*, VIII (1905), p. 148.

CHAPTER 5

Figure 5.5. The design for William Milne's ice factory in Glasgow (Bodleian: Per 193998 d.1/IV p. 251).

Figure 5.6. The Riverside Cold Storage and Ice Company, Liverpool, 1900 (Bodleian: Per 193998 d.1/II p. v).

Storage and Ice Company, located on a bank of the Mersey in a large four-storey structure, complete with the word 'ice' emblazoned in giant letters on its gable end.

Nevertheless, the city continued to import 12,000 tons of Norwegian block ice a year and some local commentators considered that it was overprovided with ice plants. Except during the three hottest months of the year, there was not the demand to sustain such an ice-making capacity, so it was argued.[188] Even so there were still summer seasons when Liverpool experienced an ice famine, resulting in spiralling prices, especially for natural ice.

Elsewhere, Newcastle-upon-Tyne acquired a large cold store and ice factory in 1904 which was doubled in size inside four years. It was housed in striking five-storey premises on the quayside, a beacon of early-twentieth century factory design.[189] For the manufacturers of ice-making plants, the buoyancy of artificial ice manufacture brought rich rewards. In 1909, The Linde British Refrigeration Company, based in East London, supplied new plants at Paddington, Blackburn, Manchester, Southampton, Bournemouth and Croydon. At Grimsby, it was to install the largest refrigeration machine ever put to work in Britain up to that time, turning out 200 tons of ice a day.[190]

Some ice-making companies quickly expanded their initial operations to take in neighbouring towns. The Cardiff Pure Ice Company, for instance, established branch plants at Newport, Barry and Milford Haven, the last two directly alongside the docks. In 1900, the four plants together had a potential output of up to 500 tons of ice a week. And the company was confident enough of its success to take a full-page advertisement in the *Cold Storage and Ice Trades Review* setting out the range of its activities.[191] These included substantial cold storage space for cargoes of foreign meat. There was also, significantly, a continuing importation of Norwegian ice, much as in London and in Liverpool.

The ice trade's capacity for occasional boom ensured that there were times when it displayed a propensity to attract capitalist speculators. In June 1901, the *Cold Storage and Ice Trades Review* carried details of the sale at auction of an ice factory at Hanley in the Potteries. It was an entirely new plant and had plainly been commissioned with a quick

---

188 Ibid.
189 Ibid., XI (1908), p. 195.
190 Ibid., XIII (1910), p. 8.
191 Ibid., II (1900), p. x.

CHAPTER 5

Figure 5.7. Newcastle's cold store and ice factory, 1908 (Bodleian: 193998 d.1/XI p. 195).

profit in mind. The Potteries district then had a population of 300,000 and the auction notice was at pains to emphasize that the plant had no competition.[192] From time to time, the *Cold Storage and Ice Trades Review*

---

192 *Ibid.*, IV (1901), p. 89.

itself played up the speculative opportunities, as in March 1900 when it observed how the town of Blackburn in Lancashire was ripe for an ice and cold storage capitalist. The borough was made up of some two dozen townships and its butchers were counted in their hundreds.[193]

The impressive financial performance of some earlier ice factories, as already seen in the case of those at Aberdeen, strengthened the belief that ice-making was a potentially lucrative venture. The Fleetwood Ice Company started at the turn of the century with a big dividend and was able to wipe off its purchase money. Within a few years, though, its dividend was only five per cent, well down on the wildly successful Aberdeen enterprises that managed to sustain dividends in double figures.[194] In February 1906, an advertisement regarding the sale of Eastbourne's diminutive 8-ton ice works described it as a 'very good investment for capitalist or syndicate'.[195] Its existing owners had clearly struggled to make a going concern of it, despite there being no competition. The *Cold Storage and Ice Trades Review* made a habit of regularly publishing share lists that included companies' rates of return. Most struggled at around five per cent and a few produced no dividend at all. Thus ice-making was clearly a risky venture. In January 1904, the *Review* editor bemoaned in verse the tense relationship between ice factory promoters and the investing public:

> We plan as the experts direct us,
> Ice-cold you remain, and unmoved:
> With such a convincing prospectus
> Our arguments should be approved!
> Concessions we have quite abundant,
> Firm options in populous towns;
> Alas! you declare they're redundant –
> And all that we get is your frowns!'[196]

Within such a speculative investment climate, it comes as no surprise to learn that there were new ice companies that failed not many years after their being established. This was the fate of the Liverpool Cold Storage and Ice Company in 1907. Fuel and engine costs had advanced significantly

---

193 *Ibid.*, II (1900), p. 175.
194 *Ibid.*, IV (1901), p. 175; V (1902), p. 63.
195 *Ibid.*, IX (1906), p. 63.
196 *Ibid.*, VII (1904), p. 4.

over the year, but the demand for ice had also been much depressed by the cold and wet summer. The directors saw no other course than to go into voluntary liquidation. The company's share capital had been £100,000, so it was no mean venture.[197] Another casualty, this time in 1908, was the Swansea Steam Fishing and Ice Company, its plant snapped up at auction by a local competitor.[198]

As the wider public benefits of the availability of artificial ice became clearer, especially the preservation in cold stores of wholesale food perishables, municipal corporations up and down the land began to consider starting up ice-making on their own account, particularly in order to serve city food markets. By 1899, Bolton Corporation, for instance, was manufacturing ice for this purpose and selling surplus to the value of £1400 to the general public.[199] Much the same prevailed at nearby Burnley where, in the year ending March 1908, the corporation sold 1,910 tons of ice, valued at £2,131.[200] For pre-existing ice factories, however, such municipal forays, underwritten by local taxation, were viewed with deep suspicion. It was typically claimed that market cold stores could rarely in themselves justify maintaining a dedicated ice plant. In other words, such enterprises could not really be viewed as anything other than unnecessary and unwelcome competition in the face of private capital. When municipal ice-making was in the offing at Blackburn in 1907-8, a local ice manufacturer complained that ratepayers' money would be being used to 'run him off'.[201] In Wolverhampton, an especially fierce battle had raged in 1900 between supporters of a municipal ice plant and cold store there and a group who opposed it, including many local ratepayers and the companies that already supplied Wolverhampton with ice.[202] The latter, however, were located in Birmingham and in Dudley, with the result that the retail price of ice in Wolverhampton was generally half as much again as in those two places. Wolverhampton's butchering trade was, predictably, fully behind the municipal operation; it would obviate

---

197 Ibid., X (1907), p. 349.
198 Ibid., XI (1908), p. 98.
199 Ibid., IV (1901), p. 125.
200 Ibid., XI (1908), p. 320.
201 Ibid., p. 37.
202 Ibid., III (1900), p. 105.

meat being wasted on warm summer days and save carting costs to and from more distant cold stores. In due course, the town did get its cold store and ice factory (in 1902), the two compressors producing between them 16 tons of ice each day in one-and-a-half-hundredweight blocks.[203] It was a largely hollow victory for the municipal lobby, for so small a scale of output was hardly a threat to ordinary ice factories. But 'municipalism' had by then grown into a powerful political movement across the growing industrial wealth of midland and northern towns. It revealed itself as a counter to the free march of capital and profit, gaining most traction in the eyes of the public through its creation of urban parks, art galleries, libraries, museums and swimming baths.[204] But at a somewhat more mundane level, the regulated food markets of growing city centres like Wolverhampton (which gained municipal borough status as early as 1848) were equally part of the municipal offering.

Given the increasing scale of artificial ice manufacture by the first decades of the twentieth century and the progressive refinement in the quality of the ice produced, it comes as a surprise to discover how far there remained a preference among many users for natural ice from Norway. However, this preference continued in some measure right up to 1914. The preference for natural over artificial ice reflected a continuing suspicion that the factory product was some kind of chemical concoction. One of the first ways that ice plants attempted to counter this view was to describe themselves as makers of 'pure ice'. Thus when ice-making began in Leeds in 1899, it was the Yorkshire Pure Ice Company that produced it – up to 50 tons a day from 12 ice tanks. This particular appellation subsequently became widely used, with plants often emblazoning the words 'Pure Ice' on their rooftops or on their engine chimneys.[205]

For users of artificial ice, one of the features that repeatedly attracted comment was its poor lasting quality alongside Norwegian ice. It was reputed by some to endure only half the time of natural block ice. When the London Butchers' Trade Society in 1901 sought to break the combined monopoly of the city's ice companies, they were sure that natural not

---

203 Ibid., V (1902), p. 68.
204 F.M.L. Thompson, op. cit., pp. 324–5.
205 Cold Storage and Ice Trades Review, II (1899), p. 30.

machine ice was the best product. Not only could it be obtained in much larger blocks, but it lasted longer.[206] The artificial ice producers themselves tended to lend credence to this view because most of them imported Norwegian ice alongside the factory output. They never stated as much, for it would have been counterproductive to sales of manufactured ice. But the scale of their Norwegian imports could not be explained merely as a way of meeting summer peaks in demand. Moreover, the artificial ice producers who also imported Norwegian block ice typically offered both products for the same price, even though the latter was by far the more expensive. They did this largely because so much of their ice sales were on regular contract, and stored natural ice allowed flash surges in demand to be met, something that was beyond the production capacities of ice-making plants.[207]

Among fishmongers, both wholesale and retail, it was found that artificial ice sometimes failed to preserve their fish stocks in the same condition as did natural ice. Salmon and haddocks, for example, boxed and stored under exactly similar conditions, using natural ice in one case and artificial in another, came out completely differently. The latter emerged yellow about the gills and soft, the former in near perfect condition and capable of commanding a far higher price.[208] Much the same applied in the transit of fish to cities and large towns. Towards the close of the nineteenth century, some of the leading British railway companies began constructing special refrigerated vans with double doors, zinc linings and ice tanks as well as tanks for meltwater. They were fitted with passenger carriage wheels and automatic vacuum braking so that they could be worked on fast trains.[209] These vans soon helped to boost the nascent 'fish and chip' retail trade that had started to become a food staple of many northern industrial towns, using cheaper fish like cod that had previously been dried, salted or smoked and sold in and around fishing ports.[210]

---

206   *Ibid.*, IV (1901), p. 246.
207   See R.G. David, 'The Ice Trade and the Northern Economy, 1840–1914', *Northern History* 36 (2000), p. 123.
208   *Cold Storage and Ice Trades Review*, V (1902), p. 74.
209   See, for example, *Ibid.*, I (1898), p. 15.
210   See the discussion in R.G. David, *op. cit.*, p. 124.

The fish for the vans would be packed using natural ice, but the ice used for cooling the vans would usually be factory-produced.

In November 1898, the *Cold Storage and Ice Trades Review* published a report of an American chemist in which were listed a whole sequence of potential contaminants of artificial ice. Metallic substances could find their way into the ice blocks in the freezing process. In summer, ice made from day to day could become contaminated by bacteria and other foreign matter getting into the freezing tanks. The water used for ice-making plants could also become contaminated through leaks in the supply pipes.[211]

The famous lasting quality of Norwegian ice derived directly from the average size of its ice blocks, normally 20 to 24 inches in thickness. A block cut in this way presented less melting surface in proportion to its bulk than the average block of artificial ice which, as a general rule, came less than half as thick. To manufacture ice of the same thickness as natural ice would require an extremely lengthy freezing process. In a factory ice-can, the first four inches froze or became congealed inside 24 hours, but the average time taken in freezing the rest of the ice slab increased progressively with each extra inch.[212] The economics of artificial ice-making permitted the production of ice blocks that were up to 10 or 12 inches thick, but, beyond that, diminishing returns applied. On this basis, in other words, Nature's factory could not be bettered.

Of course, there were factory producers who tried hard to undermine the alleged quality of Norwegian ice, arguing that it was drawn from lakes and fjords that could readily be contaminated by effluents. One correspondent of the *Cold Storage and Ice Trades Review* claimed in 1902 that natural ice, generally, was liable to be contaminated with disease germs and other noxious matter, stating that its use was condemned by most sanitary experts. The only safe ice was that made from water of known purity – that is, from distilled water.[213] The medical journal the *Lancet* had earlier tackled the issue in a study in 1901. Testing the Norwegian ice supplied to London shops, they deemed it of excellent quality, pure,

---

211 *Cold Storage and Ice Trades Review*, I (1898), p. 96.
212 Ibid., VIII (1905), p. 8.
213 Ibid. V (1902), p. 74.

sparkling and clear. The ice-water approached very nearly to the composition of distilled water or water from a mountain stream. The one concern expressed was the way Norwegian ice could become contaminated if allowed to melt in a leaden vessel, a function of the legendary softness of the water from which the ice was formed.[214] In 1902, a Glasgow water analyst compared a sample of ice taken from Baardsrud Lake, south of Kristiania, with one from Loch Katrine. It had only the slightest traces of organic matter compared with five grains per gallon for Katrine water and it was almost entirely free from lime and magnesia – in other words very soft compared with Katrine water.[215]

Contamination, though, was not a charge from which factory-made ice could necessarily claim immunity, as we have previously seen. In 1903, Bermondsey Borough Council invited its Medical Officer of Health to inquire into the purity of ice from a public health point of view.[216] The officer observed that factory ice was made with water derived from three sources: distilled water; water supplied by metropolitan water companies; and well water. The last-named source was very certainly liable to contamination by bacteria via leakage from sewers. Moreover, contrary to some popular perceptions, freezing merely inhibited the growth of disease pathogens; it did not kill them. There were few ice-making plants that used distilled water. One London plant that did was the Shingleton Ice Company, and in the provinces there was an ice plant in Devon, the Brixham Pure Ice Company, that used it, although not, presumably, for use in fish packing.[217] In by far the majority of ice-making plants, water was drawn from municipal supplies – that is, from mains drinking water. Its quality, then, met the standards that public health officials deemed appropriate for general public consumption. Even so, many ice-plant managers were soon seeking independent testing of the water they used to make ice. It became a vital part of their selling apparatus. London's large North Pole Ice Company drew its supplies from the Kent Water Company. When the ice it manufactured was melted in laboratory tests,

---

214 *Ibid.*, IV (1901), p. 136.
215 *Ibid.*
216 A summary appeared in *Cold Storage and Ice Trades Review* VI (1903), pp. 233–4.
217 *Cold Storage and Ice Trades Review* XI (1906), p. 269.

it resembled distilled water more closely in composition than almost any other.[218] In Hull, local ice plants drew supplies from the chalk basins of the Yorkshire Wolds. Its purity was beyond reproach. All the ice-makers did was correct for the water's legendary hardness.[219] Occasionally, municipal supplies could fail for quite other reasons. In 1903, for instance, a London ice factory had to destroy 200 tons of its ice stocks. The public water supply in this case had become discoloured when the Thames was in flood and the brown silt had coagulated in the freezing process, making the ice-blocks streaked and unsightly.[220]

Ice merchants who dealt largely or exclusively in imported Norwegian ice repeatedly dwelt upon the softness of the lake or fjord water from which it was made. It was claimed to form a preventive and curative in cases of kidney, liver and kindred disease. As for pureness, at Southampton in 1905 Thomas Mowat Ltd. sought the Borough Medical Officer's opinion on samples of its stocks of Norwegian block ice. He found that it contained only one forty-fourth part of the average solid matter contained in water taken from Southampton's own Corporation Water Works.[221] In the war of words and of scientific evidence, then, it was six of one and half a dozen of the other. Natural ice importers and artificial ice-makers engaged in a constant struggle to influence consumers in the type of ice that they chose. All kinds of stratagems were used to try to curry favour. One particular argument that did sometimes strike home against natural ice was the way ice-carrying ships could be used for other purposes on their return passages across the North Sea. Where coal or coke was a back-cargo, no amount of hosing down or washing out of holds could remove all residues. And the regular sight of filthy collier brigs on the Thames could hardly have been a more evocative reminder of this. The counter to this argument was the way, by the early 1900s, some ice-carrying was done in new wooden-hulled steamships specially built for the trade. The likelihood was that these returned in

---

218 Ibid., p. 268.
219 Ibid., p. 269.
220 Ibid., VIII (1905), p. 8.
221 Ibid., XI (1906), p. 269.

ballast, particularly when they were making weekly voyages in the vital summer export season.

At various times, the operators of ice factories lobbied Parliament to get a duty placed on imported ice.[222] There had been such a levy in the past, amounting to 20 per cent of the value of the cargo, but it had been repealed in 1845 under the momentum of free trade.[223] With a duty re-imposed, the hope was that Norwegian imports would be stopped in their tracks and a splendid impetus given to the home ice industry. Some parliamentarians backed the idea, but, fortunately for those involved in the Norway trade, no such policy was taken up in peacetime.

The nadir in the war of words between natural and artificial ice came in a High Court action for slander in 1910.[224] It was between the two giants of the London ice trade: The North Pole Ice Company, and United Carlo Gatti, Stevenson, and Slaters Ltd. The plaintiffs, the North Pole Ice Company, alleged slander on the part of the United Company in respect of natural ice supplied to a leading London hotel. The basis of the slander was that a representative of the United company had claimed the ice to be artificial, not natural. The jury found for the plaintiffs and the judge awarded damages of £200. The story had an even more bizarre twist in that, in the course of evidence, it came out that the two firms competed with each other in the supply of ice to the hotel in question. The plaintiffs supplied ice for one half of the week, the defendants for the other. It might have been a script for a music-hall comedy act.

An entirely different feature of artificial ice manufacture that sometimes placed limits on its expansion was the environmental nuisance to which it could give rise. It was not just the familiar problem of smoke and soot from the plant's steam engines, but the periodic leakages of ammonia gas which, allegedly, gave food a nasty taste. Some witnesses also complained of perpetual dampness, arising, it seems, from the ice stores. The difficulties were potentially most acute in the case of ice factories located in central urban areas, particularly those associated with municipal markets. In 1904, the environmental problems created by a

---

222 *Ibid.*, VII (1904), p. 46.
223 This was part of the same campaign that shortly led to the repeal of the Corn Laws in 1846.
224 *Cold Storage and Ice Trades Review*, XIII (1910), p. 331.

Leicester ice factory came before the local county court.²²⁵ The Midland Ice Company was subsequently required to make modifications to its plant and operations or face assessment for damages. A similar case at Hanley in the Potteries involved the excessive vibration from the plant of the Stoke-on-Trent Pure Ice Company.²²⁶ Here an injunction was granted, suspended for two months to allow time for remedial action.

In the final analysis, of course, artificial ice production could work only as long as the economics of the enterprise were viable. In March 1907, at a meeting of the Cold Storage and Ice Trades Association, a Grimsby plant manager treated delegates to a show of lantern slides in which the difficulties of running a large ice-making plant were made disarmingly plain.²²⁷ Aside from the capital costs of plant and machinery, and the costs of maintenance and labour, the price of coal was critical to viability. It was here that natural ice really had no peer. Apart from the rental costs involved in securing access to lakes, ice from Norway cost nothing to produce. The costs were all in labour, storage, shipping and insurance. The annual reports of ice factories in Britain repeatedly comment on the problems posed to their operations by the fluctuating price of coal and of the continued efforts that engineers were making to try to raise the efficiency of energy use. In the year 1900, the Croydon Ice Company had spent £500 more on coal than it had anticipated, representing almost a third of its entire annual profit.²²⁸ In Lowestoft in 1909, the directors of the once successful East Anglian Ice Company commented on the implications of Parliament's Eight Hours Bill for the increased price of coal and, in consequence, the plant's production costs.²²⁹ Within the trade, it was generally reckoned that it required one ton of coal to make 20 tons of ice. A shilling a ton on the coal price could make the difference between profit and loss. So it was hardly surprising that there were proprietors who started looking for alternative sources of heat like town gas.

---

225 *Ibid.*, VII (1904), p. 87.
226 *Ibid.*, XIII (1910), p. 15.
227 *Ibid.*, X (1907), p. 125.
228 *Ibid.*, III (1901), p. 433.
229 *Ibid.*, XIII (1910), p. 15.

In an effort to cut their specific labour costs, many ice factories naturally sought to mechanize further the range of their operations. For example, in 1908 the Burnley ice factory installed an electrical ice cutter to saw its standard five-hundredweight ice blocks into the hundred weight sizes that it sold to customers. Previously it had taken three men half a working day to saw seven tons of ice with hand cross-cut saws. With the ice cutter, one man could saw the same quantity in 30 minutes. The machine also used circular saws which gave a more even cut to the ice blocks and better satisfaction to customers.[230]

Figure 5.8. Giant, translucent ice blocks from Bradford's ice factory, 1923 (Bodleian: Per 193998 d.1/XXVI p. 171).

Ultimately, it is not easy to measure the scale of actual ice consumption in Britain and the relative contributions accounted for by natural and by artificial ice. The tonnages of ice imported and the productions of ice

---

230 *Ibid.*, XI (1908), p. 122.

factories are no guides in themselves, especially when long-term storage of ice is contemplated as part of the calculation. The 1907 Census of Ice Factories had put total ice manufacture in Britain at 597,000 tons, 250,000 tons ahead of imports from Norway.[231] However, in early 1915, the *Cold Storage and Produce Review* gauged London's annual pre-war ice consumption at around 300,000 tons, of which only slightly over a third comprised artificial ice.[232] There were then three principal companies producing artificial ice, with an aggregate potential output of around 365 tons a day. In other words, as far as potential consumption of artificial ice went, London appears to have had more than sufficient productive capacity. In 1910, though, at the time of the High Court case between the North Pole Ice Company and the United Company, these two principal firms were, between them, actually producing only 30,000 tons of artificial ice each year, a surprisingly low figure, even allowing for expansion of productive capacity in the intervening five years up to 1915. At the time of the court hearing, moreover, the United Company stated that it imported 120,000 tons of natural ice a year, twelve times its artificial output. Thus, for one leading firm of London ice merchants, factory ice appears to have made only limited inroads into its business, even by the time that imports of Norwegian ice were well and truly in decline. This almost certainly had something to do with its customer base in which hotels, clubs, restaurants and the houses of the upper classes featured prominently. Chefs also used natural ice for all kinds of fancy work, in that they cut table decorations from it. Artificial ice was quite unsuitable for this purpose: the ice was brittle and would not sculpt properly. Once more, then, one registers the remarkable subtleties there were in the distinctions between the artificial product and the natural material which one wit referred to as from 'Norroway across the foam'.[233]

---

231 *Ibid.*, XIII (1910), p. 309.
232 *Ibid.*, XVIII (1915), p. 48.
233 *Ibid.*, IX (1906), p. 261.

CHAPTER 6

The Iceman Cometh

> O Iceman! My Iceman! summer at length is here,
> The gladdest, gayest time for you of all the circling year;
> For when beneath a sultry sun the milk is turning sour,
> And butter's rank and meat goes bad, then is the Iceman's hour.
>
> O Iceman! my iceman! pray daily bring to me
> A solid block of crystal ice from faultiness quite free.
> I'll put it in my ice-safe – refrigerator called –
> And then before no magistrate shall I ever be hauled![234]

The second half of the nineteenth century was the age of the telegraph. For Victorian and Edwardian economy and society, it formed a precursor of the modern internet. Telegraphic communication revolutionized the conduct of business, the exercise of law and order, the operation of the military, not to mention the lives of people. For the ice trade, the telegraph could hardly have been more critical. It was the means by which London ice merchants, for example, were able rapidly to re-stock their stores when high summer temperatures caused a surge in demand, especially from among the general public. Messages to Norway requesting prompt steamer cargoes pulsed down the telegraph wires. In the same way, the telegraph was a means by which customers at home could place orders for ice with the local merchants. And so conscious were such merchants of the role of the telegraph for their businesses that they were endlessly inventive when it came to selecting telegraphic addresses.[235] Some went for the obvious, such as the Cardiff Pure Ice Company, with simply 'Ice Cardiff', 'Ice Newport', 'Ice Barry' and 'Ice Milfordhaven' to cover its four premises. The Liverpool Imperial Cold Stores was more imaginative, though, choosing 'Hoarfrost Liverpool'. The Bolton Pure Ice Company

---
234 *Cold Storage and Ice Trades Review* III (1900), p. 101.
235 Addresses are taken from advertisements in the *Cold Storage and Ice Trades Review*.

CHAPTER 6

used 'Icecold', while among other memorable telegraphic addresses were 'Polar', 'Snowcap' and 'Icicle'. However, telegraphic communication could have its downsides. Messages could become garbled in transcription. In 1866, for instance, a London ice importer wrote to a Hull ice merchant inviting him to offer a price for a 100-ton cargo of ice then aboard a schooner at Grimsby. The purchaser replied by telegraph that they would offer 23/- a ton, but a telegraph clerk subsequently mis-transcribed this as 27/-. Having ordered the schooner captain to proceed to Hull, the ice importer then found that the purchaser refused to receive the cargo on the grounds that he had offered 23/- not 27/- for each ton of ice. The matter ended in a court case, in the process raising important general points of law.[236]

The sudden surges in demand for ice that telegraphic communication was so vitally important in meeting had an allied contingent in the shape of the need for extensive storage capacity. All commodity trades require storage, but its scale varies according to the periodicities and synchronicities of demand and supply, and the extent to which prices vary from month to month and from year to year. Of all commodities, the ice trade necessitated very extensive storage capacity. In Norway, this was because ice was inevitably harvested in winter at the time when it was in least demand. In Britain, it related to the way ice demand was characterized by an acute summer peak, a few weeks in June, July or August when consumption grew exponentially, and in a manner that no conventional trading capacity could go anywhere towards meeting. Extensive storage was also necessary because most English traders in natural ice obtained their supply during the months from early spring to early summer when contract cargoes could be obtained at relatively cheap rates. The report on ice and cold storage in London, prepared for the London County Council in 1904, gave details of one ice well that was all of 104 feet deep, had a diameter of 40 feet, with perhaps the whole available space in constant use.[237] Occasionally, pickaxes or other tools fell down in the crevices between the ice blocks and were not recovered for several years. Leftwich and Company, ice merchants at Little Albany Street in London,

---

236 *The Times*, 22nd April 1869.
237 W.H. Hamer, *Ice and Cold Storage: Report for London County Council* (London, 1904) – a detailed summary appeared in *Cold Storage and Ice Trades Review* VIII (1905), pp. 4–8.

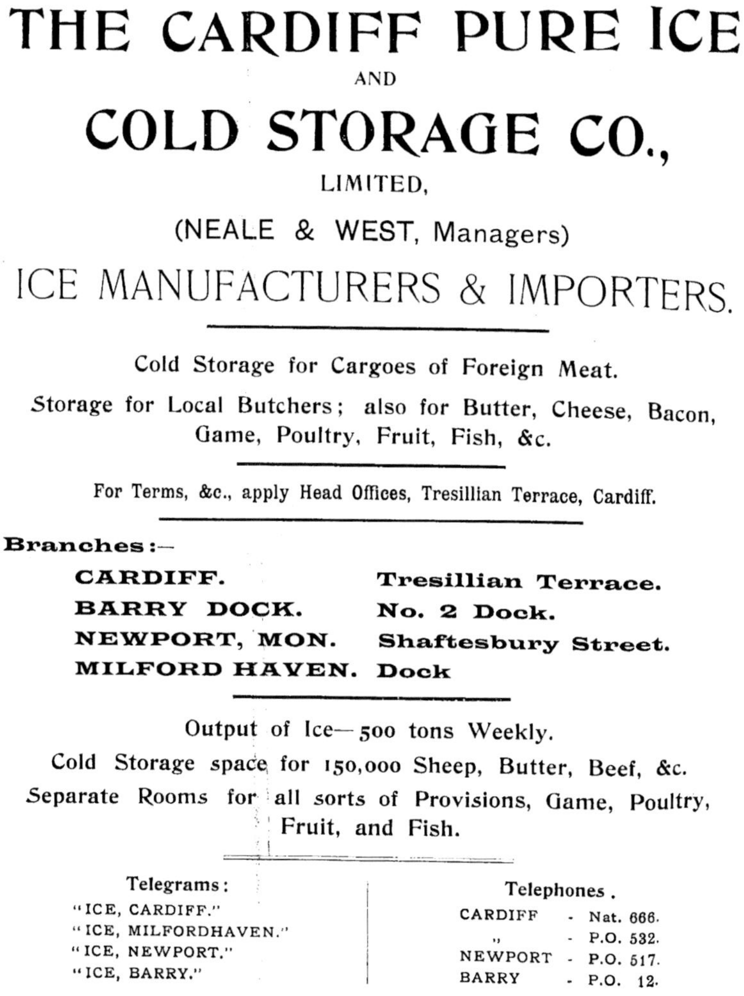

THE CARDIFF PURE ICE
AND
COLD STORAGE CO.,
LIMITED,

(NEALE & WEST, Managers)

ICE MANUFACTURERS & IMPORTERS.

Cold Storage for Cargoes of Foreign Meat.

Storage for Local Butchers; also for Butter, Cheese, Bacon, Game, Poultry, Fruit, Fish, &c.

For Terms, &c., apply Head Offices, Tresillian Terrace, Cardiff.

Branches:—

CARDIFF.	**Tresillian Terrace.**
BARRY DOCK.	**No. 2 Dock.**
NEWPORT, MON.	**Shaftesbury Street.**
MILFORD HAVEN.	**Dock**

Output of Ice—500 tons Weekly.

Cold Storage space for 150,000 Sheep, Butter, Beef, &c.

Separate Rooms for all sorts of Provisions, Game, Poultry, Fruit, and Fish.

Telegrams:	Telephones.
"ICE, CARDIFF."	CARDIFF - Nat. 666.
"ICE, MILFORDHAVEN."	,, - P.O. 532.
"ICE, NEWPORT."	NEWPORT - P.O. 517.
"ICE, BARRY."	BARRY - P.O. 12.

Figure 6.1. The Cardiff Pure Ice Company's advert from the *Cold Storage and Ice Trades Review* of January 1900 (Bodleian: Per 193998 d.1/II p. x).

had an 82-feet-deep ice well with a capacity of 1500 tons of ice. According to an account given by one of the family members, Richard Leftwich, in 1899, the well resembled an egg in shape, some 34 feet in diameter at its widest part. Originally a water well that extended 600 feet down to the chalk stratum, the residual well-shaft provided an easy means of drainage for ice that melted.[238] The same firm had further ice wells in

---

238 *Cold Storage and Ice Trades Review* II (1899), p. 35.

CHAPTER 6

Camden Town, one of which was cylindrical in shape and reputedly had a capacity of 3,000 tons.[239] At London's Cumberland market, built in 1830, there was, as we have seen, an underground ice-store 82 feet deep with a capacity of 1,500 tons. Towards the close of the nineteenth century, as London's leading ice businesses expanded and as combination brought larger and larger firms into being, the size and range of ice storage facilities increased. The North Pole Ice Company, for example, founded in 1899, had stores at Waterloo, Camden and Greenwich by 1905.[240] Together these could hold 14,000 tons of ice. The Waterloo store was the biggest, comprising all of the railway arches under Waterloo Railway Junction. The North Pole Company's great rival, United Carlo Gatti, Stevenson and Slaters, had some half a dozen ice stores by 1901. The principal one was at Ransome's Dock, Battersea, the others at Westminster, King's Cross, Commercial Road, Shadwell and Stepney. Together they could accommodate 11,700 tons.[241] In 1898, the *Cold Storage and Ice Trades Review*, in its news column, recorded the unfortunate death of a lighterman in charge of an ice-barge in Ransome's Dock. He was drowned in the basin there.[242]

Large ice stores were no strangers to cities and towns outside London. At Liverpool, the ice merchant, H.T. Ropes, maintained an extensive store at their premises in North John Street. The business had started life in 1847 and was first known as the Wenham Lake Ice Company. At that time the ice was imported from America, from Lake Wenham in Massachusetts. After 1869, however, the firm's ice imports were exclusively Norwegian. It became a limited liability company in 1899 and had been run by successive generations of the Hinchliff family who maintained that it was the oldest ice importing business in Britain. In fact, the firm had a remarkable record for the length of service of its various employees. Thomas Kearney, the warehouse keeper in 1909, had worked for H.T. Ropes for 40 years, and there were other men of his age who had started as errand boys and who, by 1909, had sons who were also employed in the business. The company's founder was a shipowner from

---

239 *Ibid.*
240 *Ibid.*, VIII (1905), p. 98.
241 *Ibid.*, IV (1901), p. 131.
242 *Ibid.*, I (1898), p. 100.

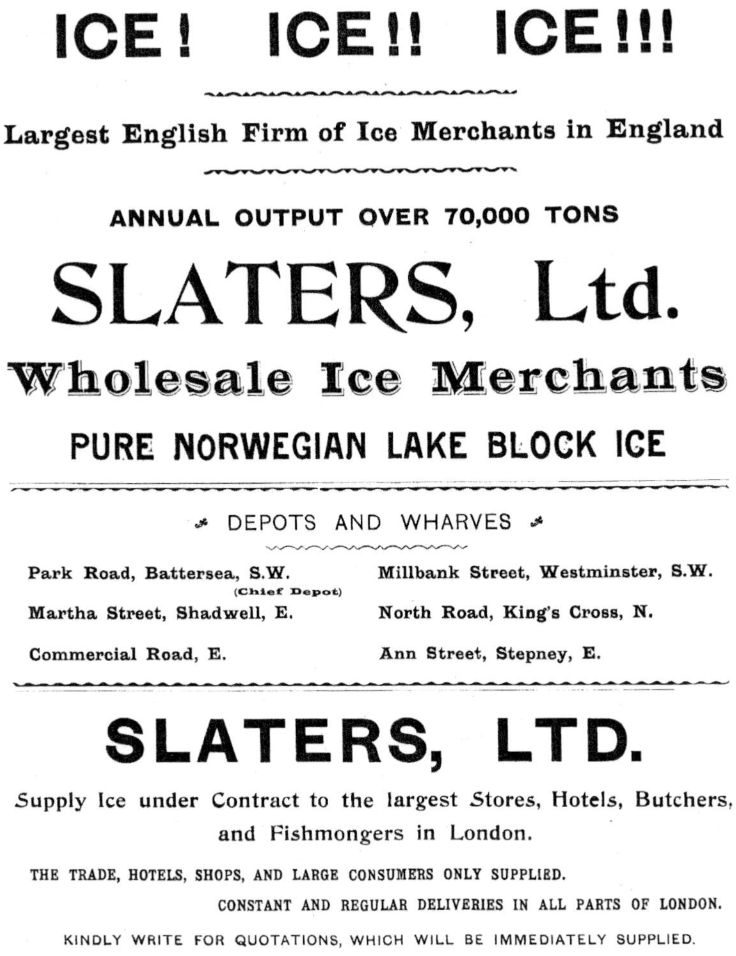

ICE! ICE!! ICE!!!

Largest English Firm of Ice Merchants in England

ANNUAL OUTPUT OVER 70,000 TONS

SLATERS, Ltd.

Wholesale Ice Merchants

PURE NORWEGIAN LAKE BLOCK ICE

DEPOTS AND WHARVES

Park Road, Battersea, S.W. (Chief Depot)	Millbank Street, Westminster, S.W.
Martha Street, Shadwell, E.	North Road, King's Cross, N.
Commercial Road, E.	Ann Street, Stepney, E.

SLATERS, LTD.

Supply Ice under Contract to the largest Stores, Hotels, Butchers, and Fishmongers in London.

THE TRADE, HOTELS, SHOPS, AND LARGE CONSUMERS ONLY SUPPLIED.

CONSTANT AND REGULAR DELIVERIES IN ALL PARTS OF LONDON.

KINDLY WRITE FOR QUOTATIONS, WHICH WILL BE IMMEDIATELY SUPPLIED.

Figure 6.2. Advertisement of August 1900 for Norwegian ice supplied by the London firm of Slaters, not long before it merged with other ice businesses to become the United combine (Bodleian: Per 193998 d.1/III p. 182).

the early decades of the nineteenth century, with a fleet of sailing ships working out of Liverpool.[243]

At King's Lynn in Norfolk, natural imported ice was stored in deep cellars or vaults beneath the dockside warehouses. Once used for storing imported wine, they formed ideal ice stores, the ice blocks showing

---

243 See the respective accounts in *Cold Storage and Ice Trades Review* II (1900), pp. 153–4; idem., XII (1909), p. 127.

CHAPTER 6

Figure 6.3. H.T. Ropes's ice store at North John Street in Liverpool (Bodleian: Per 193998 d.1/IX p. 145).

only minimal loss during the winter months.[244] At nearby Lowestoft, Norwegian ice was stored in a specially thatched ice house where a quayside gantry facilitated the unloading and loading of ice blocks from and to waiting vessels.[245] The thatch plainly had insulating benefits, although how this compared with ice that was kept in underground wells or cellars is not apparent. In Southampton, there were not only half a dozen or more ice cellars in the town itself, but also ice stores outside of the town at Shirley and at Sholing. The Shirley store was under the Ice House Inn there. The Sholing store was at one time used by a steam shipping company. All were supplied with Norwegian block ice landed at Southampton's town quay.[246]

The Norwegian ice trade into King's Lynn was recalled by one of the town's older residents from the time when he lived there as a child, in 1913. His father was among a group of local businessmen who had set up the

---

244 S.P. Beamon and S. Roaf, *The Ice-Houses of Britain* (London, 1990), p. 50.
245 R. Maltster, *Lowestoft East Coast Port* (Lavenham, 1982), p. 116.
246 M. Ellis, *Ice and Icehouses through the Ages, with a Gazetteer for Hampshire* (Southampton, 1982), pp. 45–7.

Eastern Counties Ice Company and he remembered watching ice blocks being lifted from the holds of ice steamers by means of manual hoists and then taken precariously in wheelbarrows down narrow wooden gangplanks on to the wharf. Given the weight of the ice blocks, this was a feat requiring a fine balance. Otherwise, wheelbarrow, ice block and dockworker would easily tumble into the wharf basin itself.[247]

The task of excavating ice from ice-stores or ice-wells was no easy one. If individual blocks had not been stored in dry condition and if they had not been properly packed, with layers of sawdust or some other non-heat-conducting substance between them, the ice blocks could fuse into giant and almost unmanageable masses. In 1871, *The Times* reported a fatal accident at the Gatti ice-well in Islington. Six labourers were in the process of digging out a block of Norwegian ice about eight feet high and two tons in weight when part of it broke away and collapsed on one of the workmen, fatally injuring him. At the ensuing coroner's inquest, it was established that the ice-well was 72 feet deep and 40 feet in diameter. Excavated ice was raised in baskets each containing about one and half hundredweight of ice. The usual practice was for ice only to be taken from the top. It was never to be worked from below. However, the inquest made clear that undermining the ice mass from below was a common practice, even if it had not previously led to a fatal accident.[248]

The London County Council report on ice and cold storage inquired in some detail into the type and condition of ice stores in the capital. It noted how many wells rested on gravel or other 'pervious' material, and hence were self-draining. However, a few had drainage outlets that connected to sewer pipes and this meant that there was always a possibility of back flow and thus a danger of contamination. The most unsatisfactory ice stores were those above or just below ground and constructed of brick. Even when lined internally with wood and with sawdust as insulation, there was 'suction' from the bricks such that, four or five weeks after filling, you could walk right round the ice, the blocks adjacent to the walls having entirely melted away.[249]

---

247 See S.P. Beamon and S. Roaf, *op. cit.*, pp. 49–50.
248 *The Times*, 22nd November 1871.
249 W.H. Hamer, *op.cit.*

CHAPTER 6

A problem that all ice merchants faced was the best way to light their wells. Excavation and manipulation of ice-blocks was a difficult enough task on its own, but even worse given the dark conditions in which the job had to be undertaken. Tallow candles were the primary means, but they gave only feeble illumination and had to be used in large numbers, and sometimes a thick mist would rise from the ice mass and make work on the ice all but impossible. It was thus no surprise to discover that some ice merchants were soon experimenting with electricity in their wells. In Bristol a large ice well was lit by means of electric glass lanterns fixed in the roof and arranged so as to cast illumination both downward and laterally. This ensured that all wires and switches were kept outside the well and hence unaffected by the damp atmosphere.[250]

The authors of the London County Council report explored several ice wells as part of their deliberations, remarking that it was not a task to be undertaken lightly, especially when the wells were empty. They were unsurprised to learn that writers of fiction had had recourse to the ice well as a means of affording unanticipated *dénouements*. In some ways, they offered an apotheosis of the macabre, a refuge for ghosts, demons and suspect corpses.[251] When the *Daily Mail*'s reporter visited a Gatti ice well in London in June 1900, he considered it to be the coolest place in the metropolis. You reached the vast storage cellar by a sequence of ladders that appeared to penetrate to the bowels of the earth. The cold was like death's finger. It was as if you had momentarily been transported from the torrid to the polar regions.[252] It was almost the stuff of science fiction, akin to a narrative out of H.G.Wells. The *Harmsworth Monthly Magazine* offered a not dissimilar account in its feature article on Norway's ice imports in the August 1901 issue. Its reporter had been invited to inspect Slater's large wharves and depots at Battersea. Alongside the main dock there, trapdoors in the quay floor led one down into a frozen world of clear blue ice, gleaming mysteriously in the half light. The doors were

---

250 See *Cold Storage and Ice Trades Review* II (1899), p. 23.
251 W.H. Hamer, *op. cit.*
252 *Daily Mail*, 20th June 1900.

covered with layers of thick felt and a host of precautions were taken to exclude air.[253]

As well as maintaining extensive ice stores, ice merchants plainly had to have a means of distributing their goods to business and to domestic customers. Ice intended for country destinations invariably found its way there by rail. Ice blocks were packed in special hemp sacking and were either carried as small lots on passenger trains or else in larger consignments on goods trains. In 1872, the Railway Clearing House, the central agency responsible for the setting of railway freight rates, distinguished ice that was to be carried loose, ice that was packed, and ice that was made up of lots of four tons or more. In all cases, weight was specified as being taken at the starting point of the journey, clearly implying an element of melting in transit.[254] By the 1890s, at the height of the Norwegian import trade, ice conveyed on regular merchandise trains paid 2.65d per ton mile for the first 20 miles, falling in a tapering fashion to 1.5d for over 100 miles. Ice sent by passenger train, by contrast, cost 8d per ton mile for the first twenty miles, tapering to 2.4d over 100 miles.[255] Conveyance by passenger train was so much more expensive by virtue of the greater speed that it guaranteed, in other words minimizing loss through wastage. Railway companies at the time could set their freight rates according to what traffics would bear, and ice was no exception. At King's Lynn in Norfolk, just before the First World War, the Eastern Counties Ice Company was regularly importing hundredweight blocks of Norwegian ice that were subsequently despatched via passenger trains of the Great Eastern Railway to destinations all across East Anglia. The buyers were mainly inland hotels, restaurants, fishmongers and ice-cream makers. But country houses and country estates were also important users, especially if their ornamental ponds and lakes had failed to provide an adequate winter supply to re-stock their ice-houses.[256] On the south coast of England in the late

---

253 'From Lake to Lemon Squash: How Norway Lowers Britain's Temperature', *Harmsworth Magazine* VII (1901), p. 20.
254 Railway Clearing House, *List of Alterations in, and Additions to, General Classifications of Goods* (London, 1872), p. 17.
255 J. Davies, *Railway Rates, Charges, and Regulations of the United Kingdom* (London, c. 1893), pp. 96, 141.
256 S. Beamon and S. Roaf, *op. cit.*, p. 50.

1880s, the Norwegian Block Ice Company, with depots at Portsmouth and Southampton, was distributing imported ice by rail, 'securely packed in sacking and sawdust', to destinations throughout Hampshire, Wiltshire, Dorset and Sussex.[257] Some ice importers even boasted that they could have ice delivered by rail to any part of the kingdom within 24 hours of receiving the order.

Figure 6.4. Norwegian block ice being advertised in *Kelly's Directory for Hampshire & the Isle of Wight* (London, 1889).

Ice destined for consumption within city limits was mainly for hotels, clubs, restaurants and the town houses of the upper classes. In 1911, London's National Liberal Club, with 5,000 members, spent nearly £254 on ice – somewhere around 30 tons.[258] Earlier, in 1903, one London ice merchant recorded supplying to such customers some 400 'ice pyramids', consisting of columnar masses of clear natural ice, weighing from 20 to 400 pounds.[259] In hot summers, though, on so-called 'dog days', the number of individual households requiring ice grew exponentially. In London and most other

---

257 See M. Ellis, *op. cit.*, p. 44.
258 *Cold Storage and Ice Trades Review* XV (1912), p. 117.
259 W.H. Hamer, *op. cit.*

towns and cities, ice was distributed in ordinary carts, wagons and vans, although some firms in due course came to adapt such vehicles for the specific purpose of carrying ice. By 1900, the firm of Scammells of Spitalfields had begun building special insulated vans for use in distributing meat from the capital's cold stores. Cork was the insulation material used and the van weighed just over two tons, with a loading capacity of up to four tons.[260] At the time, it was stated that ice merchants in general had shown no interest in using such vehicles, preferring ordinary close-panelled vans and carts. In later years, though, particularly after the 1914-18 war, such vans did appear on some city and suburban streets, as we will later see.

In 1900, Slaters was distributing some 70,000 tons annually to users within about a ten-mile radius of its Thames-side depots.[261] When London's United ice combine came into being in 1901, it became the possessor of a total of 234 ice vans and ice-carts, together with 231 horses.[262] By the summer of 1911, it was reckoned that London's principal ice merchants operated between them some four or five hundred carts or vans engaged in ice distribution on a daily basis.[263] Of course, some proportion of this ice was by now artificial ice, since a number of companies both manufactured ice and also imported it. In the summer season, though, it was Norwegian ice that predominated, simply because the artificial ice plants could not cope with the phenomenal surges in demand that spells of hot summer weather brought. The scale of ice distribution by 1911 was thrown into sharp relief when a strike of dockers and carmen paralysed much of the capital's import trade, ice included. The United Carlo Gatti ice combine, for instance, had five ice-steamers and several sailing vessels waiting to be unloaded in the first week of August. They also had a number of cargoes in passage across the North Sea.[264] But their plight was perhaps less acute than that of the manufacturers of artificial ice, several of whom had to cease production altogether because there were limits to the quantities of ice that they were capable of storing.

---

260 *Cold Storage and Ice Trades Review* II (1900), p. 171.
261 Ibid., III (1900), p. 166.
262 Ibid., IV (1901), p. 131.
263 *The Times*, 10th August 1911.
264 Ibid.

CHAPTER 6

The men who plied ice around London and other British cities were, like the sailors who brought it over the North Sea, a hardened breed. Those who worked for the United Carlo Gatti Company typically had to rise at three or four in the morning in the summer season. The first few hours were spent loading the carts from the freezing ice wells. Once on their rounds, the men had to manoeuvre the ice blocks into customers' premises. Sometimes there was old ice to be removed from safes and refrigerators, and it was sometimes necessary to clean them before they were re-filled. By late morning the men would have exhausted the two to three tons of ice that their carts carried and it was time to return to the ice wells and re-load before going out on a second round. Handling the ice was never easy, even when wrapped in sacking. On a hot day, it was melting continuously, water constantly trickling from the back of the ice-cart. The ice could be quite brittle and, in the process of unloading, small pieces were continually breaking off. If the men lost their grip on a large ice block while taking it down from the cart and it slipped to the ground, it often smashed beyond use. For small customers, the iceman had to cut the blocks into halves or quarters at the roadside. 'Sixpenny worth' of ice was about as much as an ordinary person could carry in two hands. Otherwise blocks had to be slid along the ground and then down planks or chutes into cellars. In a heatwave the icemen might make three daily rounds, not returning to depot until early evening. It was hard labour, in other words, and wages were poor. Whilst most icemen received a weekly wage, they had to account daily for the ice they sold. If there was any discrepancy between the ice they loaded at the start of a round and the money they returned at the end, it had to be accounted for. Thus icemen who were careless in handling or cutting the ice inevitably faced penalties.[265] The system, though, was also open to abuse. In July 1902, a Westminster court gaoled two icemen employed by the Shingleton Ice Company for selling ice to a Mayfair fishmonger not among the company's customers and then pocketing the money.[266]

---

265 This account of men who distributed ice for the United company is drawn largely from F. Kinross, *Coffee and Ices: The Story of Carlo Gatti in London* (Sudbury, 1991), pp. 27, 33–4; see also 'From Lake to Lemon Squash', *op. cit.*
266 *Cold Storage and Ice Trades Review* V (1902), p. 107.

THE ICEMAN COMETH

Most of the leading ice merchants in London at different times evolved distinctive liveries for the fleets of vehicles they operated. The United Carlo Gatti Company's colours were yellow and black, the North Pole Ice Company's at one time green.[267] A few of the largest firms had begun experimenting with motorized traction by this time. In 1906, for instance, the North Pole Ice Company took delivery of a German-built motor lorry capable of loading thirty of the company's two-hundredweight ice-blocks. The vehicle could travel up to eight miles an hour.[268] Outside of London, William Milne's Ice Factory in Old Wynd in Glasgow was running a three-ton Halley 24 horse-power petrol van by the same date.[269] In the quieter parts of the provinces, though, ice carriage remained very much locked into the horse-drawn era, as exemplified by William Francis Freelove's watercolour of a Richmond ice merchant's cart in the early 1870s.[270] Carlo Ferrari was probably an Italian ice-cream maker who did a parallel trade in ice in the locality of Richmond. The long flap at the rear

Figure 6.5. Motorized traction for ice transport, Glasgow 1906 (Bodleian: Per 193998 d.1/IX p. 355).

---

267 E. David, *Harvest of the Cold Months: The Social History of Ice and Ices* (London, 1996), pp. 345, 349.
268 *Cold Storage and Ice Trades Review* IX (1906), p. 153.
269 Ibid., p. 355.
270 W.F. Freelove, *Victorian Horses and Carriages; A Personal Sketch Book* (London, 1979)

of the gaily painted cart may have been for sliding ice blocks down on to the ground. For in the absence of hoists or other mechanical means of moving it, ice was always a difficult commodity to handle manually, even when wrapped in sacking or other insulating material.

Figure 6.6. Carlo Ferrari's ice cart (Freelove, Lutterworth Press, 1979).

The editor of the *Cold Storage and Ice Trades Review* was one of a number of key commentators of the time who became particularly exercised about the methods of unloading ice-carts at the roadside, and especially on town and city streets. In 1906 he remarked that the United Kingdom was among the worst countries in Europe for the extent of contamination from ice-handling during delivery.[271] Earlier, in 1902, the same journal had carried a detailed report of what it described as 'unappetizing ice'. It recalled how ice-carts were regularly dirty, comparing most unfavourably with their counterparts on the continent. The blankets or sacking in which the ice was wrapped were likewise soiled, while the carters and carmen who handled the ice were 'not overclean' either. Worst of all, however, was the way ice blocks were dragged along pavements upon which all manner of excreta were to be found. Even outside high-class hotels,

---

271   *Cold Storage and Ice Trades Review* IX (1906), p. 261.

restaurants and fishmongers, bare blocks of ice could be seen dumped on pavements before being manhandled to entrance doorways.[272] In 1905, the *Review* also observed that one London ice contractor sent ice-carts for use as platforms for public meetings.[273] This was presumably a means of maintaining cash flow at times of slack demand.

Most of the largest ice importers, as well as producers of manufactured ice, supplied their product under regular contract. In other words, theirs was largely what today we would call a 'trade' business. The London firm of Slaters typically advertised that it serviced only 'the largest stores, hotels, butchers, and fishmongers in London'. Daily deliveries were made throughout London for this category of customer so as to ensure a constancy of ice supply. Such firms would sell ice to private houses, but only if it was ordered on a regular basis. This was a pattern of dealing that had prevailed for fifty years and more. When the Wenham Lake Ice Company was importing American ice in mid-century, for example, most of its customers were business rather than household users; and when the Shingleton Ice Company began artificial ice-making in London in the 1870s, it developed its trade largely with West End clubs which took ice on annual contracts.[274] Most of the natural ice took the form of square blocks of from one to four hundredweight, in other words exactly in the form in which it had been cut from the lakes and fjords. With ice coming in this kind of size and weight, it could not be for anything other than trade sale.

In the spring of 1900, in a plain effort to enhance the sale and use of ice, an enterprising Dutchman launched the Star Ice Company from premises near London's Oxford Circus.[275] The firm specialized in manufacturing ice in small cubes for table use and the centre of each cube contained a glittering star. The ice cubes themselves were roughly an inch square and the star impression was made by a patent stamping apparatus. The idea was to use the ice in drinks. Given the appellation 'glace de luxe', it was

---

272   *Ibid.*, V (1902), p. 98.
273   *Ibid.*, VII (1904), p. 8.
274   See G. Weightman, *The Frozen Water Trade: How Ice from New England Lakes Kept the World Cool* (London, 2002), p. 144; *Cold Storage and Ice Trades Review*, II (1900), p. 154.
275   *Cold Storage and Ice Trades Review* III (1900), p. 15.

anticipated that other designs would follow. Sadly for the entrepreneur, as well as for the intrigued consumer, the Star Ice Company had an all too brief existence. By March 1902 its operations had ceased.[276]

One particularly interesting feature of the use of ice in restaurants, inns and other public places was the way it had become stimulated as a result of the demands made by American travellers in Britain. In 1900, the American consul in Birmingham filed a report to the Bureau of Foreign Commerce in Washington remarking on the incessant clamour among American visitors for ice.[277] As a result, even some country inns began placing ice in glass dishes which you picked out with sugar tongs and placed in your drink. It was invariably pure Norwegian block ice that was used for this purpose, not the artificial output of the emergent ice factories.

For Oxford undergraduates ice had by the later decades of the nineteenth century become a staple ingredient of what were then some of the most fashionable drinks. *Oxford Night Caps* described how, when the famous sherry cobbler was first introduced to the young men of the university, the ice was procured from local confectioners and fishmongers who had taken it from stagnant ponds and noisome ditches. The result was not wholly appetizing. Subsequently, Wenham Lake ice was substituted, first from America and later from Norway. To make a sherry cobbler, you pounded a small quantity of ice quite fine by wrapping it in a coarse cloth and beating it with a mallet or rolling pin. You then half-filled a large tumbler with the powdered ice, added a teaspoon and a half of powdered sugar, some pieces of lemon rind and, lastly, a wine glass and a half of sherry. The concoction was then mixed by pouring rapidly from one tumbler into another, adding more ice as needed. It was drunk through a straw. For its instructions for making mint julep, *Oxford Night Caps* took directly from the Wenham Lake Ice Company's own recipe: you mixed ice and sugar exactly as for a sherry cobbler, then added a wine glass of brandy, half a wine glass of rum and some sprigs of fresh mint before stirring well and adding a straw. Not surprisingly, Oxford ice merchants did a busy trade in term time supplying ice for such purposes.[278]

---

276   *Ibid.*, IV (1902), p. 359.
277   *Ibid.*, III (1900), p. 205.
278   R. Cook, *Oxford Night Caps* (Oxford, n.d.), pp. 8–10.

From the 1890s until 1914, the practice of using ice for decorative purposes grew considerably. The Queen's railway carriage had long been cooled in summer by placing large irregular blocks of ice, often concealed by foliage or flowers, on the compartment floor. In hotels and clubs in London and other large cities, miniature ice blocks were placed on dining tables and sideboards on hot summer days. In some of the smartest establishments, as we have seen, chefs sculpted decorative features from the ice. Only Norwegian ice was usually suitable for this purpose: it was less brittle and was longer-lasting than the factory product. The final touch was to place small incandescent electric lamps inside the ice for use at night-time.[279]

The later nineteenth century also witnessed a widening of industrial uses of ice. Alongside the fishing and cold storage industries, brewers, for instance, had discovered that by using refrigerating tanks, the 'wort' could be cooled much more quickly than before, allowing them to brew almost daily rather than once a week. Another growing use of ice occurred in hospitals and infirmaries. By 1900, London's principal hospitals were consuming thousands of tons every year. It was especially used in surgical operations.[280] In each case, though, in brewing as well as in medicine, it was generally factory ice rather than natural ice that was being used. In the summer of 1911, during the dock strike in London, which paralysed the unloading of supplies of Norwegian ice, the hospitals became one of the few institutions that continued to receive ice on a daily basis.[281] London's ice factories then had an output of some 500 tons a day.[282]

Supply of ice to domestic users was, on most authorities, a near monopoly of the fishmonger trade. One commentator writing on London in 1904 reckoned that as much as 95 per cent of ice sold for domestic purposes came from fishmongers.[283] In 1907, the *Fish Trades Gazette* offered advice to fishmongers on how to cut ice blocks. The saw was regarded as the most economical means, since it minimized chipping and hence waste. After sawing down two or three inches, it was usually possible to split the ice

---

279 See *British Refrigeration and Allied Interests* III (Jan-June 1900), p. 187.
280 Ibid., p. 163.
281 *Cold Storage and Ice Trades Review* XIV (1911), p. 220.
282 Ibid., p. 221.
283 Ibid., VII (1904), p. 305.

with a pick, particularly if care was taken to see in which direction the grain ran. Cutting ice to sell by weight required a good deal of practice, but it could normally be cut to within about half a pound, especially if the grain was right.[284] A few milk-dealers and butchers also dealt in ice for domestic use, but they were very much a minority. A critical difficulty with door-to-door delivery of ice was its bulk, weight and wetness. This is what made handling it alongside milk so problematic. Certainly it was beyond the capacity of ordinary dairy carts to deal in ice in any significant quantity. Besides, most dairymen delivering from door-to-door already had their work cut out just supplying milk.[285] There was still no *general* demand for ice within English households. Domestic demand was entirely contingent upon hot weather, hence helping to explain why the ice trade was such a volatile one. For ten and perhaps even eleven months of the year, the suburban middle classes required no ice at all. Come a heat wave, though, all were clamouring for ice. It was essential for food preservation. Butter, milk, meat and all manner of other foodstuffs quickly went putrid. Many of those involved in the ice trade repeatedly observed that this pattern would be altered if the public at large could be educated in the uses and applications of ice. Too few householders registered how a plentiful supply of ice was of great value for food preservation, for maintaining articles of food in a fresh and wholesome condition. Commentators pointed to the position in America and in parts of the Continent where ice was much more widely used and could be obtained with much greater ease and more cheaply. As late as 1910, a Norwegian commentator on the ice trade to Britain sagely summarized the position of domestic ice consumption. Ice was not an article people sought unless they wanted it. Cheap ice was no inducement for them to buy it. They bought it when they had to buy it. Whether it was 10 shillings or 20 shillings a ton made little difference. If people did not want ice, they would not appreciate it as a gift, so the writer claimed.[286] It was, nevertheless, true to say that small quantities of ice were more expensive to purchase than large ones. A fishmonger or butcher around 1900 would charge customers 2/6d to 3/- per cwt, the equivalent

---

284 Ibid., X (1907), p. 135.
285 Ibid., VII (1904), p. 233.
286 Ibid. XIII (1910), p. 36.

of 50 to 60 shillings a ton at a time when factory ice could be bought for a fifth of this figure and Norwegian lake or fjord ice for a quarter.[287] The added cost came from cutting the ice to the requisite size and all the wastage and melting that that invariably incurred.

In the early summer of 1902, with the warm weather approaching, retail confectioners and caterers were urged to adopt the practice of a 'keep cool' window in their premises as a means of encouraging wider use of ice. This might, it was suggested, comprise a block of ice, ice tongs, an ice cream freezer drum, lemons, a siphon and a series of fans. The entire effect could then be enhanced by creating a small waterfall. A further possibility was to display one of the American soda fountains which were already being stocked by some London confectioners.[288]

One of the ways in which the larger ice importers had long sought to address the issue of a wider usage of ice was through the sale of ice chests, ice safes and ice refrigerators, along with all manner of other contrivances or utensils intended for use in the preservation of particular items of food. The Wenham Lake Ice Company, for instance, had, almost since its formation, advertised and sold 'American refrigerators or miniature ice-houses' to its customers. And by the 1880s it had regular notices in *The Times* for American Ice Water Pitchers, Ice Butter Dishes, Ice Cream Machines, not to mention Duplex Refrigerators complete with water tanks and filters.[289] A whole variety of British firms also patented iceboxes. The smallest were just a few feet square, typically lined with zinc. Broken ice was placed in the bottom and the foodstuffs to be preserved suspended in a wire cage. A correspondent of *The Times* in August 1868 especially recommended Sorenson's patent felt-insulated ice-box, relating how, four days previously, he had placed 20 pounds of rough ice in the box, he had emptied the box of water each morning, and yet on the fourth day there was still ice left. In the interim, ice had been removed from the box for table use and various foodstuffs had been preserved in it. And all this in a room with a southerly aspect.[290] Thomas Masters's *Ice Book* of

---

287 *British Refrigeration and Allied Interests* II (July-Dec 1900), p. 11.
288 *Cold Storage and Ice Trades Review*, V (1902), p. 54.
289 See, for example, *The Times*, 6th June 1881.
290 *Ibid.*, 4th August 1868.

CHAPTER 6

1844 had described an ice-box of his own design intended for general sale. It was wood-lined on the outside, then lined inside with a patent material known as orpholithe. Within this, though, was found yet another wooden case, this time lined with lead. The wood and the orpholithe were bad conductors of heat and enabled food to be kept for quite long periods provided small quantities of ice continued to be added each day. Masters also sold wine coolers designed along similar principles.[291]

There was universal agreement among all those who dealt in ice that water was its greatest enemy, not heat. A 25-pound block of ice could be placed in a room with a constant air temperature of 75 degrees Fahrenheit and, provided it was kept perfectly drained, the ice would remain little diminished after 24 hours. However, allow the same ice block to stand in its own meltwater and much of it would disappear after five or six hours. The general maxim was that water at 40 degrees will melt ice with ten times the rapidity of air at 80 degrees.[292]

Some large ice merchants, in an effort to stimulate demand, resorted to hiring out refrigerators and ice-safes to private households. For an average-sized household in London's West End, this meant an outlay of 15/- or £1 per month. For a middle-class family in the suburbs, a much smaller ice-box would be sufficient, with a correspondingly lower hire fee.[293] In cool summers, there were always customers who, having ordered refrigerators or ice-boxes for hire, promptly sought to return them after a few weeks, usually leaving the suppliers with a financial loss in terms of the costs of delivery and collection. In hot summers, demand typically outstripped supply very rapidly. In 1899, for instance, all American ice refrigerators, either in stock or in transit, were sold within a matter of weeks once the heat wave seemed assured.[294] For some ice importers, as well as ice producers, this was exactly the springboard for widening domestic usage of ice. A succession of 'broiling hot' summers would stimulate manufacture of inexpensive ice-boxes and thereby generate the basis of a more regular domestic demand.

---

291 T. Masters, *The Ice Book: Being a Compendious & Concise History of Everything Connected with Ice* (London, 1844), p. 82.
292 *The Times*, 4th August 1868.
293 *Cold Storage and Ice Trades Review* VII (1904), p. 305.
294 *Ibid.*, III (1900), p. 205.

And with households cultivating 'a more regular ice habit', the view was that, ultimately, the price of ice would also fall. However, it was recognized that there remained a need to educate the householder much more fully in the use of ice refrigerators or ice-safes. Some made the mistake of laying fish in with the ice. Others wrongly placed jellies and blancmanges there to set. Where food items placed in the ice compartment were accidentally spilled, this often blocked the drain and so the ice, in due course, ended up standing in accumulations of water and began to melt rapidly. It was also not unknown for householders to place the refrigerators in the courtyard or garden, exposed to sun and rain. Others were just careless in failing to keep the ice compartment filled with fresh ice every three or four days.[295]

After 1918, ice trade commentators repeatedly returned to the issue of domestic ice supply, desperately keen to achieve an ice-producing industry that was in direct relation with the household consumer. The war decimated the Norwegian ice trade, as will later become clear, but the producers of artificial ice, as well as the few firms who continued to import ice, still clung to the objective of a public door-to-door ice supply. It still drew repeated comment in

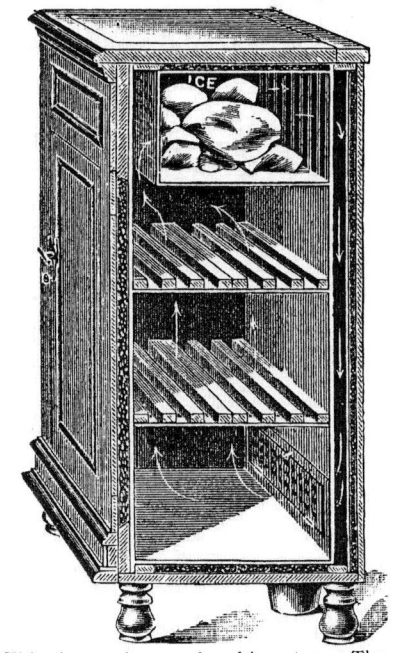

Figure 6.7. An ice refrigerator from the Army & Navy Stores catalogue of 1907 (reprinted as 'Yesterday's Shopping', David & Charles, 1969).

---

295 *Ibid.*, XXVI (1923), p. 5.

CHAPTER 6

the various trade journals.[296] However, a letter from the managing director of a leading refrigeration company to *The Times* in 1926 summarized very effectively the difficulties that remained, even by the 1920s.[297] Ice merchants and ice producers were severely hampered by the extremely variable British climate. Despite the country having a highly progressive ice industry, the trade involved high risk and great uncertainty. In one year an ice factory could be completely unable to meet local demand and yet in another not even be able to sell one quarter of its normal output. A large storage capacity was vital in all events, but it was never enough to cope with the ten days in the year when demand soared with thousands requiring ice who on the remaining 355 days never used ice at all. It was impossible for ice producers (or even ice importers) to maintain a potential scale of supply that would meet such demand peaks. For the same reason, it was hard to maintain a door-to-door delivery operation given the expenditure in vehicles and manpower that was necessary. In 1927, though, one company in London did start with a door-to-door operation. The Domestic Ice Supply Company Ltd., with a fleet of white horse-drawn vans, staffed by ex-servicemen, began delivering ice direct to households in Kensington and Marylebone. Customers had to agree to a contract of eight, thirteen or seventeen weeks that ensured ice three days a week in quantities of around 25 pounds. The company supplied customers with an ice-box (ice refrigerator) as part of the contract. The venture was a considerable success, with around 20,000 customers in its first summer season.[298] In the following year, new districts were added and the enterprise was still in operation in 1929, by which time a number of other firms had begun to organize similar services in other parts of the country.[299] In Birmingham, the Lightfoot Refrigeration Company began delivering 16-pound blocks of ice by horse-drawn van twice weekly to some of the city's suburbs.[300] A similar service was begun in Tunbridge Wells in Kent in the same year and another in Hove in 1931, in the latter instance using a

---

296 See, for example, *ibid.*, XXVIII (1925), p. 278.
297 *Ibid.*, XXIX (1926), p. 192; also XXVII (1924), pp. 459–60.
298 *Ibid.*, XXX (1927), pp. 255–6.
299 *Ibid.*, XXXI (1928), p. 244; *Ibid.*, XXXII (1929), p. 189.
300 *Ibid.*, XXXII (1929), p. 160.

Figure 6.8. A horse-drawn delivery vehicle belonging to the Domestic Ice Supply Company, 1927, based in London's West End (Bodleian: Per 193998 d.1/XXX p. 256).

motorized vehicle.[301] All of these various ventures embarked on intensive advertising forays, using such slogans as 'save it with ice'. Posters for ice refrigerators appeared in ironmongers' windows, while fish merchants were plied with extra ice for display. However, there was a spectre on the horizon: the mechanical refrigerator. As we have seen, machine refrigerators were beginning to find their way into many of the more affluent homes, sounding the death-knell for ice refrigeration and for the ice man. The one encouraging portent for ice producers was the steady expansion of the ice-cream industry bringing with it new demands for ice supply and, as the next chapter will show, enticing some ice producers themselves to engage in ice-cream making as a regular component of their business operations.

It is tempting to assume that, as the scale and range of demands for ice had expanded over the final two decades of the nineteenth century and into the first decade of the twentieth, notably as technology and organisation improved, so the price to the consumer progressively fell. In 1884, the average price for Norwegian imported ice at dockside in Britain was some 18 shillings per ton. The parallel figure in 1899 was some 13 shillings.

---

301   *Ibid.*; *Ibid.*, XXXIV (1931), p. 182.

CHAPTER 6

Figure 6.9. An ice-chest supplied by the Lightfoot Refrigeration Company in Birmingham in 1929 (Bodleian: Per 193998 d.1/XXXII p. 160).

But this was no steady fall. The fickle nature of supply and demand made for very uneven movement. In 1897, for instance, the price had dropped to just below 11 shillings, but in 1898 it had rocketed to almost 15 shillings.[302] There could, likewise, be very significant price movements from month to

---

302 *Ibid.*, III (1900), p. 134.

Figure 6.10. One of three motor lorries used for household ice delivery in Hove in 1931 (Bodleian: Per 193998 d.1/XXXIV p. 182).

month. In February 1899, for instance, ice was selling at dockside for 10 to 12 shillings per ton, but by July 1899 for over 17 shillings.[303]

In the years after the turn of the century, the price slipped further and a little more evenly, but by a fairly small margin only. In March 1904, for instance, at the start of spring shipments, ice was landed at just below 9 shillings a ton, close to a record low.[304] But over much of that decade, it hovered at just below or just above 10 shillings a ton. This relative stability may have been linked to the formation of the Society of Norwegian Shipowners which, in early 1906, had proposed an advisory scale of minimum freights for Norwegian sailing vessels engaged in the timber, coal and ice trades.[305] There were inevitably limits to the extent that freights could be squeezed. In fact, over 1913-1914, prices were creeping back up to above 11 shillings, a sign that general demand for ice was becoming greater than the capacity of the ice industry to meet it.[306]

---

303 *British Refrigeration and Allied Interests* II (July-Dec 1899), p. 11.
304 *Cold Storage and Ice Trades Review*, VIII (1905), p. 112.
305 *Ibid.*, IX (1906), p. 81.
306 *Ibid.*, XIX (1916), p. 27.

CHAPTER 7

Ice Cream

Figure 7.1. A collection of highly decorative Victorian ice or jelly moulds from Agnes Marshall's 'Book of Ices' (Bodleian: 1781 f.8, p. 59).

Ice cream has a remarkably long history, as Elizabeth David's book, *Harvest of the Cold Months,* has made wonderfully plain.[307] Her mouth-watering accounts of Neapolitan ice recipes form a stark reminder of

---

307 E. David, *Harvest of the Cold Months: The Social History of Ice and Ices* (London, 1996).

the dullness of many of the confections that today pass off as ice cream under the auspices of corporate machino-manufacture. In Britain, Victorian and Edwardian chefs produced their own mouth-watering ices, as Elizabeth David also recounts, and a perusal of some of the more popular cookery and confectionary books of the time affords an equally vivid picture of what some gastronomes might conceive of as a kind of ice cream heaven. Agnes Marshall's *Book of Ices* describes the making of banana ice: peel and pound six ripe bananas, add the juice of two oranges and two lemons, a glass of curacoa, pass through a sieve and finish with a pint of sweetened cream or custard, before finally freezing.[308] The making of water ices was equally enticing: for apple water ice, you cooked a pound of apples in a pint of water with a little lemon peel, lemon juice, cinnamon, four ounces of sugar and some sheets of gelatine. The purée was then sieved, mixed with a pint of water sweetened with sugar or syrup, before finally being frozen.[309] What is especially striking about so many books and accounts of ice cream making at the time is the startling range of flavours that were accommodated. It is not just the vast range of fruits that draw the eye, but flavours like tea, coffee, chocolate, ginger, champagne, rum, brown bread, not to mention all kinds of nuts. Brown bread ice, according to *The Pytchley Book of Refined Cookery*, consisted of half a pound of stale brown bread crumbs mixed with a pint of whipped cream, six ounces of sugar and flavoured with vanilla essence.[310]

All of these ice and ice cream confections plainly called for large quantities of ice for the freezing process. At one time, as recounted earlier, local lakes and ponds, and, later, canal cuts and dock basins, had provided the major source, especially where confectioners had ice-wells where they could store the broken ice for later use. In 1868, a leading article in *The Times* reckoned that nine-tenths of the ice then consumed by fishmongers and confectioners came from such local sources whenever there was a hard frost.[311] However, in the later decades of the nineteenth century,

---

308 A.B. Marshall, *The Book of Ices* (London, 1885), p. 10.
309 *Ibid.*, p. 28.
310 *The Pytchley Book of Refined Cookery and Bills of Fare* (London, 1885), p. 227.
311 *The Times*, 11th September 1868.

confectioners and others also started utilizing increasing quantities of imported ice. Initially this was American ice, but later it was obtained almost exclusively from Norway. From Samuel Hobbs's monthly *Kitchen Oracle* we get some sense of the prodigious amounts that might be needed from ice merchants. Menus for 16-18 people called for one hundredweight of Wenham Lake Ice (from Norway).[312] One daily menu list stipulated half a hundredweight on the second day, another half on the third, and a full hundredweight on the fourth.[313] Hobbs was plainly writing with a large upper-class household in mind, but Humphry's *Housekeeping, a Guide* made clear that delicious ices could be made in middle-class homes by investing in the necessary freezing and ice-breaking apparatus and then buying ice wholesale from the fishmonger. It was then seven pence for fourteen pounds of ice and it paid to buy larger quantities. Smaller quantities were proportionately much dearer and did not last as long.[314] In 1899, the trade magazine *British Refrigeration and Allied Interests* remarked on the hordes of Italian ice-cream and iced-drink vendors who overran London in the summer season. They consumed enormous quantities of ice, one leading Italian confectioner taking up to 120 tons a week. In this particular case, it was ice from the Shadwell ice factory by the Thames, but such ice came just as often from the many stores of Norwegian ice in the capital.[315]

London's most famous ice cream maker throughout the nineteenth century was Gunter's on Berkeley Square.[316] The establishment had existed since the mid-eighteenth century and members of the Gunter family had been running it since at least 1800. Gunter's easily dominated the other confectioners and caterers in the capital in the making of ices, helped by the royal patronage that they attracted, particularly from among George III's sons and daughters. However, what also helped to set the seal on Gunter's reputation was when Robert Gunter went to Paris shortly after the end of the Napoleonic wars in 1815 to learn the art of ice-making the

---

312 S.W. Hobbs, *The Kitchen Oracle* (July, 1886), p. 290.
313 *Ibid.*, (August, 1886), p. 335.
314 C.E. Humphreys, *Housekeeping, a Guide* (London, 1893), p. 278.
315 *British Refrigeration and Allied Interests* I (1899), p. 14.
316 See E. David, *op. cit.*, pp. 315ff.

CHAPTER 7

IMPROVED ICE BREAKER.

No. 1.

For Hotel Keepers, Confectioners, Wine Merchants, Refreshment Rooms, Ships' Cabins, Butlers' Pantries, etc., etc.

Size A.—Price £5; with Drawer, £5 10s.
„   B.—Price £6;   „   „   £6 10s.

Figure 7.2. A machine for crushing ice as used by Victorian and Edwardian confectioners (Bodleian: 1781 f.8, p. 59).

Italian way at Tortoni's in the Boulevard des Italiens. Prior to that time, some gourmets had regarded English ices, both cream ices and water ices, as inferior to continental confections. Gunter, with the experience gained at Tortoni's, soon rectified that and turned the Berkeley Square shop into a legend. The firm's recipes were committed to print in *Gunter's Modern Confectionery* which had reached a fourth edition by 1881. The shop endured for more than a century. And Elizabeth David, in *Harvest of the Cold Months*, recalls eating Gunter's famous tangerine and strawberry ices herself in the years after the First World War.[317]

Among the early confectioners at Gunter's was an Italian by the name of Guglielmo Jarrin. His recipe book, *The Italian Confectioner*, was first published in 1820 and was still being reprinted in 1861, becoming a classic guide for many more years. Jarrin set out for his readers the way to produce the highest quality cream and water ices. The nature of the quality of the ingredients was obviously part of the trick and, at Gunter's, much of the fruit came from the firm's own nursery gardens in Earl's Court, Kensington, then still a mere village.[318] For winter, fruits were preserved according to a recipe devised by the Parisian confectioner Appert, a method that did not require the use of sugar. After the ingredients, it was the freezing method that was critical to the making of the best ices.[319] If freezing occurred too quickly, there was inadequate time for the ingredients to be mixed properly. Pewter freezing pots were best for this. Tin vessels produced too rapid a 'congelation'. Badly mixed ingredients resulted in the sugar sinking to the bottom and produced ices with a sharp unpleasant taste. Poor mixing and inadequate rotation of the freezing pan in the ice mixture also gave rise to lumps. A related defect was the way ices could acquire a 'disagreeable, dirty red colour'. The effectiveness of the freezing mixture was contingent upon adding to it the right quantities of salt, nitre or soda. Agnes Marshall, in her *Book of Ices*, expanded upon the kinds of quantity that this involved. Generally it was advisable to throw over the pounded ice in the ice tub roughly half its weight in salt, before mixing thoroughly. Marshall in fact had patented a freezing apparatus for the making of ices. The pan intended for the cream ice ingredients was first removed and a layer of ice placed in the empty tub to a depth of one or one and a half inches, in turn mixed with the appropriate quantity of salt. The empty pan was then replaced on its central pivot, the lid closed and the apparatus left for a few minutes to become thoroughly cold. The lid was then re-opened and the ingredients poured into the pan, but not to a depth of much more than one inch, for

---

317 Ibid., p. 351.
318 Ibid., pp. 321–2.
319 See W.A. Jarrin, *The Italian Confectioner* (London, 1861), p. 160.

the shallower the mixture the easier it froze. The freezer handle was then rotated until, upon inspection, the mixture had attained the right consistency and flavour. If it was not sweet enough, a little syrup, such as kirsch, could be added.

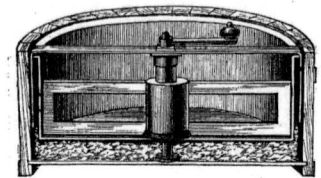

Figure 7.3. The patent freezer apparatus from Marshall's 'Book of Ices' (Bodleian: Vet A7 e.25, pp. 2–3).

For decorative ices, the frozen mixture would be scooped out of the pan and placed in the chosen mould and the mould in turn placed back on the ice mixture, with further ice and salt piled around and over it to a depth of six inches. According to *The Pytchley Book of Refined Cookery*, ices in moulds had to be overfrozen in order to retain their shape.[320] The tendency, therefore, was to remove them from the ice tub only a little while before serving. Such moulds, which were also often used for jellies, came in an astonishing array of shapes and sizes. Samuel Hobbs's *Kitchen Oracle* illustrated some of them.[321] The best were fashioned to the shape of the fruit or fruits that flavoured the ice cream inside them. They could

---

320 The Pytchley Book, *op. cit.*, p. 227.
321 S. W. Hobbs, *op. cit.*, (January, 1886), p. 45.

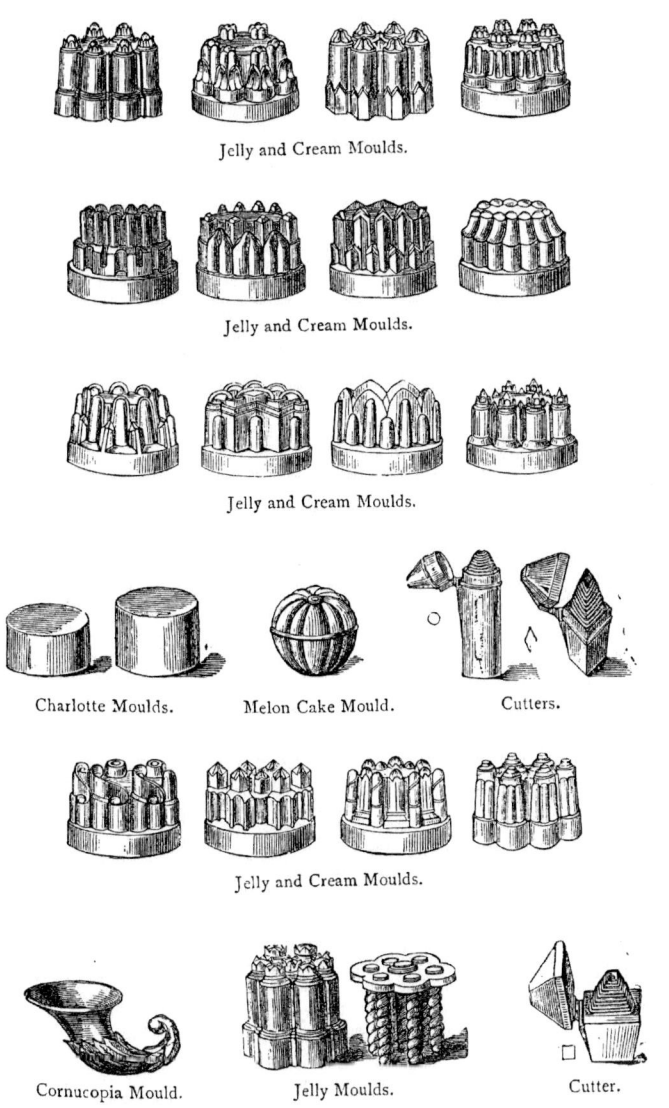

Figure 7.4. Victorian ice and jelly moulds from Hobbs's 'Kitchen Oracle' (Bodleian: 1781 e.351, p. 45).

also be surprisingly large, particularly when meant for use on grand occasions. These so-called 'bombes' or 'bomba' could contain as much as six pints of cream ice. Many were made with large numbers of egg yolks mixed with cream, lemon peel and sugar before being flavoured with fruit and sometimes also coloured. The egg yolks, cream and peel had first to be prepared over a slow fire and constantly whisked so as to form a custard. The sugar, fruit and colouring were then added and the entire confection finally transferred to the freezing apparatus.[322] It is not at all hard to see how such complex confections sometimes called for ice by the hundredweight to be available to hand. This could be met by confectioners having their own ice cellars or, better still, an ice well, much like the one at Carlo Gatti's premises on the Caledonian Road in Islington. But as the trade in imported Norwegian ice grew, and as artificial ice production expanded, particularly in the largest cities, it was more and more the big ice merchants that provided the storage, delivering ice to confectioners often several times a day in the ice cream season.

The ice trade's premier journal, the *Cold Storage and Ice Trades Review*, was very quick to notice the potential that ice cream making offered to ice merchants seeking extension of their businesses. Within six months of its first issue, it contained almost an entire page devoted to the tools and utensils needed for 'iced drinks, iced puddings and iced creams', along with appropriate recipes.[323] Its *Ice Pudding à la Princesse*, was made with a quart of fresh milk, half a pint of sweetened cream, three-quarters of a pound of granulated sugar, three-quarters of a pound of almonds, four ounces of crystallized angelica, four ounces of preserved cherries, two ounces of sultanas, two ounces of crystallized apricots, one pound of egg yolks and two wine glasses of maraschino. The ingredients, once mixed, strained and frozen, were enough to fill four moulds selling at 3/6d each. The same journal also commented on the growing practice of including ices as part of dinner menus. Whereas such offerings would once have been regarded as gastronomic heresies, diners preferring cheesecake or soufflés, increasingly they were becoming *de rigeur*. In the best restaurant establishments, the ices were served on sculptures in the shape of swans and elephants.[324] Such creations were fashioned by chefs from blocks of the finest Norwegian crystal ice. Hot smoothing-irons were used to give the final finish and polish. *Socle en glace*, as the technique was called, required great care and dexterity. If the ice cracked

---

322 See W.A. Jarrin, *op. cit.*, p. 161.
323 *Cold Storage and Ice Trades Review* I (1898), p. 62.
324 *Ibid.*, IV (1901), p. 196.

or the chef made an error, the entire process had to be started all over again. The annual dinner of the Cold Storage Association in 1901 had an ice model as a table centre, illuminated by means of electric light.[325] Creations of this sort cost £3 to £5.

Ice cream manufacture was not, of course, confined only to the cities. The business had also been growing apace in many coastal resorts. The Devon and Cornwall Ice and Cold Storage Company at Plymouth relied heavily on the summer demand for ice from local confectioners to bolster the economic viability of its ice plant. The nearby resort of Torquay, for instance, was regularly supplied with ice for this purpose. Moreover, this was alongside the activities of another Plymouth ice merchant who dealt exclusively in imported Norwegian ice.[326]

Until the mid-nineteenth century, most ices, whether cream, custard, or water-based, were a luxury confection. They were the foods of peers and princes, the fare of the best clubs and eating houses. Ices for the ordinary populace were largely unknown. It was the Italian-speaking Swiss family, the Gattis, as we have seen, who can lay claim to having introduced ices to the man on the street. Carlo Gatti and members of his extended family came to England from the canton of Ticino, from the Val Blegno, and followed in the tradition of the Ticinese in seeking their fortunes overseas. It was from Gatti's pastry and confectioner's business in the Great Hall of Hungerford Market in London in the early 1850s that 'penny ices' were first sold, and they became so popular that they were soon being sold on the streets from mobile ice-cream carts. They became known as 'hokey-pokeys', supposedly a corruption of the Italian 'ecco un poco', meaning 'here is a little'. When Hungerford Market was pulled down to make way for the building of Charing Cross station, the Gatti family relocated the business to the Adelaide Gallery, then a place of entertainment and occasional exhibitions. Stefano and Agostino eventually succeeded to this concern and expanded it by extending the premises through to the Strand. Soon the Gatti brothers had become refreshment contractors to a number of theatres and other places of entertainment.

---

325 *Ibid.*
326 *Ibid.*, III (1900), p. 137.

And, in due course, they bought the Adelphi Theatre (in 1879), launching their position in the theatrical world as managers, a position they subsequently pursued with remarkable success.[327]

In London, it is plain that the common trade in penny ices, particularly on the streets, grew in leaps and bounds in the later decades of the nineteenth century. In the Holborn area, it was Carlo Gatti, as ice merchant, who supplied the street traders with ice to make their product. According to a report for the London County Council in 1899, there were by then some 300 Italian 'ice labourers' living and working in the capital.[328] Moreover, by the 1890s, this part of the ice cream trade had grown so large that it was starting to attract the attentions of borough medical officers of health. In October 1898, for instance, *The Times* reported on a case of an Italian ice-cream vendor in Bermondsey who had been summonsed for selling ice cream that appeared to have been made from decomposing milk. Reputedly, analysis had revealed that each cubic centimetre of ice contained a million microbes.[329] In 1899, the Medical Officer of Health for Paddington recommended to his local vestry that the premises where street vendors made their ices needed regular inspection.[330] And the same vigilance was shortly being pressed by his counterpart in the City.[331] Their concerns arose from a steady accumulation of cases of people being poisoned by ices sold on the streets from carts and barrows. The members of London's Italian community that dominated the capital's penny ice trade by this time came mainly from the poor Italian colony at Saffron Hill, an area of desperately crowded, run-down tenements that had earlier in the century given Charles Dickens the inspiration for Fagin's den in *Oliver Twist*. A report for the medical journal, the *Lancet*, as early as 1879, had described finding milk, eggs and cornflour mixtures used to make penny ices 'standing in the foulest dens, where they must absorb noxious gases'. The same writer

---

327 For a detailed history of the family business, see F. Kinross, *Coffee and Ices: The Story of Carlo Gatti in London* (Sudbury, 1991); see also the obituary notice of Agostino Gatti in *The Times*, 15th January 1897; also E. David, *op. cit.*, pp. 347–50.
328 *Cold Storage and Ice Trades Review* I (1899), p. 134.
329 *The Times*, 13th October 1898.
330 *Ibid.*, 16th August 1899.
331 *Ibid.*, 5th September 1902.

found ingredients being mixed in the same saucepans and cauldrons used to wash dirty linen.[332] In 1885, *The Times* gave an account of the detaining by the authorities of an Italian ice cream vendor in Lambeth Walk. It emerged that a whole variety of people had succumbed to severe vomiting after consuming ices bought from his barrow. When the case came before the local court, the magistrate was at a loss to know what to charge the vendor with and hence the man was released.[333] In another case heard at Greenwich in March 1901, it was alleged that an Italian ice cream vendor had been making ices with bad eggs. The Town Clerk of Deptford, in prosecution, was very concerned to identify the individual who, he claimed, caused all the stomach disease in his district. He remarked how a great deal of mischief was done with 'dirty ice cream'.[334] Cities outside London were in no way immune from the phenomenon either. In 1905, in Birmingham, some 200 cases of poisoning attributable to ice cream sold from a street vendor's barrow came to light. Chemical analysis established that the cause was probably the result of contamination with arsenic and antinomy, presumably occurring at some stage in manufacture.[335]

What all these different incidents and reports highlighted was the desperate need for some kind of local authority supervision and control. And by 1900, a number of cities around the country (though not London at the time) were acting to bring the sale of ices on the same footing as the sale of milk.

In Liverpool, in the year following the passing of the Liverpool Corporation Act of 1898, over 300 people had applied for permission to sell ice cream under the Act's provisions and inspectors had closed down 56 premises as being a threat to public health. Altogether the inspectors made 1600 visits in the city, resulting in two court convictions. In one of these cases, the presiding magistrate suggested that the defendant be made to live on his own ice cream for a time.[336] Within a few years, Glasgow

---

332 A summary account was provided in *The Times*, 20th October 1879.
333 *Ibid.*, 9th June 1885.
334 *Ibid.*, 30th March 1901.
335 *Ibid.*, 18th and 19th July 1905.
336 See the account in *The Times*, 2nd September 1899.

CHAPTER 7

Figure 7.5. A busy ice cream stall on Hampstead Heath as depicted for the *Illustrated London News* in 1872 (*Illustrated London News* LV, May 1872, p. 12).

Corporation followed the example of Liverpool where, according to an account of August 1905, the number of ice cream vendors had doubled in just one year, more than justifying regulation in terms of public health.[337] At about the same time, Aberdeen was reported to have at least 700 ice cream shops within its burgh. And at premier seaside resorts, ice vending in the summer months seemed by then to know few bounds judging from

---

337   *Cold Storage and Ice Trades Review* VIII (1905), p. 234.

the inflated sums that individual vendors were prepared to pay for stands or stalls adjacent to the beaches. Some local councils resorted to letting such sites by auction, in the process trebling or quadrupling the sums they had received in earlier years by means of private tender.[338]

In Hull in 1908, the local medical officer of health came across a rather different problem. It had come to his notice that ice cream makers were using old fish salt and old ice previously used in packing and storing fish in the port. This he viewed as a potential hazard to public health, notwithstanding the fact that the ice cream mixture should never have come into direct contact with the freezing mixture.

In the worst cases of ice cream contamination, typhus fever had been reported. In October 1900, for instance, the Medical Officer of Health in Newington in London had come across 16 cases of typhus in just a five-week period, all appearing to have been connected to ice cream obtained from street barrows.[339] Some medical officers were also at pains to point out that the better class of ice cream makers were not necessarily immune from contamination. Street vendors often boiled their ingredients prior to freezing, thus reducing the likelihood of micro-organisms being present in their ices. In the better establishments, the principal ingredients were cream, fruit and sugar which were not treated in the same way. The fruit might be cooked, but not the entire ingredients. In this case, the cream was a potential source of contamination.[340]

The size of the Italian community in Britain involved in the ice cream trade and in selling ice on the streets, in particular, attracted official interest and oversight for reasons other than contamination. In the first place, many Italian 'colonies' were extremely poor, and this applied not just in London but in provincial cities as well. Many poor young Italians were being brought to Britain to work in the ice cream and related trades, but on very low or even no wages. In the early 1890s, a case before Brompton County Court highlighted the measure of exploitation that some of these immigrants faced. A young Italian immigrant vendor, working for a local Italian ice cream merchant, had suffered starvation wages and been made

---

338 Ibid.
339 *The Times*, 11th October 1900.
340 *Ibid.*, 16th August 1899.

to go out on the street in rags, despite an agreement made by his employer that he would be lodged, boarded and clothed.[341] In 1902, Parliament debated the destitute condition of many recently-arrived aliens, with the member for Bethnal Green remarking on the large colony of Italians, chiefly ice cream vendors and organ grinders, in Hatton Garden, most of whom struggled on the edge of poverty.[342]

Immigration officials later had powers to turn back at entry ports any persons who appeared to have no means of supporting themselves, but the numbers of actual expulsions were relatively few.[343] In 1913, for example, against 21,393 immigrant entrants, only 311 removal orders were made. Of the total entrants, some 13,000, that is around 60 per cent, were headed for London, with Italians among the commonest nationalities. For those entrants destined for Wales, Italians were by far the largest national group, perhaps a reflection of the rising popularity of ices among the youth of the principality.[344]

Poverty and destitution, of course, are traditional breeding grounds for petty crime and disorder, and Italian ice cream vendors seem to have afforded a cardinal example. The pages of *The Times* in the decades up to the First World War are replete with court reports of vendors involved in affrays of one form or another, a few of them with fatal outcomes. They also seem to have had a predilection for running illegal lotteries or for organizing gambling from their street barrows. In June 1904 in London, for instance, a street vendor of Lisson Grove was charged with having 20 or 30 boys around his barrow gambling for ices.[345] Sometimes, though, it was the street urchins themselves who were the culprits of disorder. Mobs of 'roughs' would attack the vendors' barrows and carts, removing and sometimes breaking the freezer lids. Given the increasing public health concerns over ices sold on the streets, it was thus perhaps no wonder that, by the end of the First World War, there was pressure even within the trade to take ice cream off the streets.

---

341   *Ibid.*, 3rd October 1891.
342   *Ibid.*, 30th January 1902.
343   See the account of the parliamentary debate in *The Times*, 24th March 1910.
344   *Ibid.*, 27th April 1914.
345   *Ibid.*, 14th June 1904.

One of the more startling features of the ice vending trade towards the close of the nineteenth century was the floating in 1893 of a company set with the task of acquiring, working and developing a machine for vending ices, in effect a coin-operated apparatus that was refrigerated and filled with ice creams.[346] The Horton Ice Cream Company established in London in 1888 was behind the scheme. The company was already a well-known refreshment contractor, supplying theatres, exhibitions, balls, garden parties, not to mention the shipping lines that frequented London docks. The intention was to install the machines in places of amusement, for example in the pits and galleries of theatres, so that ordinary people could obtain a confection that had hitherto been available only to a restricted few. It was also anticipated that much business might be done on the concourses of railway stations, at race meetings and at holiday resorts. Supplementary to their mechanical ice dispenser, the company also anticipated door-to-door selling of its ice cream in and around London by means of tricycles specially designed for the purpose. It is not apparent how the automatic ice machine fared, if at all. But the fact that it was being contemplated is illustration of the scale of the trade in ices to the population at large at this time.

The size of the ice cream trade by the first decades of the twentieth century became yet more apparent when, in 1917, the wartime government, anxious to conserve the national food supply, especially milk and sugar, issued an order restricting the making of ice cream. All categories of ice cream makers were immediately up in arms about this order since it was potentially destructive of their livelihoods. By that time, London had an association of ice cream manufacturers, and 300 members of the trade attended an emergency meeting in January 1918 at the Italian Club in Saffron Hill. The effect of the order was more or less to annihilate the trade, and members sought to bring pressure on the Ministry of Food to modify its provisions. In this they were supported by many provincial ice cream makers, as well the operators of a great majority of the small ice factories that traditionally supplied them. Between 40 and 60 per cent of the ice output from such plants went into making ices. This included the ice required in the premises

---

346 *Ibid.*, 25th March 1893.

where ice cream was made, in the shops that sold ice cream, as well as the ice that street vendors needed to fill the freezers on their barrows. Without the sale of ice for these purposes, it was reckoned that many plants would be forced to close down, in the process also losing vital cold storage capacity at a time when it was becoming in desperately short supply.[347]

The armistice late in 1918 plainly signalled hope for a relaxation of wartime restrictions, but not before many ice factories had lost up to three quarters of their custom, according to the editor of the *Cold Storage and Produce Review*, in some cases resulting in enforced closure.[348] In the spring of 1919, though, The Ice Cream Restriction Order was revoked and within a few years the ice cream trade was starting to stage a full recovery. The London firm of J. Lyons & Co. opened a new ice cream plant in West Kensington as early as 1921 and within a year were supplying their 200 or so tea-shops around the capital with ice cream on a regular footing, helped by a fleet of new Leyland motor-vans.[349] By 1923 the company was turning out 12,000 gallons of ice cream per day and already had plans for extending production.[350] The company utilized best American practice in their method of manufacture, producing much of the ice cream in 'bricks' that were retailed in thin card-board boxes at 1/6d each. The plant had the capacity to make 80,000 bricks a day, in addition to its output of more ordinary ice cream. When sold, the bricks were quite hard, softening only very slowly and capable of being cut like a cake, much in the manner of ice cream blocks today.[351]

A number of ice plants around the country were themselves shifting towards the making of ice cream. The economics of ice production on its own, especially in the smaller ice factories, were far too dependent on a bumper summer demand. An investigation for the *Cold Storage and Ice Trades Review* in 1924 revealed graphically the strains under which a small 10 tons a day ice plant operated. For most months of the year, low

---

347 For accounts of the hardships that the Order presented for the ice trade, see *Cold Storage and Produce Review* XXI (1918), p. 40; pp. 82–3.
348 Ibid., p. 181.
349 Ibid., XXV (1922), pp. 133, 168.
350 Ibid., XXVI (1923), p. 315.
351 Ibid., XXV (1922), p. 133.

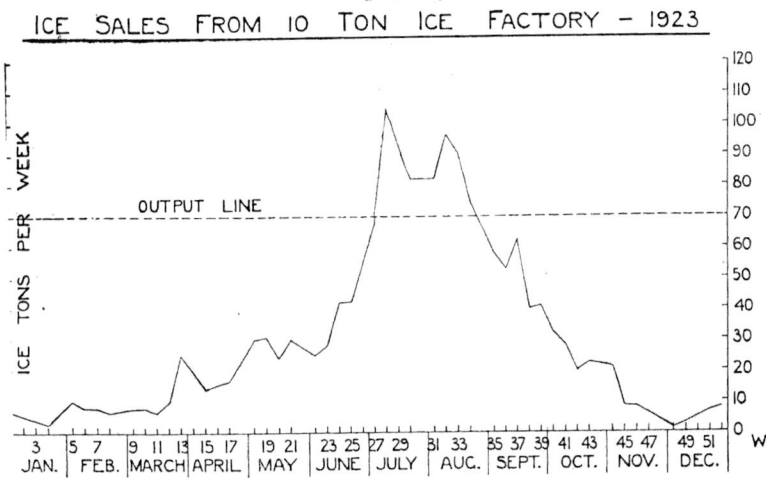

Figure 7.6. The difference between profitable and unprofitable operation for a small ice plant (Bodleian: Per 193998 d.1/XXVII p. 459).

demand left it operating way below capacity, with all that that meant in terms of balancing income and expenditure.[352]

As ice plants added ice cream making to their activities, the result was that ice cream started to become available in places where it had been unknown either before or during the recent war.

In 1921, for example, in the small seaside town of Bognor Regis, an ice-making and cold storage plant had been erected, known by the name of the Antarctic Ice and Cold Storage Company Ltd. By 1926 it had opened its own ice cream saloon selling 'cream ices', 'cream ice bricks' and supplying shops, fêtes and garden parties.[353] In city department stores, American-style soda fountains were being opened as an adjunct to ice cream sales. Selfridges in London had a soda fountain by late 1935 that seated 186 customers.[354] Earlier, in April 1934, the *Cold Storage and Produce Review* had provided its readers with an account of what was then Britain's largest soda fountain: at Lewis's department store in Leeds.[355] Whereas once the premier ice trade journal had carried

---

352 *Ibid.*, XXVII (1924), p. 459.
353 *Ibid.*, XXIX (1926), p. 231.
354 *Ibid.*, XXXVIII (1935), p. 215.
355 *Ibid.*, XXXVII (1934), p. 99.

CHAPTER 7

Figure 7.7. The premises of the Antarctic Ice and Cold Storage Company in Bognor (Bodleian: Per 193998 d.1/XXIX p. 231).

a monthly column on the state of the natural ice market, it now carried a monthly report of 'ice cream progress', of which the installation of soda fountains was part. It noted how, nationally, ice cream sales in winter had risen such that they fell only 40 per cent below the summer average. Ordinary provincial towns were also sharing in the ice cream industry's growth. In 1929, *The Times* carried an advertisement for the disposal of a flourishing ice cream business at a town in Kent, valued at £1,750. The turnover in season was £150 a week, 'at exceptional profit'. The business included ice-cream plant, motor ice cream barrow, three pony barrows with ponies, freezers, soda fountains and much more.[356]

What had changed to make the ice cream trade so vibrant was the public's attitude to it. It was becoming less and less a mere hot weather trade and more an acquired habit. There was also a steadily growing Americanisation of the trade, in terms of the mode of manufacture as well as the mode of consumption. This was at the expense of the traditional Italian dominance. The day of the tawdry street ice cream barrow was soon sealed, even if descendants of the Italian makers continued to be found selling ice cream for many more decades.

---

356   *The Times*, 11th April 1929.

CHAPTER 8

A Trade Decays

> 'O, how I long to travel back,
> And tread again that ancient track!
> When no one had an ice machine,
> And modern stores were not foreseen'.[357]

In 1908, the editor of the *Cold Storage and Ice Trades Review* remarked that the palmy days of the Norwegian ice trade to Britain had gone, never to return.[358] He was referring above all to the ice farmers and ice shippers in Norway's lakes and fjords and at the various loading ports. They had been party to an almost uninterrupted expansion of the trade from its diminutive beginnings in the early 1860s to the record exports of over half a million tons by the turn of the century. From 1901 until 1911, export levels in most years settled in the range 340-380,0000 tons. Then, from 1912 to 1914, the figure slipped from 262,000 to 200,000 tons. And with the outbreak of war in August 1914, the trade by and large collapsed.

Although artificial or factory ice was a factor in the rapid decline of the natural ice trade, the seeds of its destruction lay in the highly volatile form of the business right from its inception. This related not just to weather conditions in a Norwegian winter or a British summer but, equally, to the speculative character of the trade as part of modern capitalist enterprise. At times, price-cutting among British ice importers attained insane proportions. In Liverpool in the early 1900s, even the importers themselves accepted that there were too many players in the field.[359] Ice consumption was rising but receipts were falling against the backdrop of an incessant price war. As competition was succeeded by combination, Britain's ice importers more and more squeezed the suppliers and shippers, especially

---

357 *Cold Storage and Ice Trades Review* X (1907), p. 330.
358 Ibid., XI (1908), p. 25.
359 Ibid., VI (1903), p. 125.

CHAPTER 8

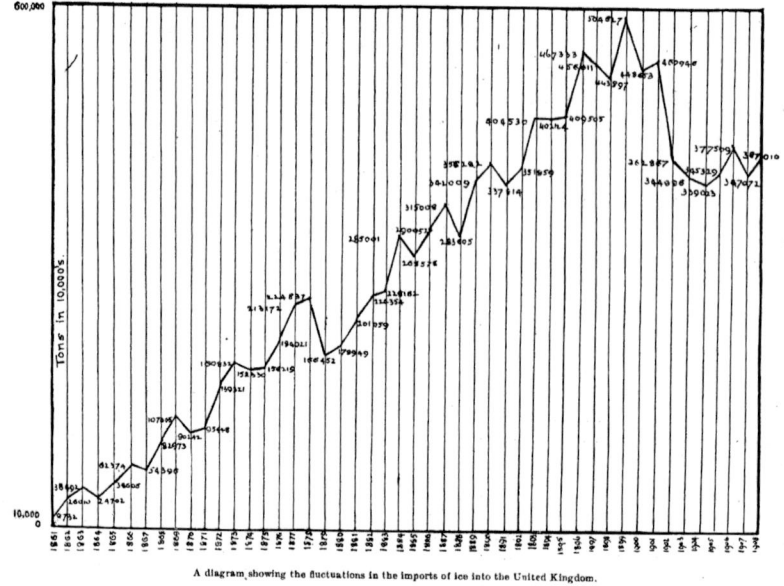

Figure 8.1. Graph showing time-series of Norwegian ice imports to Britain, 1861–1908, published in the *Cold Storage and Ice Trades Review* in July 1910 (Bodleian: Per 193998 d.1/XIII p. 185). The peak year was 1899, with 504,627 tons landed. The original data series upon which the major part of this graph is based is unknown. See Appendix for ice imports by port, 1899 to 1903.

in the prices obtained on spring contracts. As we have seen, by the early years of the new century, these contracts were barely paying their way, even in an easy ice harvest when wages were low. They present an interesting foretaste of the modern futures market, with contracts being agreed on quantities of ice that farmers and merchants in Norway merely hoped to be able to harvest. Bargains were thus made without knowing the quality or thickness of the ice in the coming winter, or the costs of obtaining it. They were speculating on an imaginary good. For the ice importers, of course, this was immaterial. Their one concern was getting a succession of ice cargoes into port, and unloading them to store. Sometimes the exporters in Norway contracted to despatch as spring cargoes more ice than it proved possible to obtain. They would then find themselves short by May or June and be forced to buy from other Norwegian merchants at inflated prices. Sometimes, though, as we have seen earlier, farmers and export merchants were granted temporary deliverance in their otherwise precarious economic lives, for if the British importers had misjudged the coming summer season and made insufficient spring contract provision, then they were forced to buy large numbers of individual shipments in a steadily rising market, much to the favour of the Norwegian suppliers and shippers. Similarly, if it turned out to be an exceptional summer in Britain, the suppliers and shippers would gain all the benefits of a seller's market. July 1904, for example, brought high temperatures and prompted the *Cold Storage and Ice Trades Review* to pen a trade fable:

> 'But iceman! O iceman! Rise up and hear the bell;
> Rise up – for ice there's still a demand – there's come a muggy spell;
> The butcher bawls, the milkman calls, the fishmonger is vocal,
> Clear as a bird each voice is heard, in ev'ry dialect local.'[360]

Three years later, in 1907, there had been a general fall in the tonnage of ice imported into Britain from Norway and so less ice was stocked all round for the 1908 season. In the event, stocks for 1908 proved quite inadequate to meet demand and the price of ice outside of spring contracts quickly went up five or six times above the level of previous seasons.[361] The Norwegian suppliers and shippers thus had another windfall. Sometimes, though, the ice trade actually failed all the parties involved in it, exporters, importers and shippers alike. A below average harvest, coupled with high summer demand in Britain, compounded by abnormal demands for Norwegian ice in Germany, could exhaust all Norway's ice stocks prematurely. A few exporters might hold back supplies in expectation of higher prices, but that always ran the risk that, if demand slumped, ice would be left unsold.

The Norway ice trade was therefore one of quite exceptional uncertainty. In 1910, the British vice-consuls at Kragerø and at Porsgrunn reported a very profitable year for the business.[362] In fact, it had proved one of the best years since 1899. This was in stark contrast to 1909 when there had been in excess of 50,000 tons of ice remaining unshipped by the close of the exporting season. At times the ice importers in Britain had a similar roller-coaster

---
360 Ibid., VII (1904), p. 336.
361 Ibid., XII (1909), p. 210.
362 Ibid., XIII (1910), pp. 251–2.

ride. At its AGM in early 1914, the giant London combine, United Carlo Gatti, Stevenson and Slaters Ltd., bemoaned the adverse trading conditions for Norwegian ice, which were reflected in the company paying no dividend to its shareholders in 1910, 1912 and 1913.[363] They were caught between a continuing growing demand for ice at home and rising prices of ice on the dockside. Even though artificial ice was making large inroads into the domestic ice market, many of its customers still retained a preference for the Norwegian product. In Norway, moreover, some regular correspondents on the ice trade with Britain felt certain that Norwegian block ice would never be found superfluous. The editor of the *Cold Storage and Ice Trades Review* was much more sanguine, however. He wrote in 1910 that it was obvious to most that factory ice was ousting ice from 'Nature's factory'.[364] Already artificial ice-making plants were producing over a quarter of a million tons more ice than was being imported from Norway in any one year. In 1910, it became apparent from the preliminary results of the Census of Production Act of 1906 just how far the ice-making industry had progressed.[365] The census of ice factories revealed a workforce of some 1,100 persons. The value of the ice produced amounted to almost £400,000 in 1907 (597,000 tons deadweight). And these figures did not include ice made by cold storage firms or by fishmongers for their own use. But perhaps the most telling portent of the decline of the natural ice trade was the re-naming of the *Cold Storage and Ice Trades Review*, the trade's premier journal since 1898. Towards the close of 1910, it was re-titled *Cold Storage and Produce Review*. The change was not trumpeted in the editorials, rather it crept in by the back door, with the running page-head continuing to display the old title for some while.[366] In its content, however, the journal had for some time been reflecting the vastly increased importance of factory-made ice, with articles on the technology of the business and detailed coverage of the commissioning of new plants. The change of name in effect reflected an emphasis that was already a fact of life.

---

363 *Ibid.*, XVII (1914), p. 106.
364 *Ibid.*, XIII (1910), p. 309.
365 *Ibid.*, p. 323.
366 To avoid confusion, the original name has been retained when footnoting the journal as a source after 1910. Volume and issue numbers continued in sequence.

In the 1911 summer season, the Norwegian suppliers and shippers enjoyed an unexpected boom when record temperatures affected northwest Europe in the months of July and August.[367] In England, the mean temperature for the two months breached 18°C. London was consuming 2,000 tons of ice a day. In some provincial cities and towns it became difficult to obtain ice at all. Across the Channel, in Paris, ice consumption jumped from 1,500 to 3,000 tons a day. Train-loads as well as boat-loads of ice were being despatched by the score, at greatly increased prices, from Norwegian rail-heads and ports.[368] The losers in this were those ice importers who had contracted to supply the retail trade at fixed prices. Some were ruined and even the biggest firms found profits squeezed. In London, matters were made worse by a dock strike. Even the ice factories had difficulty responding to the inflated demand, despite working day and night. In Switzerland, glacier ice was being exported to Germany, France and Italy, such was the scarcity of supply.[369]

With the outbreak of war in early August 1914, there was the prospect that the North Sea would become, in the technical jargon, a *mare clausam*: it would become closed to trade under threat of enemy interception, including submarine warfare. However, the timing of the start of the war was fortunate for both ice exporters and ice importers. By August, most ice stores in Britain were well stocked after five months of shipments from the fjords and lakes. Some of the Norwegian merchants had also built up stocks at home in anticipation of a possible interruption to trade. As late as early 1915, the prospects for British consumers did not appear bleak either, for stocks from the previous year's shipments remained considerable.[370] The summer of 1914 had broken no meteorological records and so demand had been tempered. In Norway, though, ice exports were by this time in a state of collapse. In the first three months of 1915, only 3,000 tons were despatched from the fjords for Britain. This compared

---

367 *Cold Storage and Ice Trades Review*, XIV (1911), pp. 220–1; see also *The Times*, 10th August 1911; Juliet Nicolson's book, *A Perfect Summer* (London, 2006), purported to address the phenomenon of the extraordinary heat of 1911, but in the event gave very little attention to it, or to the extraordinary demands for ice that season.
368 *Cold Storage and Ice Trades Review* XIV (1911), p. 221.
369 Ibid., p. 241.
370 Ibid., XVIII (1915), p. 48.

with 33,000 tons in the first quarter of 1914.[371] It was a catastrophic fall. Shipments in April 1915 were a quarter of those in April 1914.[372] What aggravated the position was the fact that ship-owners who had formerly handled much of the ice traffic and who continued to operate in wartime were turning to more lucrative traffics. Inevitably, retail prices of Norwegian ice in London were soon rocketing, with rates ten shillings above the levels of the year before, and as high as 30 shillings a ton in a few outlets.[373] Outside London, in parts of Kent, ice had become in such short supply that military authorities had prohibited its sale except to dealers in perishables.[374] Even in October of that year, the dockside price of ice was still averaging 23/5d a ton, despite the 1915 summer season having been cool.[375] In some east coast ports, however, there was a rather different story. Demand for Norwegian ice from the fishing trades had fallen dramatically. The threats from enemy shipping had locked much of the fleet up in port. West coast fishing ports, including those in Ireland, were similarly affected. The upshot was that, over the year 1915 as a whole, only 54,883 tons of ice were exported from Norway to Britain, a quarter of the total for 1914 and a tenth of the record export year of 1899.[376] For the merchants, both in Britain and in Norway, though, the situation was not quite as dire as it appeared. The value of the 1915 ice imports, at £58,321, was one half, not one quarter, of the value of the ice imported in 1914. The ice that was traded in 1915 had double its value.

By the early spring of 1916, the *Cold Storage and Produce Review* was anticipating 'ransom prices' for Norwegian ice in the coming summer season, given the reduction in the trade and the exhaustion of most natural ice stores in Britain. In March 1916, no ice was recorded as having been landed in Britain at all, the first time that this had happened for over a quarter of a century.[377] Then, in May 1916, the British government announced the prohibition of ice importation from Norway, except

---

371 Ibid., p. 98.
372 Ibid.
373 Ibid., p. 122.
374 Ibid.
375 Ibid., p. 249.
376 Ibid., XIX (1916), p. 10.
377 Ibid., XIX (1916), p. 75.

under special Board of Trade licence.[378] It was the trade's death-knell. Most commentators were very surprised by the move. They could see little to be gained by the decision. The kind of shipping tonnage engaged in carrying ice across the North Sea was by then small beer, negligible as a factor in the maritime war. In the Irish fisheries, the news was greeted with dismay. The valuable salmon catches of the south and west ports had already experienced chronic ice shortages and factory ice was much less easily procured in Ireland than on the British mainland. Then, to add to the impact of the ban, the summer of 1916 turned tropical.[379] The average temperature for the month of August reached 16.4°C, the highest since the record-breaking summer of 1911. Ice in London and the south of England become positively scarce. Fishmongers and butchers ended up paying as much as 35 shillings a ton. London importers somehow managed to evade the trade embargo and secured over 3,000 tons of Norwegian block ice in the month of July, with an average dockside price of 26 shillings a ton. Even so, the total ice imports into Britain from Norway over the months from January to July were only 5,877 tons.[380] By the year's end, the total had climbed to some 10,000 tons, two thirds of that quantity landed in London. Elsewhere, ice traffic more or less disappeared altogether. After London, only seven ports landed cargoes in 1916.[381]

For the artificial ice producers, particularly those outside the fishing ports, the virtual disappearance of Norwegian block ice as a competitor product, opened up a potential marketing coup. Notwithstanding the residual belief among some consumers, including many fishmongers, that Norwegian ice was superior to factory ice, the ice factory managers began talking of petitioning the government to forbid any resumption of the Norwegian trade following the end of hostilities, whenever that might come.[382] The trade was not in fact banned, but it never recovered, as will shortly be seen.

---

378   Ibid., p. 95.
379   Ibid., p. 178.
380   Ibid.
381   Ibid., XX (1917), p. 8.
382   Ibid., p. 24.

CHAPTER 8

At one point during the war, a Billingsgate observer came up with the rather novel idea that the Norwegian ship-owners who had regularly carried ice across the North Sea should be persuaded to collect factory ice made at the ports of Fleetwood, Milford Haven, Swansea and Cardiff and convey it for use in the salmon fisheries in Ireland where the scarcity of ice was presenting such a serious economic problem.[383] But the idea does not appear to have been acted upon. If it had been, perhaps the parlous condition of many Irish fishing communities, especially in the south-west, would have been alleviated.

If the ice factories thought they were on a rising tide of prosperity, they were soon to face a rude awakening. For as we have already seen, in late 1917 the wartime government passed an Ice Cream Restriction Order which entirely stopped the business of the ice cream trade. Not only were ice cream makers and ice cream vendors mortified by the decision, as the preceding chapter made plain, but so were many operators of ice-making plants and their allied cold stores. Increasingly, small-scale ice-making plants had obtained most of their annual profit from ice sold to ice cream makers in the summer months. In a heat wave, they could expect profit levels to rocket, with nearly two-thirds of daily output going to the ice cream trade. One proprietor, in evidence to the Food Ministry, observed that in Bath and Swindon the plants were run at a loss in the months of December, January and February. They started to move into profit in March, with July and August providing the best returns, sometimes as great as 500 per cent.[384] Petitions by the various trade associations to the Food Minister met with relatively little success and plants that had already been struggling to survive quickly closed their doors. In February 1918, the entire equipment of the Potteries Pure Ice and Cold Storage Company was advertised for public auction, including one Lancashire and one Cornish boiler, two compound steam engines, two ammonia compressors, as well as ice-making tanks and ice moulds.[385] Soon ice plants in other towns were going the same way, with the result that ice production began to fall to quite an alarming extent, according to an editorial in the

---

383 *Ibid.*, XIX (1916), p. 33.
384 *Ibid.*, XXI (1918), p. 82.
385 *Ibid.*, p. 46.

Cold Storage and Produce Review.[386] That summer, considerable quantities of fish arriving at southern destinations from Aberdeen were ending up in very poor condition through want of sufficient ice. More widely, the country's fishing industry was by then struggling with shortages of ice, especially among fleets operating in Irish waters. Nor were the ice factories helped by the fact that their operatives were liable to conscription after 1916. It was not until August 1918 that the Ministry of National Service conceded that managers, foremen, tankmen and engineers in ice factories should be exempt from call-up.[387]

The problems of the availability of ice during the last years of the war were matched by an equivalent problem in cold storage capacity. The victualling needs of the armed forces and the exigencies of wartime food supply had placed enormous demands on cold storage facilities. It quickly became apparent that storage space was hopelessly deficient and, worse still, no policy seemed to be in place for any concerted expansion of capacity. Some of the larger ports found themselves having to leave food cargoes, including meat, undischarged because they had no cold storage left. Even where new capacity was on the drawing board, there were major difficulties in acquiring the necessary construction materials, particularly steel and concrete. Construction labour was likewise a problem. In Liverpool, the port's regular manual and clerical workforce had been so reduced by the War Office that it was barely able to operate its existing facilities. Another difficulty was a chronic shortage of refrigerated railway wagons, vital for moving the increasing imports of Canadian fish, for example, that were being carried across the Atlantic to west coast ports to try to ease domestic food shortages.[388]

Increased cold storage capacity, whether in situ or mobile, naturally required increased ice-making capacity. But, as we have seen, ice-making was contracting during the last years of the war, partly at the instigation of government. Eventually, with the help of Treasury loans, the position began to be rectified. From 1918 to 1919, cold storage capacity in the UK

---

386 *Ibid.*, p. 181.
387 *Ibid.*, p. 182.
388 Some of the main problems of cold storage at the time are dealt with in *Cold Storage and Ice Trades Review* XXI (1918), pp. 87, 110–2.

was anticipated to grow by a quarter.[389] At Bristol's Avonmouth docks, the cold stores were being trebled in capacity by means of a ferro-concrete building over 200 feet long and over 100 feet wide, equipped with six one and a half ton lifts.[390] Amidst the food shortages of the last months of the war, of course, it was by and large too late.

By the late summer of 1918, most commentators were clear that there was a 'national ice question' that needed urgent attention on the part of the Ministry of Food. London suffered serious ice shortages in the summer of both 1918 and 1919.[391] At Grimsby, the re-emergent fishing industry was found desperately short of ice, with trawlers forced to call in at Aberdeen on their outward voyages in order to replenish ice stocks. Grimsby's local ice factories were working flat out, but their capacity fell short of the local fleet's needs, and this was quite aside from the ordinary demands for ice within Grimsby and its environs.[392] In other towns and cities, municipal corporations became so exercised by summer ice shortages that they began making urgent expansion plans. At Burnley, the weekly demand during the summer season was around 80 tons, but the local municipal ice plant could barely manage 30 tons.[393]

One might have expected that Norwegian ice would have quickly filled the lacuna in ice supply. But there was little ice to be had from the Norwegian stores. In August 1919, it was reckoned that there were barely 5,000 tons of ice in all Norway.[394] The explanation was that the infrastructure of ice farming and ice storage there had progressively collapsed during the later years of the war. Initially, Norwegian ice had found markets in the expansion of the country's own fish trades.[395] However, British investors in the ice exporting business in Norway had been steadily withdrawing over the course of the war. The United Carlo Gatti company finally wound up its operations there in 1920–21.[396] In April 1920, the *Cold Storage and Produce Review* had estimated that there were

---

389 *Cold Storage and Produce Review* XXI (1918), p. 257.
390 Ibid., p. 182.
391 Ibid., p. 181.
392 Ibid., XXII (1919), pp. 198, 227.
393 Ibid., XXIII (1920), p. 222.
394 Ibid., XXII (1919), p. 198.
395 See R. David, 'The Demise of the Anglo-Norwegian Ice Trade', *Business History* 37 (1995), p. 65.
396 *Cold Storage and Ice Trades Review.*, XXIV (1921), p. 95.

Figure 8.2. Ice-loading at Kragerø in February 1919 (Norsk Folkemuseum NF.W 20461).

only 18,000 registered tons of ice available for export that season.[397] In the first six months of 1921, a paltry 2,776 tons of Norwegian ice entered Britain. The prevailing view in the British press seemed to be that the trade had by and large decayed altogether.[398] However, that judgement proved a trifle premature. In the years following, signs of a sort of revival emerged. The winter of 1921–2 produced an exceptional ice harvest, better than many could remember. The ice was 15 to 20 inches thick and crystal clear. Editors quickly swallowed their earlier words. They reported how Norwegians were coming back into the trade. By spring 1922, it was estimated that around 30 firms had become so engaged. A London business, A.E. Martin Ltd., had for several years maintained an interest in Norwegian ice imports to the capital. In the course of 1921, in fact, it had landed more than 10,000 tons. For 1922, the firm anticipated

---

397 *Ibid.*, XXIII (1920), p. 86.
398 *Ibid.*, XXIV (1921), p. 189.

an even bigger trade, not just on account of the excellent ice crop, but because freight costs were falling and suitable shipping was becoming available once more.³⁹⁹ However, what was not falling were wages. The costs of manual labour in Norway rose markedly in 1918–1920, a feature that slowly rising levels of mechanisation only partially offset.⁴⁰⁰

Figure 8.3. Machine-cutting of Norwegian lake ice in 1921, a means of reducing the costs of harvesting when wage costs were rising (Norsk Folkemuseum NF.WB 14615).

The ice harvest of 1922 in due course yielded some 80,000 tons, with somewhere around half of that total maintained in store to meet the 1923 season.⁴⁰¹ Even so, Norwegian ice was still costing over 30 shillings a ton on the dockside in London, well up on the price before 1914.⁴⁰² Other ports were not long in resuming Norwegian ice imports. In June 1922, Ipswich celebrated the arrival of its first cargo of Norwegian ice since the start of the war. It arrived on board the 177-ton Danish brigantine,

---

399 *Ibid.*, XXV (1922), p. 50.
400 See P.T. Sandvik, *Nasjonens velstand, Norges økonomiske historie, 1800–1940* (Oslo, 2018).
401 *Cold Storage and Ice Trades Review* XXV (1922) p. 304.
402 *Ibid.*, XXVI (1923), p. 7.

Seierkransden, interesting evidence of the continuing attraction of sail tonnage for the ice trade.[403]

Two factors seem to have been driving the revival of ice farming and exporting. One was the growth in demand for ice on the continent, particularly in France and in Germany. The second factor in the trade's revival, particularly as far as Britain went, was the impact of the hot, dry summer of 1921 when ice was in desperately short supply in some towns and cities.[404] The mean July temperature that year was 18.5°C, breaching even the record figures for the summer of 1911. The capacities of British ice factories were severely tested. When the final tally of Norwegian ice imports to Britain over 1922 was done, it emerged that nearly 40,000 tons had been landed, the bulk of it to ports in England, with London taking over 23,000 tons.[405] The trade's speculators, however, were severely disappointed with the scale of the recovery. They had banked on the summer season of 1922 being a match for 1921. But in time-honoured tradition the English climate failed to oblige. The summer proved cool and damp, with July and August temperature means of 13.7 and 13.6°C, a bleak five degrees below the level in 1921.[406] The ice that entered London in 1922 was mostly handled by A.E. Martin Ltd., with the dockside price between 27/6d and 30/- a ton. Wooden steamers, mostly Norwegian or Danish owned, carried the ice from the Norwegian ports. The smallest were just 200 tons on the net register, the largest up to three times that figure.[407]

The 1922-3 winter season in Norway did not begin well. By mid-January 1923, it was reported that the winter there had been as mild as that in Britain. What little ice that had formed had also been spoiled by heavy snowfall.[408] Cold weather set in in mid-February, with ice developing to a thickness of 18 inches in some places, but cutting and storing the ice was subsequently very slow. It was not just that there were far fewer participants in the trade, but even where exporters remained in business, there was the separate problem that many of the old ice stores were in varying

---

403 *Ibid.*, XXV (1922), p. 160.
404 *Ibid.*, XXIV (1921), pp. 189, xxvi.
405 *Ibid.*, XXVI (1923), p. 7.
406 *Ibid.*, XXV (1922), p. 304.
407 *Ibid.*, XXVI (1923), p. 7.
408 *Ibid.*

CHAPTER 8

states of decay, with limited incentive to repair them. Nor were any new storehouses being erected. Lower shipping rates might have tipped the balance, but in 1923 many classes of shipping became involved in carrying coal from British ports to the Ruhr, a situation that arose from the French occupation of the Ruhr which had dislocated Germany's supplies.[409] The start of the summer season in Britain did not augur well for the ice trade either. June came in with 'arctic' temperatures according to one commentator.[410] The mean temperature for the month was 12.5°C, the second lowest for over a century. Rather than a perspiring public clamouring for ice, those involved in the trade found themselves sitting on their stocks, the artificial ice-makers included. Come July, though, the thermometer abruptly turned and the ice trade boomed, the monthly mean hitting 17.5°C. There was a sudden all-round demand for ice from whatever source. Whilst up until the end of June, less than 6,000 tons of Norwegian ice had been landed in Britain in 1923, the month of July alone saw as much unloaded in port or in transit across the North Sea.[411] By the year's close, England had imported around 25,000 tons, valued at nearly £30,000. The figures were down compared with the 1922 import year, and London took only 12,000 tons. But this was unsurprising given the season's slow start and the fact that ice stocks were still high from the poor summer season of 1922.[412]

Weather conditions in Norway the following winter (1923-4) were highly favourable for ice formation and, by mid-February, British ice traders were getting news that the ice crop was already in the ice-stores and that it was of fine quality.[413] Even so, the scale of the harvest remained limited by the diminished storage capacity besides lakes and fjords. There was probably no more than 60,000 tons of ice, whereas ten times that figure would have been in store around the turn of the century.[414] But even 60,000 tons turned out to be overproduction. British demand for Norwegian ice plummeted in 1924, total imports by the year's end

---

409 *Ibid.*, p. 92.
410 *Ibid.*, p. 208.
411 *Ibid.*, p. 263.
412 *Ibid.*, XXVII (1924), p. 2.
413 *Ibid.*, p. 48.
414 *Ibid.*, p. 88.

Figure 8.4. An ice-making plant installed by the London-based Lightfoot Refrigeration Company in the early 1920s. The ice-cans and ice blocks are small compared with those from earlier days of artificial ice manufacture (Bodleian: Per 193998 d.1/XXVI p. xxvi).

reaching only 10,882 tons.[415] It proved to be a cool summer and ice factories in London and other cities more and more had the productive capacity to meet summer peaks, unless temperatures turned exceptionally hot. London's leading ice importer saw gloomy prospects for the trade. Indeed, the capital's imports had all but collapsed, with less than 1500 tons landed in 1924. Southampton and Portsmouth each imported greater tonnages than London.

Nevertheless, it was not events in Britain that finally all but extinguished the Norwegian ice trade. It was a disastrous harvest season in Norway in the winter of 1924-5. The weather was exceptionally mild. There had been no winter like it for a hundred years. The 'ice-growers' faced the real prospect of the ice crop failing. In none of the lakes and fjords where ice was systematically 'cultivated' was there any ice to speak of.[416] Twenty years earlier, had such a condition prevailed, the ice merchants would have moved their operations inland to waters that were always frozen during the winter season. But such was the state of depression in the trade that this was no longer an option. Soon commentators were talking of the

---

415   *Ibid.*, p. 310; XXVIII (1925), p. 50.
416   *Ibid.*, XXVIII (1925), p. 50.

'failure' of the Norwegian ice harvest. For parts of Norway, it had been an 'iceless' winter. Cargoes ordered from British buyers under spring contracts had to be cancelled. What little ice Norway had was of very poor quality, much of it 'needle-ice', fit only for local consumption.[417] The editor of the *Cold Storage and Produce Review* likened writing about the Norwegian ice harvest that year to writing the famous chapter on snakes in Ireland: there are none.[418] Norway's importers of coke for central heating had traded one twentieth of their usual quantity that season, such was the extraordinary mildness of the weather. For the timber exporters, too, the absence of heavy snow resulted in there not being enough meltwater in the rivers to float timber down to the sawmills.[419] The meteorological explanation was that, over much of north-west Europe and Scandinavia, the winter months had been dominated by a south-west airflow. The synoptic conditions that had perennially provided Norway with one of its staple export trades had failed spectacularly. It was a freak of nature, but one that did irretrievable damage to what remained of the trade. When the tally of Norwegian ice imports into Britain in 1925 was finally done, London turned out to have landed no ice at all. Across Britain, less than 7,000 tons was traded, some of it comprising ice stored in Norway from the preceding year.[420]

With a relatively normal winter season in 1925-6, the trade recovered to a little above its 1924 level, buoyed by an unusual rise in demand from Scottish ports which actually imported more than English ports, 6,648 against 5,509 tons.[421] In London, though, the import trade remained dead. The metropolis that in prolonged summer heatwaves had once generated small fortunes for natural ice traders had now become solely reliant upon artificial ice. Over 1927 much the same pattern prevailed, with Scottish ports ahead of English ones in the tonnages they landed. Stornoway in the Western Isles imported over 2,000 tons that year, Lerwick in the Shetlands some 1,600. In England the trade was becoming highly localized, largely

---

417 Ibid., p. 92.
418 Ibid., p. 35.
419 Ibid., p. 50.
420 Ibid., XXIX (1926), p. 6.
421 Ibid., XXX (1927), p. 2.

at the south coast ports of Portsmouth and Southampton.[422] In July 1928, the *Cold Storage and Produce Review* was remarking that 'the trade had shrunk until it had almost melted away'. Its remnants were confined almost exclusively to remote ports where artificial ice was either expensive to buy or hard to obtain quickly.[423] Neither Lerwick nor Stornoway had ice factories according to the census of cold stores and ice factories of 1926.[424] Portsmouth and Southampton, though, which continued importing small quantities of Norwegian ice in the years to come, did have ice factories. In 1926, they had daily output capacities of 48 and 80 tons respectively.[425] The continuing need for Norwegian imports may have been related to the twin demands of the Navy and of ocean passenger shipping. Portsmouth was a leading naval dockyard and Southampton a growing liner port. In summer, these activities may have absorbed all the factory output, leaving little ice for ordinary public sale. Portsmouth, or Southsea to be more specific, was also a major holiday resort, adding further to ice demand in summer.[426]

One might be forgiven for thinking that owners of ice factories were by the late 1920s looking to improve their prospects given the collapse in the import of natural ice. Between 1907 and 1924, employment in Britain's ice factories had more than doubled, according to the National Census of Production.[427] However, the reality was otherwise. The editor of the *Cold Storage and Produce Review* in February 1928 talked of 'the ice man's lament'. The ice factories that expanded on the ashes of the Norwegian trade were far from secure. Yet again, cool summers were knocking their fragile profit margins.[428] The year 1927, for instance, was a very poor one, the month of June bringing a mean temperature of only 12.6°C. But supplementary to cool weather, the sale of small machine refrigerators was starting to stunt ordinary demand for ice in season. Many more butchers

---

422 *Ibid.*, XXXI (1928), p. 2.
423 *Ibid.*, p. 210.
424 *Ibid.*, XXX (1927), pp. 173-4.
425 *Ibid.*
426 This was despite the fact that Portsmouth had witnessed a major extension of its ice-making facilities in 1922 – see *Cold Storage and Ice Trades Review* XXV (1922), pp. 199-200.
427 *Ibid.*, XXX (1927), p. 223.
428 *Ibid.*, XXXI (1928), p. 39.

CHAPTER 8

Figure 8.5. An Electrolux refrigerator, run on gas or electricity, as advertised in 1928 (Bodleian: Per 193998 d.1/XXXI p. xxv).

and fishmongers were now investing in such appliances, and so too were some of the better-off households. Both business and domestic customers were becoming 'proselytized in thousands to the small machine'.[429]

---

429 *Ibid.*

Electrolux and other companies began advertising campaigns to get their refrigerators into the smarter homes.

It was hardly surprising, then, when some operators of ice plants found themselves struggling. While artificial ice-making capacity was now sufficient to cope with the often insatiable demand for ice in a prolonged summer heatwave, the industry was otherwise plagued by overcapacity and, as an inevitable corollary, cut-throat competition. As we have seen, to make a profit, or to break even, the industry had to have three months in the summer where its plant was more or less working flat out. Meeting peak hot weather demand meant large, even gross, surplus capacity for most of the other months of the year, with all the attendant cost penalties. Unfortunately, the fickle English weather performed its usual tantalizing act. The years 1928 through to 1931 produced a run of cool summers, the August mean temperature dropping to as low as 14.4°C in 1931. In an early act of desperation, the *Cold Storage and Produce Review* announced in 1928 a competition among ice businesses for 'the best accounts of the summer campaign'. Its declared object was to try to stimulate local self-help and up-to-date business methods.[430]

There appears to have been no definite point at which Norwegian ice ceased to be imported into Britain. Imports in 1933 amounted to 2,544 tons, valued at £2,076;[431] and occasional cargoes continued to arrive for some years after. Norway had maintained a trade in natural ice with Denmark, Germany, France and Belgium, so there were still a small number of exporters and shippers participating in the business. But few at the time would have imagined that, seventy years on, natural ice (this time from Sweden) would once more find its way to London as the capital opened its first ice bar, even if this was merely one of the more perverse facets of 21st-century conspicuous consumption.

---

430 *Ibid.*, XXXI (1928), p. 210.
431 *Ibid.*, XXXVII (1934), p. 24.

References

Museums and Archives

Berg-Kragerø Museum, Norway
Bodleian Library, Oxford: John Johnson Collection
London Canal Museum
Norsk Folkemuseum, Oslo

Newspapers and Periodicals (British)

British Refrigeration and Allied Interests
Chambers's Journal
Cold Storage and Ice Trades Review (Also published as *Cold Storage and Produce Review* from 1910-11. However only the original title is cited in this book's footnotes, as issue and volume numbers follow on in sequence; moreover, the running page head continued to use the old name for some years after the main title changed.)
Daily Mail
Harmsworth Magazine
Illustrated London News
Lloyd's Universal Register of British and Foreign Shipping
Longman's Magazine
Pearson's Magazine
Penny Cyclopaedia
Punch
The Kitchen Oracle
The Times

Books and articles

Aase, J., 'Norges Siste Istid', *Fortidsvern* no. 3 (1999), pp. 24-7.

Admiralty Hydrographic Dept., *Norway Pilot* (7th ed., London, 1948).

Anderson, C., *An Eight Weeks Journal in Norway etc in 1852* (London, 1853).

Anon., *The Pytchley Book of Refined Cookery and Bills* (London, 1885).

Atkinson, D., 'Following the Icy Thing: When Natural Ice Was a Commodity', *International Journal of Maritime History* 34, 1 (2022), pp. 112-123.

Bagle, E., 'Ice from "Nature's Factory"', *International Journal of Maritime History* 34, 1 (2022), pp. 123-132.

Beamon, S.P., and Roaf, S., *The Ice-Houses of Britain* (London, 1990).

Bell, A., *Port of London, 1909-1934* (London, 1934).

Bell, W.G., *The Thames from Chelsea to the Nore* (London, 1907).

Belloc, H., *The River of London* (London, 1912).

Belloc, H., *The Cruise of the Nona* (London, 1925).

Blain, B.B., 'Melting Markets: The Rise and Decline of the Anglo-Norwegian Ice Trade, 1850-1920', *Working Paper of the Global Economic History Network, London School of Economics* no. 20 (2006).

Bowden, J., *Norway: Its People, Products, and Institutions* (London, 1867).

Bradshaw, J., *Norway, Its Fjords, Fjelds, and Fosses* (London, 1896).

Brown, M., *Coalhouse Fort Wing Battery, East Tilbury, Essex* (London, 2003).

Campbell, J.R., *How to See Norway* (London, 1871)

Cook, R., *Oxford Night Caps* (Oxford, 1893).

Coton Risley, W., *Early Victorian Squarson: The Diaries of William Coton Risley, Vicar of Deddington, Oxfordshire*, 2 vols. (Banbury, 2007-12).

Cowper, F., *Sailing Tours: Part I: The Coasts of Essex and Suffolk* (London, 1892).

Cowper, F., *Sailing Tours: Part II: The Nore to Tresco, Isles of Scilly* (London, 1909).

David, E., *Harvest of the Cold Months* (Harmondsworth, 1994).

David, R., 'The Demise of the Anglo-Norwegian Ice Trade', *Business History* 37 (1995), pp. 52-69.

David, R.G., 'The Ice Trade and the Northern Economy, 1840-1914', *Northern History* 36 (2000), pp. 113-127.

Davidson, H.C. (ed.), *The Book of the Home*, 8 vols. (London, 1900-1).

Davies, J., *Railway Rates, Charges, and Regulations of the United Kingdom* (London, c. 1893).

Dickens, C., *Dickens's Dictionary of the Thames, from Oxford to the Nore* (London, 1880).

Du Chaillou, P.B., *The Land of the Midnight Sun*, 2 vols. (New York, 1882).

Ellis, M., 'Ice and Icehouses through the Ages, with a Gazetteer for Hampshire',
    Southampton University Industrial Archaeology Group (1982).
Faulkner, A., *The Regent's Canal: London's Hidden Waterway* (Burton-on-Trent, 2005).
Freelove, W.M., *Victorian Horses and Carriages: A Personal Sketch Book* (Guildford and London, 1979).
Fussell, G.E. 'Natural Ice', *Architectural Review* 112 (1952), pp. 187-190.
Gillett, E., *A History of Grimsby* (Oxford, 1970).
Gothesen, G., *Med is og plank i Nordsjofar* (Oslo, 1986).
Høy, C., *Vinden ere n lunefull venn. Seilskuteliv* (Oslo, 1972).
Humphry, C.E., *Housekeeping, a Guide* (London, 1893).
Jarrin, W.A., *The Italian Confectioner* (rev. ed., London, 1861).
Jeanes, W., *Gunter's Modern Confectioner* (13th ed., London, n.d.).
Jungman, N., *Norway* (London, 1905).
Kinross, F., *Coffee and Ices: The Story of Carlo Gatti in London* (Sudbury, 1991).
Klovland, J.T., *Contributions to a History of Prices in Norway: Monthly Price Indices, 1770-1920* (Oslo, 2013).
Konow, S., and Fischer, K., *Norway: Official Publication for the Paris Exhibition* (Kristiania, 1900).
Liddell, C., and Weir, R., *Ices: The Definitive Guide* (London, 1995).
Linney, A.G., *The Port of London* (London, 1927).
MacGregor, J., *The Voyage Alone in the Yawl 'Rob Roy'* (London, 1867).
Manley, G., 'Central England Temperatures: Monthly Means 1659 to 1973', *Quarterly Journal of the Royal Meteorological Society* 100 (1974), pp. 389-405.
Marshall, A.B., *The Book of Ices* (London, 1885).
Maltster, R., *Lowestoft: East Coast Port* (Lavenham, 1982).
Martin, R.G., 'Ice houses and the Commercial Ice Trade in Brighton', *Sussex Industrial History* no. 14 (1984-5), pp. 18-24.
Masters, T., *The Ice Book: Being a Compendium & Concise History of Everything Connected with Ice* (London, 1844).
Middleton, E.E., *The Cruise of 'The Kate'* (2nd ed., London, 1888).
Mockler-Ferryman, A.F., *Peeps at Many Lands: Norway* (London, 1909).
Moore, S.A., *The Thames Estuary: Its Tides, Channels, Ports and Anchorages* (London, 1894).
Murray, J., *Murray's Handbook for Denmark, Norway and Sweden* (London, 1871).
Norseng, P.G., 'Naturisen i norsk sjøfartshistorie', in E. S. Koren and F. Kvalø, eds., *Hundre å over og under vann: Kapitler om maritime historie og maritime arkeologi i anledning Norsk Maritimt Museums hundreårsjubileum* (Oslo, 2014), pp. 153-192.
Norseng, P.G., 'Ferskfisk og kald pils i den siste istid: Om naturisens rolle i kystøkonomien og det moderne gjennombruddet i Norge', *Heimen* 56 (2019), pp. 214-237.

Norseng, P.G., 'The "Last Ice Age" in Maritime History: An Introduction', *International Journal of Maritime History* 34 (2022), pp. 101–112.

Nygaard, K.M., 'Two Conferences in the Natural-ice Trade', *International Journal of Maritime History* 34, 1 (2022), pp.133–155.

Ouren, T., 'The Norwegian Ice Trade', in D.V. Proctor (ed.), *Proceedings of the Symposium on Ice-carrying Trade at Sea*, National Maritime Museum (1979), pp. 31–42.

Pattison, P., *Tilbury Fort, Essex* (London, 2004).

Pember-Reeves, M., *Round about a Pound a Week* (London, 1913).

Philip, A.J., *Gravesend, the Watergate of London* (3rd ed., London, 1906).

Pudney, J., *London's Docks* (London, 1975).

Railway Clearing House, *List of Alterations in, and Additions to, General Classification of Goods* (London, 1872).

Rees, A., *The Cyclopaedia; or Universal Dictionary of Arts, Sciences and Literature* XIX (Philadelphia, n.d.).

Rodwell Jones, L., *The Geography of the London River* (London, 1931).

Ross, W.A., *A Yacht Voyage to Norway, Denmark and Sweden*, 2 vols., (London, 1848).

Sandvik, P.T., *Nasjonens velstand, Norges økonomiske historie 1800–1940* (Oslo, 2018).

Saunders, A.D., *Tilbury Fort, Essex* (London, 1985).

Senn, C.H., *Ices, and How to Make Them* (2nd ed., London, 1903).

Spencer, H., *The History of the Regent's Canal* (London, 1961).

Springett, B.H., *Cold Storage and Ice Making* (London, 1921).

Stevens Cox, J., *Ice Creams of Queen Victoria's Reign* (Guernsey, 1970).

Stevens, R.W., *On the Stowage of Ships and their Cargoes* (7th ed., London, 1894).

Stoddard Eckford, E., and Fitzgerald, M.S., *Household Management* (London, 1915).

Stone, O.M., *Norway in June* (London, 1882).

Wallis Tayler, A.J., and Cracknell, J., *Industrial Refrigeration, Cold Storage and Ice-making* 7th ed. (London, 1929).

Walton, E., *The Coast of Norway from Christiania to Hammerfest* (London, 1871).

Weightman, G., *The Frozen Water Trade: How Ice from New England Lakes Kept the World Cool* (London, 2002).

Wilson, T.M. (ed.), *Norway Illustrated* (Bergen, 1889).

Worts, J.W., *Norway and Denmark Re-visited by an Old Traveller* (Croydon, 1912).

Wyllie, M.A., *Norway and Its Fjords* (London, 1907).

About the Author

Michael Freeman is Emeritus Fellow of Mansfield College in the University of Oxford. He is the author of *Victorians and the Prehistoric: Tracks to a Lost World* (Yale, 2004, and Orient Longman, 2006) and *Railways and the Victorian Imagination* (Yale, 1999) which won the *Yorkshire Post* Book of the Year prize and was shortlisted for the Sally Hacker Prize at Johns Hopkins. Since moving to the Isle of Wight on the south coast of England in 2010, he has published widely on the Undercliff coast there, including *Victorians in Search of Winter Health: Ventnor, Isle of Wight, the Mediterranean on an English Shore* (Cross Publishing, 2015).

Appendix

January 15, 1904.  9

NORWEGIAN ICE IMPORTS FOR 1903.
[COPYRIGHT.]

Our readers will find subjoined in tabular form a record of ice imported from Norway and landed at the various ports in the United Kingdom for the last five years. The ice imported into England and Wales amounted last year to 315,221 tons, value £167,264 ; into Scotland, 17,291 tons, value £9,079 ; and into Ireland, 12,916 tons, value £6,785—grand total, 345,428 tons, value £183,128, average 10s. 7d. per ton. Compared with the landings in the previous seven years, this result was as follows :—Decrease on 1902, 17,439 tons—£23,272 ; 1901, 115,518 tons—£86,769 ; 1900, 103,225 tons—£90,897 ; 1899, 159,199 tons—£133,754 ; 1898, 98,469 tons—£145,433 ; 1897, 110,583 tons—£65,543 ; 1896, 121,905 tons—£79,170. This record, although official, is not published except by COLD STORAGE.

	Tons.					Value £				
	1903	1902	1901	1900	1899	1903	1902	1901	1900	1899
London	183,460	185,257	206,978	205,390	220,430	89,393	100,364	119,486	123,463	134,528
Grimsby	26,250	23,340	68,390	74,623	84,325	12,925	11,671	31,156	37,333	42,555
Liverpool	12,917	17,296	17,117	18,760	20,212	6,911	9,559	9,805	11,944	13,832
Fleetwood	10,189	8,000	10,261	4,796	—	5,223	4,773	6,411	3,422	—
Shoreham	7,633	7,846	8,661	10,907	10,329	4,756	4,911	6,349	7,063	8,959
Penzance	7,582	7,145	4,852	3,964	3,205	4,758	4,463	3,292	2,710	2,230
Boston	7,576	7,170	7,172	5,718	—	3,794	3,565	3,588	2,947	—
Southampton	6,880	6,490	7,880	8,030	7,630	4,602	3,948	5,133	4,813	5,061
Hull	6,660	15,190	19,529	12,780	84,325	3,330	7,595	9,765	6,401	42,555
Portsmouth	5,250	3,785	3,685	3,675	—	4,078	3,407	3,187	3,509	—
Ramsgate	4,946	3,928	3,580	5,586	8,100	2,653	2,128	1,950	3,930	5,715
Goole	3,380	2,149	4,467	4,493	1,845	1,912	1,028	2,495	2,515	1,170
Bristol	3,303	3,660	4,337	3,736	4,320	3,303	3,660	4,187	3,736	4,320
Lowestoft	3,246	2,292	4,250	6,193	10,420	1,663	1,041	2,088	3,517	6,053
Hartlepool	3,170	4,221	5,610	4,670	4,846	1,531	2,158	2,782	2,879	2,715
Plymouth	3,000	3,070	4,390	3,750	4,650	2,902	3,070	4,390	3,780	4,688
Newcastle	2,958	2,275	2,101	1,770	1,580	2,103	1,869	1,855	1,770	1,590
Scarborough	2,590	2,670	3,441	2,845	2,441	1,436	1,443	2,033	1,659	1,449
Sunderland	2,371	2,630	3,006	2,734	—	1,084	1,289	1,482	1,445	—
Newhaven	1,876	2,274	2,873	1,828	1,770	1,717	2,261	2,468	1,912	1,770
Folkestone	1,630	1,260	1,320	1,170	1,175	992	796	835	934	783
Rochester	1,475	1,480	1,372	1,420	—	1,085	1,096	943	1,019	—
Lynn	1,236	1,012	1,146	787	—	683	565	780	399	—
Dartmouth	1,213	1,410	2,664	2,472	2,457	7,213	1,408	2,665	2,472	2,505
Colchester	1,074	730	—	—	—	689	460	—	—	—
Preston	932	—	250	—	—	497	—	125	—	—
Dover	820	1,216	1,270	1,050	1,390	492	707	809	720	809
Weymouth	650	613	460	320	—	325	336	230	180	—
Berwick	448	415	550	307	—	231	207	275	165	—
Exeter	205	620	—	—	—	98	880	—	—	—
Falmouth	181	200	310	155	—	95	153	210	80	—
North Shields	—	4,924	4,029	—	—	—	2,462	2,348	—	—
Yarmouth	—	1,750	3,370	3,266	5,478	—	766	1,546	1,740	3,311
Cardiff	—	600	—	158	—	—	360	—	68	—
Stockton	—	450	—	—	—	—	250	—	—	—
Milford	—	320	3,989	2,389	2,100	—	320	3,877	2,220	2,350
Glasgow	8,407	11,650	16,166	16,243	16,690	3,046	6,489	10,494	13,156	13,709
Leith	4,559	3,735	5,585	5,081	8,095	1,579	1,344	2,313	1,991	4,754
Montrose	1,255	460	615	—	—	644	180	285	—	—
Kirkcaldy	888	995	1,150	1,350	—	458	527	629	803	—
Grangemouth	770	745	620	490	330	537	437	410	331	207
Dundee	505	782	548	740	1,660	242	391	337	695	1,213
Perth	512	479	209	250	—	314	251	143	163	—
Inverness	385	574	787	698	—	239	503	560	486	—
Aberdeen	—	—	2,170	—	8,090	—	—	1,083	—	5,131
Lerwick	—	—	75	—	—	—	—	75	—	—
Peterhead	—	—	—	463	—	—	—	—	456	—
Cork	2,715	2,540	1,593	1,445	900	1,421	1,231	902	846	700
Dublin	2,096	3,200	4,752	7,472	4,790	1,115	1,750	2,547	5,452	3,165
Tralee	1,925	3,300	3,735	4,279	—	990	1,701	2,291	2,395	—
Galway	1,280	1,374	1,776	1,940	—	635	687	1,090	1,200	—
Skibbereen	1,190	1,400	2,563	2,178	6,096	605	727	1,434	1,355	4,220
Belfast	1,150	1,214	2,432	3,341	2,790	690	751	1,842	2,109	2,099
Waterford	1,000	1,080	1,030	1,180	1,950	469	486	515	590	1,090
Londonderry	960	900	1,331	825	823	505	410	1,027	559	823
Limerick	600	700	500	450	250	300	350	380	320	230

Page from the Cold Storage and Ice Trades Review showing Norwegian ice imports to Britain by port of entry in 1903, including earlier statistics for 1899–1902 (Bodleian: Per 193998 d.1/VII, p. 9)

(Wikipedia)

Index

Terms beginning with 'ice' are arranged in a single alphabetical sequence whether or not hyphenated. Page numbers in *italic* indicate illustrations and figures. References to maps have the letter 'm' following the page number; references to footnotes have the letter 'n' following the page number.

Aberdeen
    ice cream (ice-cream) vendors 162
    ice factory 106, 113
    imports 71
    shipwrecks 34
Aberdeen Ice Manufacturing Company 106
accidents *see* disasters and accidents
Achilles (sailing barque) 62, 97
advertising
    by companies 45, *110*, *127*, *129*, *134*, *137*, *138*, *147*, *148*, 168
    of door-to-door deliveries 147
A.E Martin Ltd 179–80, *181*
Albert Dock 42
American ice 18–19, 75–6, 128, 139, 153
American influences 140
ammonia, use in refrigeration 102
Amphion (sailing barque) 51
Anglo-Norwegian Ice Company 74
Antarctic Ice and Cold Storage Company Ltd 167, *168*
arsenic poisoning from ice cream (ice-cream) 161
artificial ice 101–23 (*see also* customers for ice market; ice factories)
    contamination report 117
    grades and usage 104, 108–9, *122*
    municipal manufacture 114, 178
    and natural ice preference 115–16, 123, 172
    production processes 20, 101–3, *102*, 104–5, *104*, 122, *183*
    proportion of ice company business 123
    public fear of chemicals 103, 115
    'pure ice' 115
    size and endurance 115–16, 117
    technological developments 102, 122
    tonnage produced 85, 103–4, 106, 108, 109, 111, 115, 123, 141, 172
Aston (Birmingham), local ice source 56
auctions of ice factories and storage 111–12, 113, 114, 176
average annual temperature, effect on sales 73
Avonmouth docks ice storage capacity 178

ballast for return journeys 29–30, 80–1
barques 40, 51–2, 62, 85–6, 88, 93, 96–7, *97*, *98*

197

INDEX

Battersea ice depot 44
Battlebridge basin ice storage 44
Bein (sailing brig) 35–6
Belgium, ice imports from Norway 52–3
Belvedere (steamship), collision 96–7
Berean (sailing barque) 40, 96–7
Bergen, steamships 82, 83, 86, 88
Bermondsey Borough Council, inquiry into factory ice purity 118
Billingsgate fish market, underground ice storage 56
Birmingham
    door-to-door deliveries 146
    ice cream (ice-cream) vendors 161
    local ice source 56
Blackburn, municipal ice manufacture 114
Blackwall ice factory 45, *45*, 47, 107–8, *108*
Bognor Regis, ice cream (ice-cream) business 167
Bolton Corporation, ice manufacture 114
Bolton Pure Ice Company, telegraphy 125–6
bomba/bombes 157–8
Book of Ices (Marshall) 152, 155, *156*
Book of the Home, The 17–18
Bournemouth, court case 98
Bradford ice factory 122
Brevik 51
brewery industry, use of ice 16, 141
'brick' ice cream (ice-cream) 166
brigs 34–5, 35–6, 82, 92, 96
British ice, local sources 18, 55–6, 152
British Ice Company 103
British Refrigeration and Allied Interests 24, 72, 103
Brixham Pure Ice Company 118
Burnley, ice manufacture 114, 122, 178

butchers
    cost of ice 93, 175
    meat deliveries by rail 16
    Norwegian natural ice preference 115–16
    refrigerator use 186–7

Camden ice well (ice-well) 44
Cardiff Pure Ice Company 111, 125, *127*
cargos *see* ice cargoes
cellars
    food preservation 17, 18
    ice storage 17, 21–2, 129, 130, 132, 158
Census of Ice Factories (1907) 123
Census of Production Act (1906) 172
Cliffe Fort 39m, 40
climate (*see also* heatwaves)
    average annual temperature 73
    effect on ice factories 113–14, 135, 166–7, *167*, 173, 187
    and ice farming 57, 58, 64, 65–9, 181–4
    effect on local UK ice sources 56, 152
    Norway 28, 32
    storms 29, 35, 48, 81, 89, 90–1
    effect on transportation 64, 81, 84
clubs *see* hospitality industry
coal
    cargoes 30, 79–80, 81, 89, 119
    costs of production 121
Coalhouse Fort and battery 38, 39m, 40
Coalhouse Point 38, 39m, 40
coastal resorts, ice cream (ice-cream) businesses 159, 162–3, 167
'coffin ships' 22 (*see also* sailing ships, shipwrecks and disasters)
coke, cargoes 30, 79–80, 81, 89, 119
Cold Storage and Ice Trades (later *Produce*) *Review* 23–4, *23*, 172
    advertisements 111
    on artificial ice 108–9, 123, 166, 172

competition to stimulate business 187
on demise of ice trade 185
feature on ice importers 48
on ice cream (ice-cream) and soda 158, 167, 168
on investment 73, 111–12, 112–13
poems 69, 79, 101, 113, 125, 171
on transportation 99
cold storage facilities *see* ice storage; refrigerators (ice); refrigerators (mechanical)
communications, importance of telegraphy 125–6
companies
    advertising of *45, 110, 127, 129, 134, 137, 138, 147, 148, 168*
    ice makers and factories 45, 47, 85, 103–15
    importers 43, 44, 45, *45*, 47–8, 49, 52, 85, 92–3, 109, 130, 133, 134, 135, 139, 179–80
confectioners
    ice cream (ice-cream) making *see* ice cream (ice-cream), makers and businesses
conscription, effect on ice factories 177
contamination
    ice 117–18, 119, 131, 138–9
    ice cream (ice-cream) 160, 161, 163
contracts
    and ice storage needs 126
    between importers and shipowners 88, 94
    between Norwegian and British ice merchants 87–8, 116
cool-bags and cool-boxes 18
cost of ice *see* market prices
country houses and estates, ice deliveries 133

court cases
    action for slander 120
    demurrage 51–2, 85
    exploitation 163–4
    ice cream (ice-cream) sales 161
    ice loss 47, 51–2, 98
    telegraphic mistranscription 126
crime, ice cream (ice-cream) vendors 164
Croydon Ice Company, coal costs 121
crystal (translucent) ice
    manufacture 104, 108–9, *122*
    natural ice 18–19, 20, 21, 69, 104, 158
Cumberland Market Basin, ice storage 44, 128
custard ice cream (ice-cream) 157–8
customers for ice market
    domestic customers 16–17, 134–5, 139, 141–2, 144, 145
    hospitality industry 16, 18, 133, 134, 139
    trade 51, 56, 71, 85, 93–4, 104, 106, 116–17, 133, 153, 175, 176

Daily Graphic 103–4
Daily Mail 132
dairies, ice delivery 142
David, Elizabeth, *Harvest of the Cold Months* 151–2, 154–5
deadweight (cargo) tonnage 83, 85
decorative ice 123, 141, 158–9
Deddington Manor, ice storage 56
'deeps' (Thames) 36–7
demurrage 52, 85, 85n, 95
Denmark, ice imports from Norway 52
deterioration of ice, meltwater 47, 81, 95, 97–8, 144
Devon and Cornwall Ice and Cold Storage Company 159
Devonian (liner), collision 81
Dickens, Charles, descriptions of Thames 36, 42

INDEX

disasters and accidents
   ice store fatalities 128, 131
   at sea 22, 34–5, 35–6, 40, 48, 81–2,
      90–1, 91, 96, 96–7, 99 (*see also*
      sailing ships, shipwrecks and
      disasters; steamships, shipwrecks)
   in Thames estuary 40
distilled water, use in ice making 118
distribution of ice *see* ice distribution
dock strikes 135, 173
domestic customers 16–17, 134–5, 139,
   141–2, 144
   education in ice uses and usage 142,
      145
Domestic Ice Supply Company Ltd 146,
   147
door-to-door deliveries 70, 142, 145, 146
   ice cream (ice-cream) 165
Drammen, ice loading 49–50
Drammenfjord, ice harvesting 68
drinks using ice 16, 139–40
Drøbak 49, 51
dykes 36

East Anglian Ice Company, coal costs 121
Eastern Counties Ice Company (King's
   Lynn) 130, 133
Elizabeth I, at Tilbury 40
Embla (steamship) 92
English towns (*see also* London; seaside
   resorts)
   artificial ice 106, *107*, 109–10, 111, *112*,
      113–14, 115, 121, 122, *122*
   court cases 51–2, 98, 126, 163–4
   distribution of ice 121, 133, 146
   environmental pollution 121
   fishing industry 51, 71, 72, 86, 107
   ice cream (ice-cream) 161, 167
   ice shortages 178
   ice storage 56, 128, 129–30, 178

imports of ice *195*
local ice sources 18, 55–6, 152
municipal ice manufacture 114, 178
ports 30n, 51, 52, 80, 84n, 93, 130, 185
   (*see also* Grimsby)
shipping 92–3
soda fountains 167
telegraphy 125–6
water sources 118–19
environmental pollution, ice factories
   120–1
equity sharing ship ownership 82
exports from Norway (*see also* ice
   importers; ice merchants; ice ships
   (ice-ships) and shipping)
   development of trade 16, 19, 49, 76
   peak of trade 19, 49, 133
   impact of First World War 173–4
   decline 169–87
   effect of London monopoly 94
   prohibition on imports to UK 174–5
   spring contracts 87–8, 116, 169–70
   timeline of ice imports to Britain *195*
   tonnage 19, 42, 43, 47, 49, 51, 52–3, 123,
      173, 174, 175, 179, 181, 182, 184, 187
   weather and climate 67, 70–1, 72–3,
      84, 94–5, 171

factory ice *see* artificial ice; ice factories
fatal accidents (*see also* disasters and
   accidents)
   ice stores 128, 131
Ferrari, Carlo 137, *138*
fiction references 36, 42, 132
First World War, effect on ice trade 173–8
'fish and chip' trade 116
Fish Trades Gazette 141
fishing industry (*see also* fishmongers)
   artificial ice usage 106
   fish deliveries to towns 16, 107, 116–17

ice shortages 175, 176, 177, 178
imported ice usage 51, 56, 71–2, 85
requirement fluctuation 71, 174
fishmongers (*see also* fishing industry)
   cost of ice during war 175
   natural ice preference 116
   refrigerator use 186
   requirement for ice 20, 48, 71, 133, 139
   suppliers of ice 133, 141–2
Fleetwood Ice Company 113
'Floating Republic' mutiny 38
flooding (Thames) 36
food poisoning, from ice cream (ice-cream) 161, 163
food preservation
   consumer demand for ice 142, 144, 145
   larders 17–18
forts and batteries 38, 40
France, ice imports from Norway 52–3, 92
'free from core' ice 108–9
freezing methods
   artificial ice manufacture 20, 101–3, *102*, 104–5, *104*, 122, 183
   ice cream (ice-cream) 155–6, *156*
frigorific mixtures (cooling liquids) 101

galiots 62, 97
Gatti, Carlo (*see also* United Carlo Gatti, Stevenson and Slaters Ltd)
   import company 44, 85
   local ice use 56
   restaurateur and ice cream (ice-cream) maker 22, 47–8, 159
   supplier of ice 160
Gatti, Stefano and Agostino, theatrical business 159–60
Geir (sailing brig) 92
Gem (sailing schooner) 96
General Ice Company 103

George III, ice cream (ice-cream) patronage 153
Germany
   ice farming 53
   imports from Norway 52, 92
Glasgow
   ice cream (ice-cream) vendors 161–2
   ice manufacture 109, *110*
   imports of ice 51
Goole 51
government (*see also* local government)
   immigration controls 163–4
   legislation 165–6, 172, 175
Gravesend 40–1
Great Cumberland Market, ice supplies 44, 128
Great Expectations (Dickens), description of Thames 36
Great Northern Ice Company (Grimsby) 106
Great Tower Street, ice depot 45
Greenwich 42, 45
Grimsby
   artificial ice factory and usage 72, 106–7, *107*, 111, 121
   fishing industry 71, 86, 107
   ice imports 51, 92–3, *93*
   ice shortages 178
   shipping speed premium 80
Grimsby Co-operative Ice Co. 106–7, *107*
Grimsby Ice Company 92–3
Gunter's (ice cream maker) 153–4
Gunter's Modern Confectionery 154

Hanley in the Potteries, ice factory 121
Harmsworth Monthly Magazine 15, 16, 89, 132–3
Hartlepool 51
Harvest of the Cold Months (David) 151–2, 154–5

health risks *see* contamination
heatwaves (*see also* climate)
    effect on domestic demand 17, 142, 144, 146
    and door-to-door deliveries 146
    ice farming revival 181
    effect on ice market 69–73, 84, 94–5, 135 175, 146, *167*, 171, 173, 175
    and ice storage needs 17, 69, 126, 135
    and wages 92
Henry (sailing brigantine) 91
Hobbs, Samuel 153, *156*
horses
    use in deliveries 135, *138*
    use in ice harvest 58, *59*, 60, 62, 65
Horton Ice Cream Company 165
hospitality industry
    artificial ice quality 104
    demand 18, 133, 134, 139
    ice cream (ice-cream) desserts 158
    ice deliveries 133, 134, 139
    use of ice 16, 141
hospitals, use of ice 16, 141
Hove, door-to-door deliveries 146–7
Hoy, Christian, sailor's memoir 80, 81
H.T. Ropes 128, *130* (*see also* Wenham Lake Ice Company)
Hull
    court case 126
    fishing industry 34, 51, 71
    ice cream (ice-cream) contamination 163
    ice manufacture 106
    purity of water used 119
Hungerford Market 47, 159

ice (*see also* British ice; Norwegian natural ice)
    classification for distribution 133
    cracking and splitting 60–1
    'free from core' ice 108–9
    grades of artificial ice 104, 108–9, *122*
    manufactured vs natural ice 102–3, 115–16, 123, 172
    meltwater 47, 81, 95, 97–8, 144
    'pure ice' 115
ice bars (ice-bars) 21, 187
ice block 'trains' 62, *62*, 79
ice blocks
    artificial ice construction 105, 108, *108*
    cutting (consumption) 141–2
    cutting (harvesting) 32, 58–60, *59*, 68, *180*
    endurance 117
    harvesting and storage 32, 64, 65, 68
    loading 49–50, *50*, 62–3, 79, 84, 179
    quality 69
    size 60, *183*
    transportation *see* transportation of ice
    unloading from ships 80, 89, *90*
    unloading to customers 135, 138, *138*–9
ice-boxes *see* ice chests (ice-chests) and ice safes (ice-safes); iceboxes (ice-boxes)
'ice canals' 60
ice cargoes (*see also* tonnage, ice imports)
    insurance 81
    return cargo management 30, 79–80, 89, 119
    tonnage 42, 43, 47, 49, 51, 52–3
ice carts (ice-carts) 135, 136, 137–8, *138*
ice chests (ice-chests) and ice safes (ice-safes) 17, 18, 143–4, 148
ice cream (ice-cream) 151–68
    coastal businesses 159, 162–3, 167
    contamination and food poisoning 160, 161, 163

cream ices 152
custard ice-cream 157–8
door-to-door sales 165
growth in popularity 154, 158, 159, 160, 168
Italian vendors 153, 160–4, 168
jelly moulds *151*, 156–7, *157*
makers and businesses see ice cream (ice-cream) makers
recipes 151–2, 158
restriction on sales 165–6, 175
royal patronage 153
soda fountains 167–8
sources of ice for freezing 152–3, 158, 159, 163
supply of ice 160
techniques 155–6, *156*
use of ice 16, 47, 69–70, 103, 152, 153, 158
vending machines 165
water ices 152
ice cream (ice-cream) makers
businesses 47–8, 153–5, 166–7, 168
ice deliveries 133
use of ice 16, 69–70, 70, 147
Ice Cream Restriction Order (2017) 165–6, 175
ice crushing machines *154*
ice cutting (ice-cutting)
manufactured ice 109
natural ice 32, 58–60, *59*, 68, 141–2, *180*
ice distribution
delivery men and conditions 136
delivery vehicles 135, 136, 137–8, *137*, *138*
door-to-door deliveries 70, 142, 145, 146
inland 43–4, 45, *45*, 46–7, 52, 133–9, *137*, *138*

'ice dogs' (grappling irons) 89, *90*
ice factories 101–23 (see also artificial ice)
development and expansion in Britain 19, 103–4, 105, 111
decline 185–7
coal costs 121
cold storage facilities 109, *109*–10, *110*, 111, 128
companies 45, 47, 85, 103–15, *104*, *107*, *108*, *110*, *112*, 121, *122*, *122*
effect of dock strike 135
environmental pollution 120–1
failed companies 113, 114, 176
ice cream (ice-cream) manufacture 166–7
investment 106, 111–12, 113–14
mechanisation 20, 101–3, *102*, 104–5, *104*, *122*, 183
meeting demand 72, 85
natural ice imports 116, 119
restriction order 166, 175, 176
sales of facilities 111–12, 113, 114, 176
sources of water 118
supplies for ice cream (ice-cream) 165–6
tonnage produced 103–4, 106, 108, 109, 111, 115, 123, 141, 172
and weather conditions 113–14, 135, 166–7, *167*, 173, 187
ice farming 55–77 (see also ice harvest)
competition from artificial ice 74–5
descriptions in press 62, 76–7
First World War collapse 178
Germany 53
market for ice 69–75, 85
production methods 56–61, *59*, 63–9, *64*, *65*, *67*, *68*
public interest 75–7
renewal of facilities 75
revival 179–81, *182*

203

slump 178–9, 181–2, 183–4
terminology 57, 77
tonnage *see* exports from Norway, tonnage
ice fields (ice-fields) 63
ice harvest 58–69, *59, 64, 68*
    effect of climate 65–6, *66*, 68
    descriptions 75–6
    employment of sailors 91–2
    failures 178, 183–4
    and ice export revival 1921 179
    quality variation 69
    storage 32, 60, 65, 126, 178
    tools 58–60, *59, 64, 68, 180*
ice-hooks 60, *64*
ice hotels 21
ice houses (ice-houses) 17, 22, 51, 55–6, 60, 85
ice importers (*see also* exports from Norway; Gatti, Carlo; ice merchants; United Carlo Gatti, Stevenson and Slaters Ltd)
    charters and contracts 87–8, 94, 116, 139, 170
    impact of climate 69–71, 72, 84, 94, 146, 173, 175
    companies 43, 44, 45, *45*, 47–8, 49, 52, 85, 92–3, 109, 130, 133, 134, 135, 139, 179–80
    and ice manufacture 116, 119
    London monopoly 93–4
    price wars 169–70, 171
    shipping costs 63–4, 86
    telegraphy 125–6
    timeline of Norwegian ice imports 195
    tonnage imported *see* tonnage, ice imports
'ice labourers' 160
ice-loading 49–50, *50*, 62–3, 79, 84, 179

ice manufacture *see* artificial ice; ice factories
ice market (*see also* customers for ice market; market prices)
    and artificial sources 74–5
    domestic market development 142–7
    fluctuation 69–75
    and heatwaves 69–73, 84, 94–5, 135, 146, *167*, 171, 173, 175
    and investment 72–4, 105, 106, 111–12, 112–13, 172, 178
ice merchants 84 (*see also* ice distribution; ice importers)
    contracts 87–8, 116
    export/import competition 91
    effect of heatwaves 70, 72–3
    ice for ice cream (ice-cream) making 158
    profits from demand surges 72, 73
    telegraphy 125–6
ice palaces 21
ice-ploughing 58, *59*
ice railways (trunkways) 15, 49–50, *50*, 60, 61, *61*, 79
    construction 62
    efficiency 63
ice refrigerators 143, 144, *145*, 147
ice safes (ice-safes) 17, 143
ice ships (ice-ships) and shipping 79–99 (*see also* sailing ships; steamships)
    British owned ships 80, 92–3
    conditions 22, 90
    demurrage 52, 85, 85n, 95
    hazards of journey 22, 34–5
    inspection by London County Council 88–9
    journey times 28, 80, 92
    loading 49–50, *50*, 62–3, 79, 84, 179
    maintenance 81

Norwegian owned ships 79, 80, 81–4, 82
return journeys 29–30, 80–1, 96
shipping costs 63–4, 86, 149
speed competition 91
storage of ice 32, 60, 84
unloading of ice 80, 89, *90*
West Coast/Irish route 91
wooden ships and fitments 82–3, 86, 99, 119–20
ice storage 126–33 (*see also* artificial ice; demurrage)
for demand fluctuation 126
disrepair of facilities 182
fatal accidents 128, 131
ice houses (ice-houses) 17, 22, 51, 55–6, 60, 85
lighting 132
London 17, 21–2, 44, 126–8, 132
manufactured ice 109, 109–10, *110*, 111, 128
Norway 32, 60, 64–5
effect on Norwegian trade 69
restocking 85
retrieval 131
in ships 32, 60, 65, *65*, 84, 126
underground storage 44, 56, 126–7, 128, 129–31, 132–3, 158
in wartime 177–8
ice trade (*see also individual aspects of trade and industry at main headings*)
development in 19th century 18–21
establishment in London 44
expansion 46–53, 169
decline in 20th century 169–87
new trade in 21st century 21
effect of First World War 173–8
investment in 72–4, 105, 106, 111–12, 112–13, 172, 178
literature on 22–5

newspaper and magazine articles 15, 16, 62, 70, 75–7, 89, 131, 146, 152
terminology 57, 77
ice wells (ice-wells) 44, 47, 126–8, 131–3, 158
iceberg experiment 55
iceboxes (ice-boxes) 143, 144, 146, *148* (*see also* ice chests (ice-chests) and ice safes (ice-safes))
'icemen' (delivery men) 136
Iduna (sailing schooner) 34
illuminated ice sculpture 141, 159
Illustrated London News, American ice harvest 75
immigrant workers, poverty and exploitation 161–2, 163–4
immigration from Italy, government response 163–4
importers *see* ice importers
imports of ice *see* ice importers
inundation (flooding), Thames 36
investment in ice market
imported ice 72–4, 172, 178
manufactured ice 105, 106, 111–12, 112–13
Ireland, ice for fishing industry 51, 174, 175, 176
Isbaaden (sailing briganteen) 35
Italia (steamship) 91
Italian ice cream (ice-cream)
manufacturers 22, 47–8, 154–5, 159, 166
workers 160, 161, 163–4

J. Lyons and Co, ice cream (ice-cream) manufacture 166
Jarrin, Guglielmo, *The Italian Confectioner* 155
jelly moulds *151*, 156, *157*
Julia (steamship), collision 96–7

INDEX

'keep cool' shop windows 143
Kent
    mains water supply 118–19
    rationing of ice 174
Kent Water Company 118–19
King's Lynn, ice imports, storage and distribution 129, 130–1, 133
Kitchen Oracle (Hobbs) 153, *156*
Kragerø
    exports 47, 51, 53
    ice railway *50*
    ice ships 83, *179*
    response to heatwaves 94–5
    Wiborg company 83, 92
Kristiania 33m (*see also* Oslo)
    activity in winter 32–3
    ice exports 49, 51, 52–3, 60
    loss of trade to Skiensfjord 74–5
    steamships 83
Kristianiafjorden 32, 33m, 49–50, 51, 65, 79 (*see also* Oslo fjord)
Kristiansand 30

labour costs 92–3, 180
lake ice
    from America 75
    in Britain 18
    in Norway 33–4, 49, 63, 73–4, 74, 74–5
    purity 118
Lake Oppegård 49
Lake Wenham 49
Lancet, study on Norwegian ice purity 117–18
larders, food preservation 17–18
Larvik, deposition of ballast 80–1
Lavoisier, Antoine 101–2
laying at anchor 38
leasing
    of lakes 63, 74
    of land 49

Leeds 115, 167
Leftwich, William, ice importer pioneer 48
Leftwich and Company, ice storage 127–8
Lehman (sailing barque) 51
lemon squash recipe 16
Lerwick 184, 185
Lewis's soda fountain (Leeds) 167
Lightfoot Refrigeration Company 24n, 146, *148*, 183
Limehouse, Regent's Canal Dock 43–4, 46m
Linde British Refrigeration Company 103–4, 104, *104*, 111
literature on ice trade 22–5, 76 (*see also* magazine articles; newspaper articles)
Liverpool (*see also* Wenham Lake Ice Company)
    ice cream (ice-cream) vendors 161, 162
    ice imports 51–2, 92, 94
    ice manufacture 109–10, 113–14
    ice shortages 70
    ice storage *110*, 113–14, 125, 128, *130*
    market prices 94, 109, 169
    steamship disaster 81–2
Liverpool Cold Storage and Ice Company 113–14
Liverpool Imperial Cold Stores 125
local government, municipal ice manufacture 114, 178
London (*see also* Thames)
    court cases 47, 85, 120, 123
    customers for ice market 17, 93–4, 104, 115, 123, 134, 139, 141, 144, 153, 175
    dock strikes 135, 173
    ice cream (ice-cream) makers 47, 48, 153–5

ice cream (ice-cream) vendors
   159–61, *162*
ice factories 19, 45, *45*, 47, 103–4, *104*,
   107–8, *108*
ice importers 45, *45*, 92–3, 135,
   179–80, 181, 183, 184 (*see also*
   North Pole Ice Company; Slaters
   ice importers; United Carlo Gatti,
   Stevenson and Slaters Ltd)
ice storage 44, 45, 56, 126, 131, 132
ice transportation 43–4, 45, 47, 135
import tonnage 16, 19, 42, 43, 47, 49,
   85, 175, 179, *195*
purity of ice inquiry 118
London Butchers' Trade Society 93,
   115–16
London County Council report on cold
   storage 126, 131, 132
   ice and cold storage report 88–9
Longman's Magazine 76
Lorenzo (sailing barque) 51–2
Lowestoft
   fishing industry 71, 85
   ice manufacture 85, 86, 106, 121
   ice storage 130
   journey time from Kragerø 92
   local ice sources 56
Lowestoft and East Coast Manufacturing
   Company 85
Lowestoft Ice Company 85, 121
'lying off' (ships at anchor), Thames 38

magazine articles 15, 16, 76, 89, 132–3
mains drinking water, use in ice making
   118
Manchester, ice imports vs manufacture
   105
Manchester, Sheffield and
   Lincolnshire Railway, specialist
   dock facilities 107

manufacture of ice *see* artificial ice; ice
   factories
Marie (sailing schooner) 35
market for ice *see* customers for ice
   market; ice market; market prices
market prices
   artificial ice 106, 109, 116
   deflated by monopoly 94
   domestic consumers 142–3
   freight charges advisory scale 149
   natural ice 70, 86–7, 106, 109, 116,
      147–9, 170–1, 173, 174, 175, 181
   price wars 169–70
Marshall, Agnes, *Book of Ices* 152, 155, *156*
Masters, Thomas, icebox 143–4
Matilda (sailing brig) 34–5
mechanisation of ice-making 20, 101–3,
   102, 104–5, *104*, 122, *183*
medical officers of health, control of
   contaminated ice cream (ice-cream)
   160, 163
Medway and Chatham dockyard 38
meltwater (loss of ice) 47, 81, 95, 97–8, 144
Messrs Leftwich and Co (ice importer)
   42
Midland Ice Company, environmental
   pollution 121
Milne, William 109, *110*, 137
Ministry of Food, ice cream (ice-cream)
   restriction 165–6
mint julep 19, 140
motorised transport for delivery 137, *137*,
   147, *149*, 166
municipal ice manufacture 114, 178
Murray, James (publisher) 77
*Murray's Handbook for Denmark,
   Norway and Sweden* 77

National Census of Production 185
National Liberal Club, use of ice 134

natural ice *see* American ice; British ice; Norwegian natural ice
naval defences 38, 40
navigation
    from Norway 28–30, 32, 80–1, 91, 96
    River Thames 35–42
net registered tonnage 83
Newcastle-upon-Tyne, ice factory 111, *112*
newspaper articles (*see also* magazine articles; *The Times*)
    American ice production 75
    effect on financial speculation 73
    heatwaves 17
    ice storage 132–3
    London ice factories 103–4
    Norwegian ice farming 62, 76–7
Nico (steamship) 92
Nore (sailing barque) 85–6
Nore light 38
North Eastern Ice Company (Aberdeen) 106
North Pole Ice Company 45
    competitive firm 93–4
    court cases 47, 120
    delivery vehicles 137
    ice storage 128
    manufacturer and importer 45, 123
    water testing and ice purity 118
North Sea 29, 31m
Norway (*see also* exports from Norway; ice farming; ice harvest; Norwegian natural ice)
    ports 27–8, 33m, 49–51, *50*
    tourism in 28, 29, 32–3
Norway Dock 46, 46m
Norway Lake Ice Company 60
Norwegian Block Ice Company 134
Norwegian natural ice (*see also* exports from Norway; ice farming; ice harvest)
    endurance time 20, 117
    impact of artificial ice 172
    market prices 70, 86–7, 106, 109, 116, 147–9, 169–71, 173, 174, 175, 181
    preference for 115–16, 123, 172
    purity and appeal 18–19, 102–3, 117–18, 119
    use for sculpture 123, 141, 158–9
    use in drinks and ice cream (ice-cream) 69–70, 139–40

Old Curiosity Shop 42
opaque (man-made) ice 102–3
Oslo 27–8, *27* (*see also* Kristiania)
Oslo fjord 27–8 (*see also* Kristianiafjorden)
Oxford University students, ice drinks 140

Parker, Richard, mutiny 38
Pearson's Magazine 76
Peeps at Many Lands: Norway 34, 77
'penny ices' 47, 159, 160
Perkins, Jacob, ice machine 102, *102*
petty crime, ice cream (ice-cream) vendors 164
Phoenix (sailing galiot) 62, 97
pilots
    Norwegian sea pilots 30, 32
    steamships 29
    Thames river pilots 40
ploughs for ice harvesting 58, *59*, 60
poems 69, 79, 101, 113, 125, 169
Pollux (sailing brig) 82
Pool of London 43, 47
Port of London (docks) 41, 42–7, 43, 44, 45, 46m, 55, 56, 88–9, 95, 128, 132
ports
    London *see* Port of London (docks)
    Norway 27–8, 33m, 49–51, *50*

other UK ports 51, 80, 129, 130–1, 133, 185 (*see also* Aberdeen; Grimsby; Hull; Liverpool; Lowestoft)
Portsmouth, ice imports 185
potassium nitrate (saltpetre) 101
Potteries Pure Ice and Cold Storage Company, closure and sale 176
poverty, among immigrant workers 161, 164
press *see* magazine articles; newspaper articles
Presto (sailing schooner) 90–1
price-cutting 94, 109, 169–71
production of ice *see* artificial ice, production processes; ice farming, production methods; tonnage
profits and profit-making
   from artificial ice 106
   from demand surges 72–3
   from manufactured ice 106, 113
   monopolies 93–4
public demand for ice (*see also* domestic customers)
   and distribution 69–70, 134–5, 139
   fear of artificial ice 103
   and heatwaves 17, 142, 144, 146
   municipal ice supply 114
   stimulating 145–6
pulley system (ice 'trains') 62, *62*
Punch, satirical report on ice imports 75
purchase of lakes 49, 63
'pure ice,' description of artificial ice 115
Pytchley Book of Refined Cookery 152, 156

Railway Clearing House, classification of ice 133
railways (British) 15
   cooling of Royal carriages 141
   facilities for fishing industry 16, 107, 116–17
   ice transportation 98, 133
railways (ice) *see* ice railways (trunkways)
recipes using ice
   drinks 16, 140
   ice cream (ice-cream) 151–2, 158
refrigerated transport 116–17, 135, 177
refrigerator hire 144
refrigerators (ice) 147
refrigerators (mechanical) 147, 185–7, *186*
Regent's Canal Dock 43–4, 56
restaurants *see* hospitality industry
retail trade customers 18, 93–4, 133, 139, 167–8
river pilots, Thames 89
Riverside Cold Storage and Ice Company 109–10, *110*
Rotherhithe, Surrey Commercial Docks 45, 46m
Russian ice palaces 21

sailing ships
   deadweight (cargo) tonnage 83
   favoured over steamships 30, 51–2, 83–4, 180–1
   inspection by London County Council 88–9
   involved in court cases 52, 85
   journey times 28, 80, 92
   loading *84*
   mooring 32, 66, 93
   owned by Wiborg company 83
   shipwrecks and disasters 22, 34–5, 35–6, 40, 82, 90–1, *91*, 96, 96–7, 99
   Thames 40, 41
   towing across sea 88, 89
   wooden ships and fitments 99

209

sailors
    conditions 22, 81, 90–1
    ice harvest employment 91–2
    wages 92–3
sales
    ice factories 111–12, 113, 114, 176
    lakes 49, 63
saltpetre, artificial ice production 101
saws for ice-cutting 58, 59, 60
Scammells of Spitalfields, insulated vans 135
schooners 34, 35, 90–1
Scotland
    ice cream (ice-cream) vendors 161–2
    ice imports 51, 71, 184, 185, 195
    ice manufacture 106, 109, 110, 113
    shipwrecks 34
sculptures in ice 123, 141, 158–9
sea dykes, Thames estuary 36
sea journeys (see also transportation of ice)
    between Britain and Norway 28–30, 32, 80–1, 91, 96
Sea Reach, Thames estuary 38, 39m
sea routes 28–30, 34, 80, 81, 91
seaside resorts, ice cream (ice-cream) businesses 159, 162–3, 167
Selfridges' soda fountain 167
Shadwell Basin 44, 46m
Shadwell Ice Factory 104, 104, 153
Sheerness 38, 55
'sherry cobbler' 19, 140
Shingleton Ice Company, ice factory 103, 104–5, 118, 139
shipowners
    British ships 80
    contracts with importers 88, 94
    Norwegian ships 79, 80, 81–4, 149
    profits from demand surges 72–3
    return cargo management 30, 79–80, 89, 119

shipping costs 86, 149
Society of Norwegian Shipowners 149
of wooden ships 82–3
ships see ice ships (ice-ships) and shipping; sailing ships; steamships
shipwrecks see sailing ships, shipwrecks and disasters; steamships, shipwrecks
Shoreham-on-Sea 80
Shornehouse Fort 40
Skagerrak (sea strait) 28, 29, 31m
Skiensfjord 51, 74–5
Skjolden 60
Slaters ice importers 43, 44, 135, 139 (see also United Carlo Gatti, Stevenson and Slaters Ltd)
    advertising 129
snow clearing 58
Society of Norwegian Shipowners 149
socle en glace technique 158
soda fountains 167, 167–8
Sognefjord 60
Sogns Iskompagni 60
Sønderstøen 79
Sorenson ice-box 143
Southampton
    ice imports 185
    ice storage 130
The Spring (sailing ship) 48
spring contracts 87–8, 116, 170
St Katherine's Dock 44
St. Petersburg ice palace 21
Star Ice Company 139
Stavanger 82, 86, 88
steamships
    deadweight (cargo) tonnage 83
    disasters 81–2
    journey times 28, 84, 92
    loading 79
    owned by Wiborg company 83
    vs sailing ships 30, 51–2, 83–4

210

shipwrecks 29, 91
specialised vessels 30
wooden ships 82–3, 86, 99, 119–20
steel ice 69
Stoke-on-Trent Pure Ice Company 121
storms 29, 35, 48, 81, 90–1
Stornoway 184, 185
strikes
   docks 135, 173
   fishing industry 72, 86
Surrey Commercial Docks 45, 46m, 55
Swansea Steam Fishing and Ice
   Company, auction 114
Swedish natural ice 21, 187
Swiss glacier ice 173
switchback ice railways *see* ice railways
   (trunkways)

table centre sculpture 123, 141, 158–9
taxation of imported ice 120
Telegraph (sailing schooner) 34
telegraphy, role in ice trade 125–6
Telemark 63
terminology 20–1, 57, 77
Thames
   estuary 35–8, 37m
   flood contamination 119
   hazards and disasters 40, 96
   ice formation 55
   Pool of London 43, 47
   Port of London dockyards 41, 42–7,
      43, 44, 45, 46m, 55, 56, 88–9, 95,
      128, 132
   river pilots 40, 89
   Sea Reach to Gravesend 38–41
   Tilbury/Gravesend to Port of London
      41–2, 45
The Times
   on companies 73, 74, 143, 168
   report on ice from local sources 152

reports of disasters 25, 34, 131
reports on ice consumption 17, 70,
   146
reports on Norwegian ice 76
Thomas Mowat Ltd 119
Thoreau, Henry David, descriptions of
   ice harvest 75–6
tides, Thames estuary 38
Tilbury 40, 41
tonnage
   artificial ice manufacture 85, 103–4,
      106, 108, 109, 111, 115, 123, 141, 172
   for confectionary businesses 153
   deadweight (cargo) tonnage 83, 85
   ice imports 16, 19, 42, 43, 47, 49, 51,
      52–3, 85, 123, 173, 174, 175, 179, 181,
      182, 184, 187, *195*
   of ice storage 127, 128
   London deliveries 135
   net registered tonnage 83, 85
   space needed on ships 82
Torne, River (Sweden) 21
Tortoni ice cream (ice-cream) method
   154
tourism in Norway 28, 29, 32–3
Tower Bridge, ice storage 44
Tower of London, ice storage 45
towing of sailing ships 88, 89
Tralee, ice tonnage 51
transportation of ice 123 (*see also*
   door-to-door deliveries; horses;
   ice distribution; ice railways
   (trunkways); ice ships (ice-ships) and
   shipping; sailing ships; steamships)
   costs 63–4, 84, 86–8, 89, 95, 133, 149,
      180
   disasters at sea 22, 34–5, 35–6, 40,
      81–2, 90–1, 91, 96, 96–7, 99
   loss of ice (meltwater) 47, 81, 95, 97–8
   to Norwegian ports 60

river barges 43–4, 44, 45, 46–7
sail versus steam 30, 51–2, 83–4, 180–1
sea journey to and from Norway 28–30, 32, 80–1, 91, 96
towing of sailing ships 88, 89
tramway at Greenwich 45
trunkways *see* ice railways (trunkways)
Tudor forts, Tilbury 40
Tunbridge Wells, door-to-door deliveries 146
typhus outbreak 163

underground ice storage 47, 128, 129–30, 132, 158
   wells 44, 47, 126–8, 131–3, 158
United Carlo Gatti, Stevenson and Slaters Ltd (*see also* Gatti, Carlo)
   assessment of temperature fluctuation 73
   competition 93–4, 172
   court cases 85, 120, 123
   delivery men and conditions 136
   delivery vehicles 137
   effect of dockers' strike 135
   ice storage 128, 132
   termination of imports 178
upper classes, use of ice 133, 134
urbanisation, effect on artificial ice consumption 105–6

Vale (steamship) 92
vending machine for ice cream (ice-cream) 165
Vera (sailing brigantine) 82
Veritas (steamship) 81–2
Victoria Dock 42

Waterloo railway arches storage 128
weather *see* climate; storms
wells 44, 47, 126–8, 131–3, 158
'Wenham ice' 18–19
Wenham Lake Ice Company (*see also* H.T. Ropes)
   customers 139
   domestic refrigerators 143
   ice storage 44, 128
   imports 49, 63, 75
   mint julep recipe 140
   origins at Liverpool 128
   purchase of lake 63
   'Wenham ice' 18–19
Weser district, Germany 53
Wiborg company 24–5, 52, 83, 92, 94–5
windmill pumps 89, 98
wooden ships and fitments 82–3, 86, 92, 98, 99, 119–20
Woolwich 42
working conditions
   ice cream (ice-cream) workers 160, 163–4
   ice delivery men 136
   ice harvest workers 58, 59, 60, 64, 67, 68
   sailors 22, 81, 90–1

Yorkshire Pure Ice Company 115